UNIVERSITY OF CAMBRIDGE
DEPARTMENT OF APPLIED ECONOMICS

MONOGRAPHS

16
BIPROPORTIONAL MATRICES
& INPUT–OUTPUT CHANGE

UNIVERSITY OF CAMBRIDGE
DEPARTMENT OF APPLIED ECONOMICS

MONOGRAPHS

This series consists of investigations conducted by members of the Department's staff and others working in direct collaboration with the Department. The Department of Applied Economics assumes no responsibility for the views expressed in the Monographs published under its auspices

BIPROPORTIONAL MATRICES & INPUT–OUTPUT CHANGE

MICHAEL BACHARACH

CAMBRIDGE

AT THE UNIVERSITY PRESS

1970

Published by the Syndics of the Cambridge University Press
Bentley House, 200 Euston Road, London N.W.1
American Branch: 32 East 57th Street, New York, N.Y.10022

Library of Congress Catalogue Card Number: 77–75823

Standard Book Number: 521 07594 7

Printed in Great Britain
at the University Printing House, Cambridge
(Brooke Crutchley, University Printer)

CONTENTS

TABLES

PREFACE

This book is a revised version of a doctoral dissertation presented at Cambridge University in 1965. Since then a good deal of new work has been done on the model that the book is about and several pieces of earlier work have come to my attention. I have revised the text of the Ph.D. thesis in an attempt to bring together—at least by reference—all the offshoots of Professors Stone and Brown's pregnant idea of 1961.

My interest in the biproportional model—more often called the 'RAS' model—stems from my participation from 1959–65 in Professor Stone's Growth Project at the Department of Applied Economics in Cambridge University. It was as a device to solve a practical problem of the Growth Project that the RAS model was conceived. My work on the model was founded on the patient finance of the Department of Applied Economics and on the freedom of thought encouraged by the enlightened director of its Growth Project.

In the framing and solving of problems of the model I owe much to the encouragement and help of Professor J. A. C. Brown and John Bates, my closest colleagues on the input–output aspects of the Growth Project. At a later stage I benefited greatly from discussions with Professor W. M. Gorman, who pointed out the implications of the way that the variability of the multipliers r and s depends upon their normalization. I am indebted both to Professor Gorman and to Professor K. J. Arrow for pointing out errors in an earlier version of Chapter 4. Needless to say, I am responsible for any errors that remain.

The substance of Chapter 4 has been published in 'Estimating nonnegative matrices from marginal data', in the *International Economic Review*, vol. 6, 1965. I am grateful to the editors of that journal for permission to present it again here.

Finally I would like to express my thanks to Nuffield College, where I spent a year and a half in 1966–7 and enjoyed ideal conditions for completing the book.

M. B.

Balliol College, Oxford

GUIDE TO NOTATION

In general, notations confined to single sections are not listed here. The definitions are informal.

a_i ith row of a matrix A

a^j jth column of a matrix A

a_{ij} (i,j)th element of a matrix A

A initial estimate in a constrained matrix problem; a nonnegative matrix with semipositive rows and columns; a Markov matrix (Chapter 10)

A_{IJ} partition of A with rows of index-set I and columns of index-set J

A^B solution of a biproportional constrained matrix problem

$A^B(u,v)$ solution of a biproportional constrained matrix problem, written as a function of u, v

A^{2t} matrix estimate reached after t rounds of a biproportional process

$A*$ limit point of biproportional process with vanishing (I', J) partition

$\overset{0}{A}$ nonnegative matrix whose positive elements equal corresponding elements of A

B solution of a generic constrained matrix problem; $I - (\mathscr{R}A)(\mathscr{C}A)'$ (Chapter 5)

C matrix function of A defined in Chapter 5, section 3

C^B C evaluated at A^B

$\mathscr{C}$ taking-coefficients-by-columns operator

f final demands net of competitive imports

$f(u,v,r,s)$ marginals of a biproportional transform less prescribed marginals

$f(r_i, s_j)$ projection of the series: $1, r_i s_j$

G aggregation matrix

i unit vector (as row or as column); row-index of a matrix; index of delivering industries

I identity matrix; subset of row-indices of a matrix

I_j jth partition of the set $I = \{1, ..., m\}$ (Chapter 8)

j column-index of a matrix; index of using industries

J subset of column-indices of a matrix

L observed (base-year) input–output coefficient matrix

L^P	projection of the time series: $L, L*$
$L(1)$	estimation-year input–output coefficient matrix
$L*$	generic estimate of $L(1)$
$\overset{0}{L}$	nonnegative matrix whose positive elements equal corresponding elements of L
m	row-order of a matrix;
	number of industries in the input–output model
M	observed (base-year) 'make' matrix of industries' outputs of their own and others' principal products
n	column-order of a matrix
^{0}	(right-superscript): true value (Chapter 5)
p	commodity prices in estimation year
q	observed (estimation-year) gross outputs
r	row multipliers in a biproportional relation
r^0	value of r given by (u^0, v^0)
r^t	tth round row multipliers in a biproportional process
R^t	cumulated products of row multipliers in a biproportional process
$\mathscr{R}$	taking-coefficients-by-rows operator
s	column multipliers in a biproportional relation
s^0	value of s given by (u^0, v^0)
s^t	tth round column multipliers in a biproportional process
S	$\{(i,j)\,|\,a_{ij} > 0\}$
S^t	cumulated products of column multipliers in a biproportional process
t	time;
	index of rounds in a biproportional process
$t = 0$	base year
$t = 1$	estimation year
u	prescribed row-sums in a constrained matrix problem;
	observed (estimation-year) total intermediate outputs
U	$(\bar{u}, v)$
U_I	$\sum_{i \in I} u_i$
v	prescribed column-sums in a constrained matrix problem;
	observed (estimation-year) total intermediate inputs
V_J	$\sum_{j \in J} v_j$
w	dominant characteristic vector of a Markov matrix A
x	proportional deviations in r
X	(x, y)
y	proportional deviations in s;
	net outputs of industries
$Z(1)$	estimation-year input–output transactions matrix

$Z^{①}, Z^{②}$	intermediate and final estimates of $Z(1)$ in two-stage biproportional model
$\in$	belongs to
η	column-multipliers in a Friedlander relation
ξ	row-multipliers in a Friedlander relation
σ_i	standard deviation of ith national accounting observation
$\phi(a, b)$	$b \log (b/ca)$
$\phi(A, B)$	$\displaystyle\sum_{(i, j) \in S} (a_{ij}, b_{ij})$
$\chi^2(A, B)$	$\displaystyle\sum_{(i, j) \in S} [(b_{ij} - a_{ij})^2/a_{ij}]$
$\psi(a, b)$	$\geqq 0$ for all real a, b; $= 0$ when $a = b$
Ω	covariance matrix of $(\bar{u}, v)$
$\langle \; \rangle$	(enclosing vector symbol): written as the leading diagonal of a diagonal matrix
$>$	each element greater than
$\geqslant$	no element less than, not all equal to
$\geqq$	no element less than
$\bar{}$	(overscript): deletion of first row (element) of a matrix (column vector)
$\sim$	(overscript): deletion of first column (element) of a matrix (row vector)
$=$	(overscript): deletion of first row and column of a matrix
$'$	(right superscript): transpose (of a matrix); complement (of a set)
$*$	(right superscript): observed value

Chapter 1

INTRODUCTION

1 THE BIPROPORTIONAL INPUT–OUTPUT MODEL

The main aim of this book is the thorough investigation of the properties of a certain model designed to estimate the behaviour of input–output relations through time. The model consists of two parts: a descriptive part, and a pair of identities that may be used to estimate the parameters of the descriptive part. The basic equation of the descriptive part was proposed by Leontief in 1941 in *The Structure of American Economy* [49]. It may be written

$$l_{ij}(1) = r_i s_j l_{ij}(0) \quad (i = 1, ..., m; j = 1, ..., n), \tag{1}$$

where $l_{ij}(0)$ and $l_{ij}(1)$ are the values of the (i, j)th input–output ratio at times 0 and 1. To it we add the obvious nonnegativity restriction

$$l_{ij}(1) \geqq 0 \quad (i = 1, ..., m; j = 1, ..., n). \tag{2}$$

We shall call the matrix $L(1) = \{l_{ij}(1)\}$ 'biproportional' to $L(0) = \{l_{ij}(0)\}$ if it satisfies both (1) and (2). 'Biproportional' is used as a shorthand for the more natural 'nonnegative biproportional'; we shall deal so extensively with nonnegative matrices that the latter term would be tedious to maintain. (1) and (2) together define the 'biproportional input–output model'.

In 1962 Stone [24, 67] independently suggested the relationship (1) and proposed estimating it by fitting it to single observations on total intermediate outputs and total intermediate inputs at time 1. Knowing $L(0)$, he determined r_i's and s_j's such that

$$\sum_{j=1}^{n} r_i s_j l_{ij}(0) q_j(1) = u_i(1) \quad (i = 1, ..., m), \tag{3}$$

$$\sum_{i=1}^{m} r_i s_j l_{ij}(0) q_j(1) = v_j(1) \quad (j = 1, ..., n), \tag{4}$$

where $u_i(1)$ is the observed total intermediate output of commodity i and $v_j(1)$ the observed total intermediate input into commodity j at time 1, and $q_j(1)$ is the observed gross output of commodity j at time 1. The estimation model given by (1) and (2) together with (3) and (4) will be called the 'biproportional input–output estimation model'.

Stone's own name for the biproportional model is the 'RAS' model—a code-name that comes from his notation $r_i a_{ij} s_j$ for the form on the right-hand side of (1), and that is now firmly established in the language of applied economics. The 'biproportional' terminology is not introduced in what would certainly be a futile attempt to dislodge 'RAS', but to help to abstract the mathematical characteristics from the economic associations of the model. When input–output applications are meant, we shall often talk of 'RAS'.

The estimation model (1) to (4) is not an econometric model of the familiar type in which random errors of specification are explicitly included. It could be made into one by, say, introducing an error term on the right-hand side of (1) and making appropriate alterations to (3) and (4). But there would be no point in doing so. We shall see later that, under weak conditions, one can always exactly fit (1), subject to (2), to single observations on the $u_i(1)$'s and $v_j(1)$'s; that is, one can find r_i's and s_j's such that $\{r_i s_j l_{ij}(0)\} \geqq 0$ and (3), (4) are fulfilled with zero errors. Loosely, this is because the model contains as many unknown parameters $r_1,\ldots,r_m,s_1,\ldots,s_n$ as observed elements $u_1(1),\ldots,u_m(1)$, $v_1(1), \ldots, v_n(1)$, i.e. because there are zero degrees of freedom. The price that must be paid for this wealth of parameters is to be left without confidence intervals for the true values of the parameters r_i and s_j. But to obtain them one would be obliged to adopt a simpler model in which $L(1)$ was related to $L(0)$ by a function containing fewer unknown parameters. The choice is typical of the econometric method: the more complex our descriptions, the less confidence can we place in the accuracy of our estimates. The dilemma is seldom resolved by increasing the number of parameters to the point where degrees of freedom vanish. But in few areas are data so scarce and simplistic descriptive relations at the same time so hard to accept as we shall see them to be in interindustry analysis.

In essence, the estimation problem that has just been described is to find a matrix having prescribed row and column totals. We shall adopt the name 'constrained matrix problem' for any problem of this kind. A constrained matrix problem in which the marginal constraints are nonnegative and a solution matrix is required to be biproportional to a given nonnegative matrix will be called a 'biproportional constrained matrix problem'. The given matrix often has the character of an initial estimate, and will be so referred to. The input-output estimation problem is a biproportional constrained matrix problem: its solution is an estimate of the transactions matrix at time 1 whose rows and columns sum to observed intermediate outputs and inputs $u_i(1)$ and $v_j(1)$ and which, it is easy to see, is related biproportionally to the initial 'constant-coefficients estimate' $\{l_{ij}(0)\,q_j(1)\}$ of the transactions matrix at time 1. Both the marginal constraints $u_i(1), v_j(1)$ and the given matrix $\{l_{ij}(0)\,q_j(1)\}$ are nonnegative by their economic nature.

2 Historical background

Leontief's suggestion of a biproportional form for the relationship between the values taken by an input–output matrix at different points of time does not seem to have been followed up at the time. It was only after Stone, in 1962, proposed the estimation of this form by means of the marginal constraints (3), (4) that interest was aroused. In 1963 Paelinck and Waelbroeck used the model to estimate an input–output matrix for Belgium for 1959 [59]. A directly estimated Belgian matrix for the same year enabled Paelinck and Waelbroeck also to perform an empirical test of the biproportional hypothesis by confrontation of the two estimates. Professor Stone's Cambridge Growth Project has used the model as the basis for its own input–output estimate for Britain for 1960 [26]. This estimate, in turn, was the input–output basis for the industrial gross output projections in the British National Plan for 1964 to 1970 [28]. Schneider [62] has made a detailed comparison of some properties of the biproportional model and of an alternative model for updating input–output matrices—the linear programming model of Matuszewski, Pitts and Sawyer [54]. In particular, Schneider compares the quality of estimates from the two models by confronting each with a directly observed table: these tests are made on U.S. figures for 1947 updated to 1958.

There have been two recent applications of the biproportional input–output model of slightly different kinds. For the current Japanese medium-term plan, a biproportional *forecast* of the transactions matrix for the terminal year was made by adjusting a constant-coefficients estimate to forecasts of intermediate outputs and inputs [41]. In 1966, Paelinck and others [60] used the biproportional model in an intercountry analysis of input–output structures in the European Economic Community. As in the earlier 'Belgian tests', direct observations of the biproportionally estimated matrices were used to test the model.

Meanwhile the model has been turned to use outside the study of interindustry relations. Bénard [7] in 1963, Waelbroeck [74] in 1964, and Kouevi [46] in 1965, used marginal data to estimate international trading matrices assumed to be biproportional to observed ones. The Cambridge Growth Project applied the model to estimate 'make' matrices showing the non-principal product compositions of industries' outputs [26], matrices showing the demand for labour by skill and industry, and other nonnegative economic matrices.

All of these applications were characterized by the limitation of estimation year data to observations on the marginals of the required matrices—industry and commodity outputs, countries' total exports and imports, industries' labour demands and demands for labour skills, and so on. The absence of further data, e.g. of data on the 'interiors' of the unknown matrices, ruled out the estimation of hypotheses richer in unknown parameters than the biproportional one. Moreover, an *a priori* case could in many instances be made out for a biproportional hypothesis analogous to (1) by attaching economic interpretations to the r_i's and s_j's. Each r_i multiplies a row and each s_j a column of the 'base' matrix of time 0 to give the assumed matrix at time 1. In the input–output model, for example, Stone interpreted the row multipliers r_i as measures of substitution tendencies between commodity inputs and the column multipliers s_j as measures of upward or downward tendencies in industries' 'degrees of fabrication'. In the international trading application, Waelbroeck interpreted the row multipliers as indices of countries' 'market shares' in all other countries.

In 1940, Deming and Stephan had treated as a biproportional constrained matrix problem the statistical problem of estimating an unknown contingency matrix from known marginals and an initial estimate of the matrix [23]. They had, however, proposed the biproportional form merely because it seemed to offer a mechanically convenient way of fitting the unknown matrix to its known marginals, and had made no attempt to justify it either by interpretation of the multipliers or otherwise.

The method that Deming and Stephan suggested for computing a solution was to fit rows to the known row sums and columns to the known column sums by alternate scalar multiplications of rows and columns of the base matrix. Each member of the sequence of matrices so generated would, it is easy to see, be biproportional to the base matrix. Hence if the sequence converged, the limiting matrix would be a solution. Stone independently proposed this iterative solution method in 1962. It has been used in all the subsequent applications of the model and it has always led to a solution.

3   ARGUMENT

The argument of the book will advance on two fronts: on the first, the attempt will be to establish that the biproportional model descriptive of the temporal behaviour of input–output relationships is a significant theoretical advance on the existing operational model of this behaviour; on the second, we shall consider the biproportional model as an instrument for the generation of numerical results in a field in which extreme scarcity of information is a major obstacle to economic planning. The operational model which has been in general use and which the biproportional model claims to supersede is the classical fixed-coefficients model in which input–output coefficients are assumed to be constant through time, supplemented by *ad hoc* side-models of movements in particular coefficients. The sophisticated Arrow and Hoffenberg model [**37**], which assigns several explanatory variables to each input–output coefficient, cannot be regarded as operational: its data requirements are prohibitive for most countries, and even in the United States, where data are relatively rich, it could not be satisfactorily estimated. We shall argue that of all operational models of coefficient change the biproportional model is the 'best model we have'—though the almost exclusive attention that it has recently received may lend the claim a Butlerian note.

We know already that the biproportional model has succeeded in the past in producing current input–output matrix estimates from observed 'base' matrices and information on current intermediate output and input totals. Such an estimate is necessarily nonnegative, and it is not hard to see from the nature of the iterative solution procedure we have sketched that it also necessarily preserves the zero elements of the observed matrix. The first of these features is obviously theoretically desirable, and a strong case can at once be seen for the second. But these properties alone certainly do not amount to a theoretical justification of the biproportional model. We cannot yet assert that there are not plausible circumstances in which either no solution exists to the estimation problem or an embarrassing multiplicity of solutions exists. An essential step in justifying the model must be, then, to examine existence and uniqueness properties for the solution of the system (1) to (4). Both these properties are clearly possessed by the constant-coefficients estimate. We shall succeed in establishing existence for the biproportional solution under weak conditions and uniqueness unconditionally.

The next step in strengthening the theoretical basis of the biproportional input–output estimation model is to introduce stochastic elements for the first time. Paelinck and Waelbroeck's confrontation of a biproportional with a direct estimate indicated that the biproportional specification (1) is, but for a few coefficients, an acceptable approximation. This is encouraging, but it does not rule out the possibility that slight specification error may lead to serious error in the biproportional estimate. We show, however, that not only is a biproportional estimate correct if the true matrix $L(1)$ at time 1 is in fact biproportional to the observed base matrix $L(0)$, but it remains nearly correct if $L(1)$ only approximates biproportionality to $L(0)$. Practical investigators employing the model have, on the other hand, been concerned by possible large errors of *observation* in the data, especially, in the marginals $u_i(1)$ and $v_j(1)$. What is the effect of such errors upon the associated biproportional estimate? We derive an explicit transformation from the distribution of errors in the $u_i(1)$, $v_j(1)$ to the approximate distribution of errors in the resulting estimate. This allows the question to be answered numerically for any particular problem.

Next, it is shown that there is a sense in which the biproportional estimate is as near as it can be to the 'initial estimate' while satisfying the given marginal constraints. This property gives some assurance that the model will not yield wild estimates in conflict with the widely-held view that most input–output coefficients are, if not constant, rather stable over time.

Our adoption of a model that admits temporal change in input–output coefficients does not imply that we reject Leontief's assumption of virtual invariance, namely that the coefficients ruling at a particular date would have been the same had gross outputs at that date been different. Input–output theory is empty without an assumption of this kind. The question then arises: does the biproportional estimate likewise remain constant in response to virtual variations in the gross outputs of the estimation date $t = 1$? This invariance certainly prevails if the true matrix at $t = 1$ is indeed biproportional to its observed value at $t = 0$; we establish, in addition, a weaker robustness property of the biproportional estimate in the case in which the true matrix only approximates biproportionality. We obtain, too, dual results on the behaviour of the estimate in response to variations in the prices of commodities at time 1.

The results that have been sketched in the last four paragraphs go some way to substantiating the claim that the biproportional model improves theoretically upon the model of fixed coefficients as a means of estimating a nonobservable input–output matrix. But we have not yet dealt with the possibility that some third estimation model might improve upon them both—say an alternative constrained matrix problem in which the biproportionality (1) is replaced by a relationship of a different form. Several possible formulations of the constrained matrix problem are considered in different parts of the book. Two broad categories are distinguished: in the first, a matrix is sought which satisfies the marginal constraints and, under this condition, minimizes some criterion, often a measure of 'distance' from the 'initial estimate'; in the second, the search is for a constraint-satisfying matrix which bears a prescribed form of functional relation to the initial estimate. The biproportionality (1) makes the biproportional problem a member of the second class; but by its property of 'nearness' to the initial matrix it also turns out to belong to the first.

In the prototype of one specific formulation the solution is a least-squares fit—a matrix which, among those satisfying the marginal constraints, deviates least by the sum-of-squares criterion from its base value: in input–output terms, that transactions matrix estimate for time 1 which, among those displaying prescribed intermediate output and input totals, is nearest in the Euclidean sense to the constant-coefficients estimate $\{l_{ij}(0)\, q_j(1)\}$. The least-squares estimate, however, possesses neither the property of nonnegativity nor that of the preservation of zero elements. Both these difficulties are surmounted by generalizing the least-squares model to a quadratic programme, but this—and the linear programming version of Matuszewski, Pitts and Sawyer[54] that is also considered—lose the property of the simple least-squares model that its solution may be expressed as an explicit function of the initial estimate—that is, that the problem belongs to the second category as well as to the first.

A second specification of the problem, due to Uribe, de Leeuw and Theil[73], seeks a matrix that minimizes a criterion (subject to the constraints) which, like distance criteria, is inspired by conservatism. Here the criterion is interpreted in terms of concepts of information theory, but not entirely convincingly. In any case, mathematical difficulties force the authors to resort to an approximate solution which is the same as that of the third formulation.

The third specific model is Friedlander's[32], in which (1) is replaced by the form

$$l_{ij}(1) = (x_i + y_j) l_{ij}(0) \quad (i = 1, ..., m; j = 1, ..., n). \tag{5}$$

A matrix estimated from (5) preserves zeros and there is a sense in which it is near to its base value. It is not, however, necessarily nonnegative. The biproportional estimation model is finally preferred. But the analysis of the Friedlander model turns out to be helpful in investigating the stochastic behaviour of biproportional estimates, for its solution gives the first variation of a biproportional solution in response to disturbances in the marginals $u_i(1)$ and $v_j(1)$.

The main burden of the argument up to this point has been that the biproportional estimation model possesses certain properties that seem desirable on *a priori* grounds and of which one or more are lacking in rival estimation models. It was also claimed that the biproportional model is capable of greatly augmenting the supply of useful input–output statistics. The results that have already been described show this to be so for years for which intermediate output and input data are available: for such years the biproportional model provides acceptable input–output matrix estimates while constant-coefficient estimates are liable to be widely at variance with the observed marginals. The next job is to show how biproportional estimates may in turn be employed to obtain estimates for years for which marginal data are lacking. We begin by considering the exponential projection $\{r_i^t s_j^t l_{ij}(0)\}$ as a possible estimate for a time $t > 1$: this projection has the 'natural' characteristic that the 'substitution' and 'fabrication' tendencies measured by the r_i's and s_j's continue over the interval $(1, t)$ to act as they were observed to act over the interval $(0, 1)$. It has, however, an unfortunate 'explosive' effect on the column sums of the projected matrix—i.e. on industries' projected ratios of intermediate to total input. It turns out, indeed, that there exists no projection of the form $\{f(r_i, s_j)\, l_{ij}(0)\}$ which both yields satisfactory total intermediate input ratios and fulfils certain other minimal *a priori* conditions. We finally adopt a projection in which intermediate input ratios are subjected to constraints but which otherwise retains much of the character of an exponential projection of the biproportional estimate.

Our chief concern has so far been with the biproportional model of temporal changes in input–output matrices. The excursion into alternative constrained matrix problems was necessary to eliminate rivals to the biproportional hypothesis as well as being useful in the analysis of the stochastic behaviour of biproportional estimates. We now turn to a problem that has nothing to do with input–output analysis, but whose solution by an oblique application of results for the biproportional model illustrates that model's versatility. The problem is to alter a given Markov matrix as little as is necessary for the Markov process defined by the new matrix to converge to a desired vector. Concretely, this 'Markov programming' model is applied to the problem of rescheduling a Markovian labour-training structure to produce a desired distribution of labour skills asymptotically.

Finally, the data-generating capacity of the biproportional approach is illustrated by presenting numerical input–output estimates and projections for 1960 and 1966 based on British data. We also work through illustrative examples for the training model and other subsidiary models whose theory has earlier been discussed.

4　How the book is arranged

In this quick review a good deal has been left out: we have tried only to sketch the overall shape of the book's main argument. In doing so we have, too, somewhat altered the order in which we reach our results. A comprehensive chapter-by-chapter summary is to be found in section 10 of Chapter 3. By then enough terms will have been defined and enough notation introduced to make a much more concise account possible.

The book is arranged in five parts. The first (Chapters 2 and 3) reviews past studies of the temporal behaviour of input–output coefficients, introduces the biproportional input–output estimation model against this background, describes the non-input–output empirical applications of the biproportional constrained matrix problem, and discusses other constrained matrix problems that have been proposed. The second part (Chapters 4 to 6) develops formal properties of the biproportional problem and stochastic variants of it. The third (Chapters 7 to 9) investigates further properties of the specifically input–output application of this model, including its implications for input–output projections. The fourth (Chapter 10) treats the Markov programming problem. The fifth (Chapter 11) translates the theoretical models into figures.

The emphasis that has been laid on overall conclusions and on the findings upon which these conclusions most critically rest does not mean that the book's main intention is polemical. The purpose of what follows is not, in the end, to show the superiority of the biproportional model over alternative models of input–output change. The fact is that this model has been and is being extensively used by empirical investigators both in input–output and in other fields of economics where phenomena are representable by nonnegative matrix functions of time. This fact alone calls for a thorough investigation of the formal traits of the model—beginning with the existence, uniqueness and sensitivity properties of the estimates it provides. It is this investigation which is undertaken.

Our conclusions, by and large, are encouraging. We are able to vindicate theoretically what until now has been justified only pragmatically. Having said as much, we shall from this point on make only infrequent references to the progress of the 'case for the model'.

5 SYMBOLISM

We follow Gale [22] in making no notational distinction between a vector x and its transpose. Whenever it is necessary to know which is intended the context makes it clear. There is some tendency to use the same letter to stand for different things in different parts of the book in an attempt to avoid too ornate, exotic or anti-conventional a notation. The letter i, for instance, is used both to denote the unit vector $(1 \ldots 1)$ and as an index of commodities, matrix rows, etc., but no cases of confusion arise. All the other notational conventions are either quite standard ones or are explained as they are adopted. A vertical bar $|$ is used to mark the ends of proofs and formal definitions.

CHAPTER 2

TEMPORAL CHANGES IN INPUT–OUTPUT COEFFICIENTS

1 THE ASSUMPTION OF TEMPORAL CONSTANCY

Characteristic of input–output analysis is some assumption of invariance of the (i, j)th input–output ratio with respect to changes in the jth output. Leontief himself[49] thought of such changes as virtual changes; the statement was: had the jth output been different, the (i, j)th input–output ratio would have been the same. They were not to be thought of as changes through time. Much of Part II of [49] is in fact devoted to justifying a specific hypothesis on temporal changes in input–output coefficients—a hypothesis which will be discussed at some length in Chapter 3. But no attempt was made to estimate numerical values of the parameters entering this hypothesis.

What use, then, was an observed input–output matrix? The virtual invariance hypothesis justified its application only in answering questions about alternative universes. And the hypothesis on coefficients' behaviour through time was not available in numerical form.

It seemed, however, a small and inoffensive step from an assumption of coefficients' invariance with respect to virtual changes in outputs to one of their invariance with respect to changes in outputs occurring within short periods of time. Such a hypothesis—of temporal as well as virtual invariance—would at once make input–output a powerful tool for the formation of policy, enabling one, for instance, to derive gross outputs from short-run predictions of final demands. The prospect of confirming it was so attractive as to inspire repeated empirical tests— tests which form almost the entire body of published empirical work on input–output theory from Leontief's publication in 1941 of *The Structure of American Economy* [49] until that of Arrow and Hoffenberg's *A Time Series Analysis of Interindustry Demands* in 1959 [3].

2 TESTS OF CONSTANCY

Tests of the constancy of input–output ratios through time have been of two main types. The first type of test uses a matrix of input–output ratios observed at one date to calculate gross outputs from the final demands of another date. The deviations of these estimates of gross outputs from directly observed figures are then compared with corresponding deviations in various 'naive' gross output estimates arrived at without making use of input–output methods. The second type of test of constancy is by the direct comparison of input–output ratios observed at different times. These comparisons are sometimes made for whole matrices, but more often for selected coefficients. The coefficients whose constancy is tested are in almost all cases the constant-price, 'technical' coefficients considered by Leontief. Little empirical work has been done to test Klein's suggestion[45] of constant current-price input–output coefficients arising from exponential production functions that allow substitution between physical inputs. From now on our discussion will be confined to constant-price coefficients, or else the contrary will be stated.

Christ[17], Arrow and Hoffenberg[3] and Chenery and Clark[16] have given detailed accounts of tests of the first type. It will be enough for our purpose to describe their main features. The 'naive' estimates of gross outputs that figure in these tests were made variously: (i) by multiple regressions of outputs on G.N.P. and time, (ii) by assuming a constant ratio between each industry's output and G.N.P. (the 'G.N.P. blowup' method), or (iii) by assuming a constant ratio between each industry's output and the final demand placed upon it (the 'final demand blowup' method). Leontief[49], Selma Arrow[4] and Hoffenberg (reported in [16]) carried out this type of test on backward predictions based on Leontief's 1939 U.S. matrix. Barnett[5] tested Cornfield, Evans and Hoffenberg's prediction of 1950 outputs from the same matrix [18] against predictions by the alternative methods (i), (ii), (iii), in each case using Cornfield, Evans and Hoffenberg's predicted figures for 1950s final demands. In these tests multiple regression estimates did better than input–output ones, which in turn came out about as well as final demand blowups and better than G.N.P. blowups. The multiple regression estimates were the only ones to make use of a time variable.

Hatanaka[38] has made more elaborate tests of the same type on the much more detailed and reliable 1947 U.S. matrix. He focused his tests on the coefficients whose stability was most crucial for the accuracy of the input–output projections, distinguished between short-run and long-run projections, and carried out statistical significance tests on the differences between errors in the various predictions of individual industries' gross outputs. His input–output projections were superior to projections from multiple regressions at a 25 % significance level in both short-run and long-run tests, but paradoxically showed no clear margin of superiority over alternative naive projections that did not employ a time variable. Examining the pattern over time of errors in the input–output projections revealed significant trends which implied the presence of trends in the coefficients.

Others [54, 70] have tested the stability of coefficients by the method of which Hatanaka's is the most elaborate application. In these more recent studies, however, the tests by conditional gross output prediction have usually been routine exercises to confirm the existence of temporal change as a preliminary to the proposal of some way of measuring or correcting for this change.

Chenery and Clark[16] also give a full account of tests of temporal invariance made by comparison of coefficients directly observed at different times. Leontief in the U.S.[49] and official statisticians in Japan (see [16]) compiled frequency distributions of observed coefficient changes. Helzner[39] examined variations in input coefficients in the U.S. steel industry over a nine-year period for 'significance' in the sense that a constancy assumption for these coefficients would lead to impermissible errors in gross output estimates. Phillips[61] found greater inter-firm than temporal variation in selected input coefficients in the U.S. ball and roller bearing industry. Cameron[13], using a very fine industrial classification for Australia, found considerable stability over five- to ten-year periods in coefficients other than those of fuel inputs, and concluded that much observed coefficient variation could be attributed to changes in the nature of the product of the using industry.

Sevaldson[64] suggested that a change in a coefficient over time could be additively decomposed into: a technological change; changes related to the output level of the using industry, prices, and other economic variables; changes due to changes in the product-mix of the using industry; changes related to observation errors; and residual changes. Figures for the Norwegian cork industry appeared to show volume coefficients to be more stable than value ones, contrary to the suggestion of Klein[45]; variations over time to be mainly but not entirely due to observation errors; and variations between establishments to be partly due to variations in the nature of the product. Figures for the Norwegian mechanical woodpulp industry showed significant movements over a seven-year period in the coefficients of some establishments.

Collectively, the tests we have described provide convincing evidence against an assumption of temporal constancy in observed input–output ratios.

Nerlove[56] has justly criticized the first type of test of constancy, that based on comparative gross output estimates, on the grounds that it provides no specific alternative to the invariance hypothesis which it sets out to, and in many cases does, refute. We are thus left with no way of making use of our knowledge of the structure of interindustry demand in one year to make gross output estimates for other years. Much the same goes for the studies based on the inspection of time-series of coefficients. They give, at most, qualitative indications of the factors which, through time, affect coefficients' values. They do, however, yield the information, encouraging from one point of view, that variation in product-mix is a major determining factor of the changes in observed coefficients. This implies that one could in principle get rid of some temporal variation without amending any assumption of the model, but merely by diaggregating the industrial classification on which observations are made. In practice, however, it may be harder to carry out the necessary refinement of the classification than to introduce dummy explanatory variables to represent changing product-mixes. This is the method used by Arrow and Hoffenberg in the major study which will be described in the next section.

3 TIME SERIES ANALYSES

A sequence of thirteen comparable, reliable, medium-sized tables puts the Netherlands among the countries richest in data for the study of temporal changes in input–output ratios. But the series is for consecutive years (those of 1948–60) and too short in span for an econometric analysis of the causal structure generating the ratios. The data have been exhaustively explored by Tilanus in a recent book [70]. Tilanus has the practical object of finding a way to *correct for* coefficient changes in making predictions of gross outputs conditionally on predictions of final demands. Before proposing a way of making this correction he goes through two classical exercises in the description of coefficient changes. One is a set of conditional gross output forecasts of the usual kind. The second, a standard essay in econometric method, consists of the linear regression of individual coefficients on a time variable, and of tests for significance and autocorrelation. Tilanus's analysis is in terms of the 'aggregate production coefficients' obtained by dividing the (i,j)th transaction by the total of *all* industries' gross outputs: like ordinary input–output coefficients, aggregate production coefficients make flows of widely different sizes comparable, but unlike input–output coefficients they are large if and only if the corresponding flows are large in the economy. For more than half the regressed aggregate production coefficients, the t-statistics for the estimated coefficients of time were significant at 5 %. However, for most equations estimated disturbances showed evidence of positive autocorrelation: the median von Neumann ratio was less than 1·5. This throws some doubt on the meaning of the t-statistics.

Arrow, Hoffenberg and others' 1959 *A Time Series Analysis of Interindustry Demands* [3] is the first attempt at a precise quantitative description of the causes of change in input–output coefficients. Inadequacy of data forced the authors to adopt an indirect approach to the problem. At the time of their study there existed only four input–output tables for the U.S., spread out over time. Their industrial classifications were not comparable, and the prewar tables unreliable into the bargain.

Even a time-series of four reliable, comparable tables might not have done: for the number of explanatory variables that should be included on theoretical grounds would not have left adequate degrees of freedom.

Such problems of data scarcity are typical. Most countries, indeed, are much worse off than the U.S. Even when a country has more than one matrix compiled on comparable industrial classifications, other sources of incomparability remain. One table may be expressed in purchasers' prices, another in producer's prices; the treatment of indirect taxes may vary from one table to another; and so on. The first of these difficulties stands in the way of a comparative study of, for instance, the 1948 [65] and 1954 [72] British tables (see [26]). In general, we may attribute the shortage of thorough-going econometric studies in input–output analysis as much to the minuscule supply of usable data as to a rigid attachment to the constancy theory. Chenery and Clark [16] review the meagre interindustrial data availabilities of nine countries and Latin America.

Arrow and Hoffenberg [3] bypassed this problem by using Klein's approach [45] to estimating coefficients. Klein, assuming coefficients to be constant subject to added random disturbances and putting the (i, j)th transaction $z_{ij}(t) = l_{ij}q_j(t) + \epsilon_{ji}(t)$, proposed estimating the exactly identified system

$$q_i(t) - f_i(t) = u_i(t) = \sum_j l_{ij}q_j(t) + \sum_j \epsilon_{ij}(t)$$

from time series for the $q_j(t)$ and final demands $f_i(t)$. Arrow and Hoffenberg, more generally, consider the implications of hypotheses on *changes* in the coefficients of the ith row for the total intermediate output of i, given gross outputs. Confronting this estimate of $u_i(t)$ with its known value could, in principle, yield estimates of the parameters in the change hypotheses. Clearly, however, the number of parameters to be estimated in such a regression was far greater than the number in the regression of a single input–output transaction on the variables affecting it through time. The procedure therefore depended on there being available a very long time series of intermediate and gross outputs. Arrow and Hoffenberg were able to derive from available statistics a series running from 1929 to 1950. This could not be done for most countries. The coefficients whose postulated changes were to be estimated were those of the 200-order U.S. table for 1947.

The authors considered two models of individual coefficient changes. In each of these a coefficient was made a linear function of several explanatory variables subject to an added error term. Data did not allow the first model to be estimated, but it is worth sketching for its theoretical interest. For an embodied input i, the quantity of i used in industry j was regarded as essentially proportional to the gross output of j, but as increasing with the rate of increase of that output because of the waste accompanying rapid adjustments of scale. A non-embodied input, on the other hand, might be economized by the installation of better capital equipment, but a certain quantity depending on the vintage composition of existing stock was needed to maintain this stock, independently of the level of output. These considerations made the quantity of a non-embodied input a nonhomogeneous linear function of the output of j. Both types of input were made to depend on a time variable which served, among other things, as an indicator of the possibly changing product-mix of industry j.

In Arrow and Hoffenberg's second model a typical transaction is made to depend upon: real disposable income; the ratio of defense expenditure to G.N.P.; a time variable; and the excess, if any, of the year's output of j over its previous peak value, divided by the year's output. Higher disposable incomes may lead to a shift in j's product-mix towards better-quality products which are typically more fabricated and so characterized by smaller intermediate input coefficients. The observation period covered the second world war: the defense-G.N.P. ratio serves to account for product-mix changes that gave increased weight to war-products. The time-variable should capture changes in technology, and changes in consumer tastes which exert an effect upon product-mixes. The last variable accounts for a learning effect similar to the one represented in the first model. Relative prices are left out as explanatory variables for the sake of the resulting gain in degrees of freedom. Their omission is defended on the grounds that (i) production methods are insensitive to price changes in the short run, (ii) the generally vertical aggregation in the industrial classification of the 1947 table reduces the possibility of price-induced substitutions among the aggregated commodities, (iii) physical controls made price motivations irrelevant during the war period, and (iv) some of the factors that give rise to relative price changes are partially represented by explanatory variables that are included.

Arrow and Hoffenberg attempted to estimate the balance equations for only a small number of inputs. The equations they chose were for inputs whose coefficients in a large number of industries could be set *a priori* equal to zero, leaving manageable numbers of parameters to be estimated. Other requirements were also imposed on equations retained for estimation. Only four finally remained. These four were estimated simultaneously by the limited information maximum likelihood method. A set of non-interdependent predetermined variables was sought out of which enough members could be excluded from each fitted equation to achieve identification. Such a set could not, however, be found. From an initial list of 19 predetermined variables, no large enough subset of statistically independent variables could be drawn to identify two of the four equations, and a number of the estimated relationships gave coefficient values that were either negative or implausibly large at one or more points of time.

Arrow and Hoffenberg now re-estimated the equations by a linear programme that minimized a sum of absolute deviations subject to *a priori* restrictions on estimated input–output coefficients, but they were able to attach little reliability to the results of this procedure. Finally, they estimated reduced forms in which 'constant-coefficient residuals'— the deviations of actual intermediate outputs from those implied by constant input–output coefficients—were regressed on various sets of pre-determined variables. On the assumption of an unchanged underlying causal structure, these regressions would allow the prediction of gross outputs from given predictions of final demands and of the predetermined variables. The estimated regressions showed a very close fit. But the structural constancy condition, together with other drawbacks, limits the usefulness of the reduced-form forecasting approach. These objections will be discussed in Chapter 9.

Arrow and Hoffenberg's painstaking and sophisticated study failed, then, in its main, explanatory purpose. Nerlove[56] suggests that quadratic programming techniques not available at the time of the study might make it possible to compute successful estimates of Arrow and Hoffenberg's structural equations by an application of Theil's two-stage least-squares method with restrictions on the estimated input–output coefficients. But these equations would provide explanations of changes and hence predictions of changes in only a small area of the input–output matrix. This would not be enough for the solution of the overall planning problems to which input–output is so well theoretically suited. In any case, the labour needed to process official statistics for the implementation of a model of the Arrow and Hoffenberg type is too formidable to promise the widespread application of these methods. In the long run there seems to be no good alternative to employing either an Arrow and Hoffenberg-like approach or a non-econometric method depending on industrial engineering information. But in the short run there is a need for a snappier way of making use of existing data in the analysis of coefficient changes, a method intermediate in sophistication between the qualitative studies described in section 2 and a fully-fledged simultaneous equations estimation procedure. Such methods are out-lined in the next chapter. Like Arrow and Hoffenberg's they exploit intermediate output data: the most promising of them—the bipropor-tional input–output estimation model—makes use of both intermediate output and intermediate input data to fit a temporal relation of the form originally postulated by Leontief.

CHAPTER 3

CONSTRAINED MATRIX PROBLEMS AND THEIR APPLICATIONS

1 INTRODUCTION

Let us call a *constrained matrix problem* the problem of determining a matrix whose rows and columns are to sum to prescribed magnitudes. Such a problem is trivial as it stands. We shall only be concerned with versions of it that have been specialized in three ways. (i) The first is to restrict the given matrix to be nonnegative. (ii) The second is to restrict the prescribed row and column sums to be nonnegative. (iii) The third is a determining principle which may take one of two forms. (*a*) One is to specify a simple form giving a solution matrix as a function of some given matrix. (*b*) The other is to require that a solution matrix minimize a criterion, e.g. be nearest to a given matrix, in the class of matrices satisfying the row and column constraints. Sometimes, we shall see, (*a*) and (*b*) come to the same thing.

As far as one can tell interest in constrained matrix problems was first aroused by a statistical application considered by Deming and Stephan[23]. In this application, the given matrix is a sample estimate of a contingency matrix; the prescribed row and column sums are known population frequencies of the row- and column-represented attributes. The problem is then to improve on the sample estimate by adjusting it to the known row and column sums of the population frequency matrix. In this application, the appeal of a condition ensuring that a solution be close to the given matrix is clear.

In [32] Friedlander demonstrates important properties of a constrained matrix problem proposed by Deming and Stephan as a possible formalization of the contingency-matrix estimation problem. This constrained matrix problem, which we shall call the 'Friedlander problem', will be outlined in section 7 of this chapter. Friedlander also gives a review of the statistical literature that sprang from Deming and Stephan's paper.

We note in passing that Deming and Stephan also proposed a method of adjustment of the initial estimate to its known marginals which is equivalent to the biproportional constrained matrix problem that is to be our main concern. But Friedlander does not go into this problem.

2 INPUT–OUTPUT ESTIMATION AS A CONSTRAINED MATRIX PROBLEM

We have seen how the study of changes in input–output relations through time has been frustrated by lack of data, that is, by lack of time-series of comparable input–output coefficient matrices. The Cambridge Growth Project encountered this obstacle in its earliest stages. A central purpose of the project was to estimate a detailed and comprehensive social accounting matrix for 1960[25]. An input–output transactions table forms an important part of such a matrix. But no directly observed input–output matrix was available for 1960, nor for any year close enough to 1960 for the coefficients to serve as acceptable approximations. The most recent available matrix was for 1954[71]: an assumption of constancy over the six-year period to 1960 could not be admitted. Nor did earlier matrices exist which, together with that for 1954, formed a comparable time-series that could be extrapolated to 1960.

This was the situation which prompted Stone's suggestion[24] of making an estimate of a matrix for 1960 not obtained by direct observation of transactions or coefficients. Those data were lacking. On the other hand, there were available a matrix for a recent year, 1954, and figures for industries' intermediate output and intermediate input totals in 1960, i.e. for the row and column sums of that year's transactions matrix. These marginal figures could be derived from official statistics for 1960's gross outputs, final demands, imports and values added by industries[26].

The problem of estimating a transactions matrix for 1960 could be regarded as one of adjusting some naive estimate based on 1954 data to fit 1960's known row and column sums. Specifically, a matrix of current-value transactions for 1960 could be naively estimated as that which would result from operating with 1954 input–output coefficients re-expressed in 1960 prices, at 1960's gross output levels.

But a constrained matrix approach could not itself provide a solution of another, related problem that faced the Growth Project—that of predicting the input–output matrix of a future year for which marginal figures could not be known. But the 1954 coefficient matrix together with the estimate of 1960's coefficient matrix obtained from the fitted estimate of 1960's transactions matrix would form a time-series of comparable coefficient matrices which might be extrapolated to provide forecasts.

The data situation that confronted the Cambridge Growth Project is widespread. Many countries possess either a single input–output matrix or a series of matrices whose non-comparability makes it difficult to discern time-trends in the coefficients and, *a fortiori*, to estimate the matrix of a no-observation year. But whenever such a country possesses reliable figures for industries' gross and net outputs and for final demands, constrained matrix methods offer a possibility of estimating input–output matrices for the years to which these marginal data pertain.

3 THE RAS OR BIPROPORTIONAL INPUT–OUTPUT MODEL

Henceforth we shall let L denote the value of an observed input–output coefficient matrix. The letter L (for Leontief) is used because the customary A is reserved for another use. It is assumed that the observation L is made without error: we have in mind input–output data compiled directly from census of production data. q, u, v will denote observed values, at a second date, of, respectively, gross outputs, total intermediate outputs and total intermediate inputs, on some common industrial classification. The consequences of errors of observation in these variables will be considered at length in Chapter 5. u, v will be used to denote different variables later, but no cases of confusion will arise. For the present, we take for granted a one-to-one correspondence between commodities and industries (but see section 6 of this chapter). The exact meanings we attach to the terms 'input–output coefficient', 'gross output', etc., will be explained in the next paragraph. The dates of observation respectively of L and of q, u, v will be denoted by the values 0, 1 of a time variable t. Thus in the Cambridge application, 1954 is mapped into $t = 0$, 1960 into $t = 1$. In most of our work it will be convenient to regard L as expressed in the prices of $t = 1$. A notation such as $L(0, 1)$ displaying time arguments for both the date of the matrix and the date of the prices in which it is expressed would be more explicit than the simple notation L. But it would be too cumbersome. Only in Chapter 7, which is explicitly concerned with price variation, shall we change our understanding about the meaning of the symbol L.

The coefficient l_{ij} is to be understood as including absorptions of imported amounts as well as of domestically produced amounts of good i per unit gross output of commodity j. These imported inputs, however, exclude 'noncompetitive' imports in the sense of goods that cannot be produced in the home country (see [24]). This amounts to saying that i only runs over a set of domestically producible commodities, or alternatively that no primary inputs figure in the input–output matrix. The gross output q_j measures the domestic output alone of commodity j and excludes imported amounts. These are standard conventions and are the most appropriate for the interpretation of the l_{ij} as technological parameters. Throughout, we shall also follow input–output convention in assuming that

$$L \geqq 0.$$

Theoretically, this assumption is generally valid only in the absence of by- or other joint-production. Empirically, however, it is justified by the fact that at medium levels of aggregation, such as the 31-commodity classification of the Cambridge Growth Project, 'negative inputs' representing these phenomena are usually exceeded by positive inputs in the same cells.

u, v are the vectors of the row and column sums of the transactions table $\{l_{ij}(1) q_j\}$ and so include competitive imports used in producing domestic outputs. The elements of u, therefore, are properly intermediate 'supplies' or 'expenditures' rather than 'outputs': but we shall not observe this distinction when it is not essential.

Throughout, we shall denote the diagonal matrix having the vector x on its main diagonal by $\langle x \rangle$. If $x = (x_1, ..., x_m)$ then

$$\langle x \rangle = \begin{bmatrix} x_1 & 0 & \cdots & 0 \\ 0 & x_2 & \cdots & 0 \\ \cdot & \cdot & & \cdot \\ \cdot & \cdot & & \cdot \\ \cdot & \cdot & & \cdot \\ 0 & 0 & \cdots & x_m \end{bmatrix}.$$

In the above notation, the constant-coefficients estimate of the transactions matrix at $t = 1$ is $L\langle q \rangle$. Stone's constrained matrix problem is to adjust $L\langle q \rangle$ in such a way that its row and column sums become equal to u, v. The fitted matrix will be taken as the new estimate of the transactions matrix for $t = 1$.

Let us denote the coefficient matrix for $t = 1$ by $L(1)$. Stone assumes that $L(1)$ is related to L by the biproportionality

$$L(1) = \langle r \rangle L \langle s \rangle, \tag{1}$$

as well as that $\qquad\qquad L(1) \geqq 0,$

and he requires his estimate of $L(1)$, L^* say, also to be nonnegative and of the form shown in (1). But the solution of the constrained matrix problem is to be the estimate of the transactions matrix at $t = 1$ and should therefore equal $L^*\langle q \rangle$. Hence it must have the form

$$L^*\langle q \rangle = (\langle r \rangle L \langle s \rangle) \langle q \rangle = \langle r \rangle (L \langle q \rangle) \langle s \rangle, \tag{2}$$

and of course $\qquad\qquad L^*\langle q \rangle \geqq 0.$

We have committed another notational impropriety in omitting from L^* the time argument 1. But the asterisk reminds us that L^* is an estimate; and it is always for $t = 1$ that an estimate is made.

We are now faced with a constrained matrix problem specialized in all of the three ways listed in section 1. (i) and (ii), the nonnegativity of the given matrix $L\langle q \rangle$ and of the prescribed row and column sums u, v, follow from the economic nature of the case. (iii) (*a*) follows from the simple functional relationship of biproportionality holding between the given matrix $L\langle q \rangle$ and a solution of the constrained matrix problem: this relationship is shown in expression (2) for a solution. In addition to the restrictions (i), (ii), (iii), it is required that a solution be non-negative. Given the nonnegative matrix $L\langle q \rangle$, then, our problem is to find another nonnegative matrix $\langle r \rangle (L\langle q \rangle)\langle s \rangle$ with prescribed non-negative row and column sums u, v. Any problem of this mathematical form will henceforth be called a *biproportional constrained matrix problem*, a *biproportional matrix problem*, or simply a *biproportional problem*. There is no need for the 'initial estimate' to be of the form $L\langle q \rangle$, that is, to be a constant-coefficients one. Nor, indeed, need a biproportional problem have anything at all to do with input–output. In this book, however, it usually does. When this is so, it will often be referred to alternatively as an 'RAS' problem.

We note that Stone's requirement $L^* \geq 0$ that the estimated input–output matrix be nonnegative is more strongly founded than the corresponding assumption for the observed matrix L, for without it the estimation model would be capable of yielding negative cell-values that, on *a priori* grounds, could not be interpreted as joint-production phenomena.

It will be shown in section 3 of Chapter 4 that if a matrix $L(1)$ is non-negative and of the form $\langle r \rangle L \langle s \rangle$ then r and s may always be chosen to be nonnegative. The (i, j)th element of the matrix equation (1) may then be written

$$l_{ij}(1) = r_i s_j l_{ij},$$

with

$$r_i, s_j \geq 0.$$

Stone interprets r_i as a measure of the extent to which, during the time-interval $(0, 1)$, the input i has substituted for other inputs—or has been substituted by them. r_i's independence of j implies that this substitution effect is uniform over using industries, in the sense that it induces proportional changes in all industries' coefficients of input of i. s_j is interpreted as a measure of a 'fabrication effect' in the production of commodity j—the extent to which the industry that produces j has decreased —or increased—its consumption of intermediate inputs per unit of gross output. s_j's independence of i implies that this effect induces proportional changes in every one of industry j's input coefficients.

It is worth emphasizing that the substitution and fabrication effects measured by the r_i's and s_j's are only partial effects. r_i, for instance, shows what would have happened to l_{ij} if the j-producing industry had been subject to no fabrication effect, i.e. if s_j had been equal to 1. Conversely, equality of say the total intermediate ratios $\sum_i l_{ij}$ and $\sum_i l_{ij}(1)$ at times 0 and 1 does not imply the absence of a fabrication effect on industry j. A tendency to increase the degree of fabrication ($s_j < 1$), for instance, might have been offset by a tendency throughout the economy to substitute-in certain goods which bulked large in j's input structure.

It is easily seen that

$$\langle r \rangle L \langle s \rangle = \langle \lambda r \rangle L \langle \lambda^{-1} s \rangle \tag{3}$$

for any nonzero scalar λ. The arbitrariness of λ means that one may not interpret certain values of r_i as indicating substitution-in (e.g. those greater than one) and others as indicating substitution-out, until one has applied some normalization itself having an appropriate economic meaning. Otherwise, Stone's substitution-fabrication interpretations attach only to relative values of the r_i's and s_j's.

To overcome this problem Paelinck [60] has proposed the formula

$$\rho_i = \frac{r_i i l^i}{r l^i},$$

where i is the unit vector and l^i the ith column of L, as a measure of the substitution effect along the ith row. ρ_i has the properties that (i) it is independent of the normalization of (r, s), (ii) it increases with r_i. The formula for ρ_i may be rewritten as

$$(r_i s_i) \Big/ \left(\frac{r l^i s_i}{i l^i} \right),$$

in which the divisor is the ratio of the ith industry's intermediate input ratios in the two periods. When the iterative method of solving biproportional problems has been described, this ratio will be recognized as the first-round multiplier of the ith column in a solution process that begins by adjusting columns. It may be thought of as a first approximation to s_i. Denoting it by s_i^1, we may write ρ_i, finally, as

$$\rho_i = r_i \left(\frac{s_i}{s_i^1} \right).$$

The arbitrariness of λ in (3) seems at first sight to rule out an answer to the question: do the row effects measured by the r's or the column effects measured by the s's make a larger contribution to the change from L to $\langle r \rangle L \langle s \rangle$? A natural approach is to compare the Euclidean distances of $\langle r \rangle L$ and $L \langle s \rangle$ from $\langle r \rangle L \langle s \rangle$; but it is clear that for large enough λ, $\langle \lambda r \rangle L$ can always be made more remote than $L \langle \lambda^{-1} s \rangle$. This problem may be overcome by making use of an angular type of distance function, e.g. by first normalizing each of $\langle r \rangle L$, $L \langle s \rangle$ and $\langle r \rangle L \langle s \rangle$ to be points on the simplex, and only then making the above comparison of Euclidean distances.

The hypothesis that changing input–output coefficients obey a relationship of the form (1) was first made by Leontief in [49]. His interpretation differs slightly from Stone's. r_i is regarded as a measure of the increased productivity of i in all uses. s_j is regarded as a measure of the joint effect of increased 'productivity' in industry j—i.e. increased efficiency in the use of all its intermediate inputs—and of a decrease in its rate of investment—i.e. in the extent to which its outlay on all inputs exceeds the value of its gross output. Neisser[55] sums up Leontief's interpretation as follows:

Any economies occurring (*a*) in a given industry or (*b*) in the use of some equipment good or material in production are considered as affecting *proportionally* all coefficients of production in the industry in which the good is (*a*) produced or (*b*) used productively...

Defining savings and investment in a gross fashion, as an excess of current receipts in an industry over, or their falling short of, the industry's total current outlay, it is assumed that investment increases *proportionally* all outlay items of a given industry...

There is nothing absurd about the idea that earlier capital formation may exert proportionate productivity effects on different intermediate inputs. But the assumption of this proportionality over all an industry's intermediate inputs in the operation of the contemporaneous investment effect described by Neisser seems very implausible. It is moreover unnecessary, as its object, to justify the assumption of proportional variation of all j's intermediate input coefficients in response to productivity changes in j and contemporaneous investment in j taken together, may be achieved instead by assuming that investment outlays are confined to primary inputs, so that there is no investment effect on intermediate input coefficients. This assumption still introduces some error, as certain intermediate input requirements may in fact be increased with capital formation, and the failure of the hypothesis (1) to account for such distortions in input structure will no doubt be revealed by empirical tests. But it does less violence to reality than Leontief's and accomplishes as much.

Gorman has pointed out [36] that changes of type (1) in process coefficients would affect relative prices: the relative price changes might in turn induce substitution of the changed processes by yet other processes. The coefficients of the processes finally adopted would themselves be related as in (1) to the original coefficients provided that industries' production functions are of the constant elasticity of substitution type[2], viz.

$$q_j = (\sum_i c_{ij} z_{ij}^d)^{1/d} \quad \text{(all } j\text{)}, \tag{4}$$

where z_{ij} is the input of good i into industry j, the c_{ij} are constants, and $1/(1-d)$ is the common value of all elasticities of substitution. CES implies RAS: but only if the elasticity of substitution $1/(1-d)$ is constant not only for all pairs of inputs into a given industry, but also for all industries. The result depends upon producers' minimizing the costs of producing given outputs at given relative input prices. The row multipliers representing induced substitution effects are simple functions of the corresponding prices: they are proportional to the quantities p_i^{q-1}. Gorman proposes generalizing this formulation of the technology in a way that keeps the effects of price changes biproportional. The arguments of (4) are replaced by measures of the aggregate inputs of subsets of commodities; these aggregates of groups of inputs would be related to their components less restrictively than q_j is in (4), though still uniformly over using industries.

In a recent study of changes in Canadian input–output relations through time [53] Matuszewski, Pitts and Sawyer assume proportional trends in the elements of a row of the coefficient matrix, but make no analogous assumption about the elements of a column. The coefficient matrix they consider is L exclusive of the imported components of its elements; let us denote it by L_D. Such a domestic input–output matrix was observed in 1949; a naive estimate of the corresponding transactions matrix of 1956 based on assuming constant coefficients is adjusted to fit row sums observed in 1956, i.e. to intermediate absorptions of domestic outputs in that year, subject to the requirement that

$$L_D^* = \langle r \rangle L_D, \tag{5}$$

where L_D^* is the final estimate for 1956. The series L_D, L_D^* is now extrapolated to give estimates of input–output matrices for 1957 and 1958. Matuszewski, Pitts and Sawyer find that these estimates lead to substantially smaller errors in the estimates of those years' gross outputs given their final demands than do naive constant-coefficients estimates. But they question the realism of (5), recalling the observation of Stone [66] and Chenery and Clark [16] that changes in input–output matrices are characterized by substantial movements in a few elements and very small ones elsewhere. The point recalls the discussion in Chapter 1 in which we suggested that the biproportional hypothesis $L(1) = \langle r \rangle L \langle s \rangle$ is in some sense the least complex that can be accepted. The introduction of column-multipliers s into the simple proportional-row hypothesis (5) liberates the input–output estimate for time 1 from the objectionable rigidity to which Matuszewski, Pitts and Sawyer call attention. This is not to say that a biproportionality assumption does not have some other constraining effect that goes against our empirical knowledge of input–output change. That it in fact does so emerges from our account in the next section of Paelinck and Waelbroeck's Belgian tests. These tests show, however, that the resulting distortion is not widespread enough through the estimated matrix to undermine the usefulness of the biproportional hypotheses.

Matuszewski, Pitts and Sawyer also experiment with a variant of the above constrained matrix model in which the assumption yielding (5) is replaced by the corresponding assumption applied to the 'Leontief matrix':

$$I - L_D^* = \langle r \rangle (I - L_D). \tag{6}$$

In this case, the rows of the transactions analogue of $I - L_D^*$ are made to sum to the final demands met out of domestic production in 1956. (6) implies a uniform substitution effect r_i on all elements of row i but the diagonal one; and that, when for instance this substitution effect exceeds 1, the diagonal element should increase by a factor smaller than 1. These implications of (6) are not justified by the authors. But they find that predictions for 1957 and 1958 based on it show smaller errors than those based on (5). In both these proportional-row models a provisional estimate is adjusted to a single set of marginal constraints. 'Half-constrained' matrix models of this type will be discussed again in later chapters.

The same authors tried a third method of estimating interindustrial relations based on a different type of relation. Leontief's assumption of a proportionality between an input and the output of the using industry that possibly changes through time is replaced by an assumption of an unchanging but non-homogeneous relation between inputs and outputs, viz.:

$$q = \langle r \rangle L_D q + k + f_D. \tag{7}$$

Here L_D is some observed matrix of domestic input–output ratios, say that of time $t = 0$, r and k are vectors of constants and f_D is the vector of final demands met out of home production at time 1. r, k may be determined by subtracting from (7) the corresponding equation for time 0. This is clearly not a constrained matrix problem proper. But it makes first differences in intermediate sales depend on first differences in gross outputs in a way analogous to the dependence of the corresponding state variables in (5). Estimates for 1957 and 1958 based on (7) were slightly better than those based on (5), but less good than the ones based on (6).

Leontief's productivity interpretations of the r_i's and the s_j's are not in conflict with Stone's interpretations of them as measures of substitution and fabrication effects. Indeed putting the two interpretations together strengthens rather than weakens the case for a hypothesis (1). But this hypothesis is not to be judged only on its *a priori* merit, but also by empirical tests of the input–output coefficient estimates it yields. In the next section we shall describe such empirical tests in some detail. In the rest of this section we recapitulate the formal properties of bi-proportional estimates to which we have already drawn attention, and sum up the arguments for and against them.

First, a biproportional estimate L^* of $L(1)$ is a function of $m + n$ parameters of change r_i and s_j, when the matrix L is of order $m \times n$. In a loose sense this is as large a number of parameters as we could estimate from the $m+n$ row and column sum restrictions, so the method allows maximum flexibility in estimating changes in various elements of the matrix. From one point of view this is a virtue. It has the drawback, however, that so many parameters can be estimated only by imposing all the marginal restrictions, so that we are left with no degrees of freedom with which to assess the estimate L^* by confronting it with data not already 'used up' in the estimating procedure. We have already drawn attention in Chapter 1 to this disadvantage of the biproportional esti-mation model. We there suggested that the absence of measures of the statistical reliability of our estimates was to be preferred to the alterna-tive of adopting a hypothesis of input–output change even simpler than the biproportional one, (1): we have seen, for instance, that the simplistic proportional-row hypothesis of Matuszewski, Pitts and Sawyer has consequences which conflict with dependable views on coefficients' temporal behaviour. Measures of the statistical reliability of estimates of hypotheses in which we have little *a priori* belief are not worth much. In any case, even though we are without reliability measures for a biproportional estimate L^* we may still resort to testing this estimate against freshly gathered data. This is the approach of Paelinck and Waelbroeck's Belgian tests.

Secondly, by virtue of the hypothesis of biproportionality, L^* tends to show a rough and ready, 'structural' similarity to L. E.g. important items in industry j's input vector will remain important, at least in the absence of quite dramatic falls in their aggregate intermediate con-sumption. To this extent the hypothesis (1) is a conservative one, attri-buting inertia to the pattern of interindustrial relations. This view is also advanced by Bénard in a discussion of a different application of a biproportional constrained matrix model [7].

In particular, it is clear from (1) that zero elements of L are preserved in L^*. This is what we would generally want. If zero is the value at time 0 of the consumption of i in the production of j, this is likely to be because positive consumption is unthinkable, as the consumption of Railway Locomotives, etc., products in the Drink and Tobacco industry is un-thinkable. In such cases the appearance of positive elements in the $t = 1$ estimate would be embarrassing. In other cases, however, a recorded value of zero might be an approximation to a small positive value capable in principle of being substantially increased. In yet others, a radical technical change might turn positive at time 1 a coefficient that was truly zero at time 0. A way out of these two difficulties would be to substitute an arbitrarily small positive value in the zero-valued cell of the given matrix L whenever one suspected an instance of such cases. In this way the estimation method would, by an arbitrarily small distortion of observed data, be freed from its previous formal constraint and enabled in principle to estimate upward changes in the initially zero elements of L: such estimated changes, however, would almost always be small.

A strong *prima facie* case for the model of biproportional temporal change in input–output matrices has now been made. We have seen that a biproportional estimate fits all estimation year data whenever these consist only of the marginals of the transactions table; it is non-negative, by definition; it preserves zeros; and it is suitably conservative. There certainly exist infinitely many other estimates that share these properties. But the biproportional estimate stands out by the simple functional relationship that it bears to its predecessor: this relationship admits an interpretation that is economic, if a little wishful; and its simple form opens the way to the mathematical investigation of further properties of the model that we shall presently undertake.

4 TESTS OF THE BIPROPORTIONAL INPUT–OUTPUT MODEL

In [59] Paelinck and Waelbroeck describe tests of a biproportional estimate L^* of an input–output matrix $L(1)$ made by confronting L^* with a comparable direct estimate of $L(1)$. The data are for Belgium, and distinguish 21 industries. The values 0, 1 of t represent the years 1954 and 1959 respectively. The estimate L^* was computed by the standard method of iterative adjustments of rows and columns, discussed in detail in Chapter 4. A straightforward comparison of L^* with the direct estimate, which it will be convenient to denote as the true value $L(1)$ of the matrix, produced the frequency distribution of errors in coefficients

$$e_{ij} = l_{ij}^* - l_{ij}(1)$$

shown in the third column of the table below.

It ought to be pointed out that the 'direct' estimate of the 1959 matrix was not based on a full census of production, but was arrived at by the detailed extrapolation of the 1953 matrix 'sur la base des données statistiques disponibles et des avis donnés par des experts'. The biproportional estimate, then, is here tested against a standard estimate whose reliability is neither obvious from the nature of the statistics that it is drawn from, nor is otherwise supported by its authors. The 1953 matrix was compiled by Kirschen and Falleur [44] on a 51-order classification. It was aggregated before being extrapolated.

Inspection of the matrix's worst estimated cells revealed three important causes of error. (i) First, overaggregation in the industrial classification. This might take its effect through failing to distinguish either (*a*) different inputs, or (*b*) different using industries. In neither case could the resulting errors be attributed to the biproportional form of the estimated matrix. Aggregation errors arise in all input–output

Interval	Frequency of errors d_{ij}	Frequency of errors e_{ij}	Frequency of errors e'_{ij}
$(-\infty, -0.0095)$	7	3	1
$(-0.0095, -0.0085)$	1	2	—
$(-0.0085, -0.0075)$	4	2	3
$(-0.0075, -0.0065)$	1	1	1
$(-0.0065, -0.0055)$	5	1	1
$(-0.0055, -0.0045)$	5	6	4
$(-0.0045, -0.0035)$	4	2	3
$(-0.0035, -0.0025)$	9	10	6
$(-0.0025, -0.0015)$	23	9	29
$(-0.0015, -0.0005)$	26	36	23
$(-0.0005, 0.0005)$	132	117	128
$(0.0005, 0.0015)$	19	41	38
$(0.0015, 0.0025)$	12	14	16
$(0.0025, 0.0035)$	5	6	9
$(0.0035, 0.0045)$	—	4	2
$(0.0045, 0.0055)$	3	5	4
$(0.0055, 0.0065)$	2	1	1
$(0.0065, 0.0075)$	2	3	—
$(0.0075, 0.0085)$	—	1	—
$(0.0085, 0.0095)$	—	—	—
$(0.0095, \infty)$	10	6	—

Source: [59].

work. We have, for instance, seen in Chapter 2 that changes in the product-mix of an industry aggregated of establishments making different products are a major cause of variation in observed coefficients. (ii) Secondly, errors sprang from variations in substitution (or input productivity) effects over using industries in violation of the assumed uniformity of these effects. (iii) Thirdly, a false estimate of any one cell would force offsetting errors in other elements of its row and column, which in turn would do the same. Such errors would spread ripple-like over a wide area of the matrix.

A few cases of large proportional errors $e_{ij}/l_{ij}(1)$ may serve to illustrate these points. For Coal to Coke the proportional error was -8%. This error occurred because coal is in general a fuel input, which in Belgium was being substituted-out over 1954–9; but for the coke industry it is also a material input whose coefficient stayed about constant. This may be considered either as a case of (ii), i.e. of dependence of r_i upon j for $i =$ Coal, or of (i) (a), i.e. of failure to distinguish two in fact different inputs, coal for fuel and coal for coke.

For Metal-using to Coal the proportional error was 29%. This was due to a substantial substitution of metal for wooden pit-props in the coal industry in contrast to only a slight upward tendency in the economy-wide use of metal-using industries' products as a whole. This is an example of (i) (*a*), a failure to disaggregate inputs with different r's.

For Electricity to Building Materials $e_{ij}/l_{ij}(1)$ was 21 %. The delivery of electricity to Building Materials is chiefly to the cement sector of that industry. This sector stagnated over (1954, 1959) because of a rapid growth in brick house-building at the expense of large-scale building. The error arose from aggregation of using sectors (i) (*b*). In fact it was a 'good' error in that, in the long run, the cement sector is likely to grow in importance in the Belgian building materials industry.

For Coal to Electricity $e_{ij}/l_{ij}(1)$ was -9 %. The true coefficient was affected by government controls on the use of fuel in the electricity industry. Institutional factors were thus responsible for this instance of (ii).

Numerous errors were attributed by Paelinck and Waelbroeck to complex interdependencies among cell estimates induced by the nature of the biproportional model (iii). s_j's often played the role of compensatory factors for errors due to (i) or (ii) rather than measures of fabrication effects. But they did not always reach their corrective goal. For instance, s_j for Coal was high enough to be implausible as an estimate of a fabrication effect, yet too low to give a true estimate of the increase in metal inputs due to the switch to metal pit-props. Several errors in the Transport row, in particular, were ascribed by Paelinck and Waelbroeck to ripple effects springing from errors elsewhere in the table.

Paelinck and Waelbroeck noticed that many of the worst estimated elements might well have been identified in advance as ill-suited to estimation by a biproportional model. This is true, for instance, of the Coal to Coke and Coal to Electricity transactions discussed above. Moreover, if these elements could be removed from the estimation procedure, errors elsewhere in the table were to be expected to diminish. These considerations led Paelinck and Waelbroeck to carry out a second test, in which the coefficients in six unsuitable cells of L were assigned zero values in place of their observed positive ones, and in each such case the directly estimated value $l_{ij}(1) q_j$ of the corresponding transaction at time 1 was subtracted from each of the sums u_i, v_j. This move left the hypothesis (1) to apply only to *a priori* suitable cells, and meant that substituting back the values $l_{ij}(1)$ of the six special coefficients for the zero values estimated for them in L^* yielded a final matrix conforming with the originally given marginal data. In general, of course, no direct estimates $l_{ij}(1)$ are available for such special cells; separate side studies would be needed to obtain them. Several of Paelinck and Waelbroeck's six, however, relate to industries which in Britain and other western countries are dominated by public enterprises with relatively good data-collecting machinery.

The fourth column of the table shows the distribution of errors e'_{ij} in the estimate of $L(1)$ obtained in the second Belgian test by the 'quasi-biproportional' method just described. The expectation was fulfilled that the refinement of the biproportionality hypothesis would decrease secondary errors due to ripple effects. For the record, the second column of the table shows the distribution of errors in the naive estimate L of $L(1)$, i.e. the estimate that coefficients were unchanged between 1954 and 1959.

The Belgian tests leave the impression that the distortion induced by the rigidity of the biproportional assumption—by its rigid insistence on the uniformity of row- and column-effects—is mainly confined to a few elements. If these are singled out in advance for special treatment, encouragingly good estimates may be obtained. Paelinck and Wael-broeck conclude: 'L'emploi de cette procedure en conjonction avec un minimum d'information sur l'évolution des techniques donne des resultats [qui] sont assez bons pour qu'on puisse envisager des applica-tions pratiques.' This assessment, however, clearly depends on the judgment that the results of the tests are relevant to other countries and periods than those which they studied. This seems reasonable enough as long as the conclusion is not applied to developing countries in the course of 'changing technologies', not to long periods spanning techno-logies so distinct as to undermine the assumption of a stable 'structure' of input–output relations.

In [60], Paelinck and others tested the degree of biproportionality of input–output matrices relating to different countries rather than to different times. The tests were done on the French and Belgian matrices from the set of comparable 1959 matrices of the countries of the E.E.C. (estimated from non-comparable national tables by the Statistical Office of the European Communities in [57]). Each matrix was trans-formed into a biproportional estimate of the other. If the observed matrices—L_1, L_2, say—were indeed biproportional, products of corre-sponding multipliers in the two directions of estimation would be constant in the sense that

$$\langle {}^1r \rangle {}^2r = ki, \quad \langle {}^1s \rangle {}^2s = \frac{1}{k}\, i,$$

where $\langle {}^1r \rangle L_1 \langle {}^1s \rangle$ and $\langle {}^2r \rangle L_2 \langle {}^2s \rangle$ are the biproportional estimates of L_2 and L_1 respectively, k is some nonzero scalar, and i the unit vector. Hence deviations of the ${}^1r_i\,{}^2r_i$ from constancy measure deviations of the pair of interindustry structures from a relationship of biproportionality. Paelinck obtained a coefficient of variation of the ${}^1r_i\,{}^2r_i$ of 0·59, certainly too high to make the simple biproportionality hypothesis a satisfactory explanation of differences in national structures.

5   BIPROPORTIONAL MATRIX MODELS OF INTERNATIONAL TRADE

The second main field of economic application of the biproportional constrained matrix model has been the study of international trading relations. In [7] Bénard, on a suggestion of Waelbroeck, used the model to predict trade matrices from given predictions of the row and column sums of these matrices, i.e. of world sums of the exports and imports of individual countries or groups of countries. Bénard tested the model by comparing such biproportional estimates of past matrices with their observed values. In [74] Waelbroeck used the model in an attempt to reveal the 'Common Market effect', the distortion of trading patterns brought about by the lowering of internal tariffs and raising of external tariffs by the E.E.C. block.

Bénard [7] predicted countries' (or blocks of countries') export and import totals from estimates of relevant elasticities, published export plans and various other data. Clearly no trade matrix could be found to fit the marginals so obtained unless the sum of predicted export totals were equal to the sum of predicted import totals; Bénard describes alternative methods of reconciling provisional predictions of these marginals.

He argues for the stability that he claims a biproportional prediction ascribes to the structure of trade in terms of slow-to-change levels of industrialization and patterns of international specialization. The r_i's he interprets as (partial) export 'supply' indices and the s_j's as (partial) import 'demand' indices. In testing the model by retrospective estimation of observed past matrices Bénard confines it to the trade of industrialized capitalist countries, on the grounds that the exports of underdeveloped countries are unlike those of industrial countries in being largely supply-determined, and the exports and imports of socialist countries obey different laws from those of capitalist countries, being the outcome of planning decisions. In two tests he finds no proportional error of more than 20 % in the estimate of an element, save for two transactions very small in absolute amount (Japan to Common Market and Japan to Rest of Europe), and mean square proportional deviations of 7 % and 10 % when these two transactions are excluded. The results for the second test, carried out over the period 1953–60, are slightly worse than those for the first, made over 1953–7. The error in the estimate for 1960 for intra-Common Market trade is negative—as one would expect since by 1960 any effect of Common Market tariff policies had had time to make itself felt—but quite small. Waelbroeck deals more fully with this kind of measure of Common Market effect. Bénard concludes positively: 'Ainsi, à condition que les échanges atteignent un volume suffisamment important et que de sérieuses mutations institutionelles n'interviennent pas, la méthode R.A.S. est un procédé valable et commode de projection du réseau des échanges internationaux sur un horizon de dix à quinze ans.'

Bénard notes an interesting contrast between the biproportional prediction of a trade matrix and a related method discussed by Tims and Meyer zu Schlochtern [71] and by Waelbroeck [74]. This method begins by predicting countries' imports alone, next adjusts the initially given trade matrix to these column sums by diagonal post-multiplication, i.e. by multiplying each column by a scalar. This adjustment gives the final prediction, and thereby determines predictions of countries' total exports. It is essentially the method for forecasting input–output coefficient matrices that is proposed in Chapter 9 on the grounds that we can make sensible predictions of the economically meaningful column sums of such matrices, but not of their row sums. Formally, of course, it is also very similar to Matuszewski, Pitts and Sawyer's method of fitting an interindustry transactions matrix to a single set of marginals, in their case to given row totals by diagonal premultiplication.

Waelbroeck's [74] main object is to assess the distorting effect of Common Market policies on world trade by comparing with the actual trading matrix of some year of the Common Market's existence, a 'comparison matrix' or extrapolation to that year of a pre-Common Market time-series of corresponding matrices. This aim was incidental to Bénard's main purpose. Waelbroeck criticizes methods of forming comparison matrices that have been proposed. It does not make sense, for instance, simply to compare the ratio of intra-Market to total Market trade in two appropriate years unless one would expect all row and column totals to have varied proportionally in the absence of the Treaty of Rome. Nor is it correct to assume, in constructing a comparison matrix, that each country's import pattern (the proportion in which its imports are provided by various countries) would have remained fixed. Such a rule implies catastrophe for any one country that increases its import total, as it can never increase its 'market shares' in other countries. A third method, proposed by Lamfalussy [47], obtains indices of various countries' market shares in the non-Common Market world over an appropriate span of time, then to get a comparison matrix assumes that their shares in the Common Market countries would have changed in the same way had there been no Treaty of Rome. This method may give rise to an index-number adding-up problem.

Waelbroeck takes as his comparison matrix a matrix biproportional to an observed pre-Common Market one and with rows and columns summing to the observed marginals of the Common Market year. The uniform row-effects r_i are interpreted as Lamfalussy-like indices of countries' market shares; the uniformity of the column-effects s_j is justified by appeal to the stability of other countries' relative shares in a given country's market in response to whatever it is that tends to change that country's total imports. The constrained matrix approach, it is worth noticing, yields no measure of the trade-creating effect of the Common Market as distinct from its trade-deforming effect.

His results show a slight Common Market effect as from 1951–2 to 1959–60, i.e. a negative error in the estimate of 1959–60 intra-Market transactions, but one which is smaller than other trade-deformations, e.g. that which shows itself in a negative error in the estimate of American exports to certain countries and is due to their decolonization and to American aid to them during the period. From 1960 to 1962 a Common Market effect is shown for certain classes of manufactured goods whose internal Common Market tariffs were effectively reduced between those dates. Waelbroeck concludes that the estimates establish a definite Common Market effect but not a startling one. Slighter 'E.F.T.A.' effects are observed.

Kouevi[46] reports an empirical investigation that generalizes Waelbroeck's, tracing the time profiles of the ratios of observed trade flows to the elements of 'comparison matrices' given by a biproportional model.

6 BIPROPORTIONAL METHODS FOR MAKE MATRICES AND MARKOV MATRICES

As well as for the estimation of input–output matrices the Cambridge Growth Project has employed the biproportional matrix-adjustment model in another interindustrial problem, that of estimating 'make' matrices showing industries' production of non-principal products. A detailed account of this work appears in [26]. Let us for the time being define an 'industry' as the set of establishments whose principal products are a certain commodity (more strictly, belong to a certain group of commodities). Reasons are advanced in [26] for placing more confidence in predictions of input–output coefficients showing absorptions of commodities by producers of single commodities—i.e. of the coefficients defined by Leontief in [49]—than ones of coefficients showing absorptions of commodities by mixed-product industries. It is, accordingly, a commodity input–commodity output matrix that the Cambridge Growth Project forecasts for its projection year 1966, and so it is forecasts of gross outputs of pure commodities rather than of industries that are obtained for that year. But forecasts of production functions in 1966 are, for reasons explained in [26], cast in terms of industries' outputs; hence in order to calculate the factor requirements for 1966's commodity outputs it is first necessary to transform these into industry outputs. For this a prediction of the 1966 make structure is needed. It is got by observing the make matrix of 1954, estimating one for 1958, then extrapolating from this series of two matrices a 1966 matrix consistent with given commodity gross outputs for that year. The method of extrapolation will be described in Chapter 9.

For 1958 it is possible to obtain estimates of both industry and commodity gross outputs. These estimates provide marginals for an estimate of 1958's make matrix. The estimate is a biproportional one, i.e.

$$M^* = \langle r \rangle M \langle s \rangle, \tag{8}$$

where M and M^* are respectively the make matrices observed at 1954 and estimated for 1958. The (i, j)th element of M shows the production in industry i of commodity j in 1954, and that of M^* has a corresponding meaning. r_i is interpreted as the extent to which, over the period 1954–60, the ith industry uniformly increased its domination of all lines of production. It may be regarded as partly a measure of processes of vertical and horizontal integration by industry i. s_j is interpreted as the extent to which the jth commodity uniformly assumed increased importance in the make patterns of all industries—a measure, that is, of processes of integration *of* the production of commodity j. An example of such an effect would be a trend in many industries towards carrying out their own packaging. These interpretations, however, were not so much the motivation for adopting a biproportionality assumption (8), but rather were *ex post* justifications of a convenient statistical fitting procedure giving a result which kept the 'look' of the observed matrix.

Except in section 5 of Chapter 9, which also deals explicitly with make matrices, the term 'industry' will from now on signify the collection of producers of a certain commodity or group of commodities. This is the sense that is usual in input–output theory and also the one that we have used so far in this book. It allows one to speak of the element l_{ij} of the input–output matrix L, the input of commodity i per unit output of commodity j, as, instead, the input of i per unit output of industry j, and of q_j as the gross output of industry j.

In Chapter 10 a biproportional constrained matrix problem will be formulated whose solution provides an answer to the question: knowing the matrix representing a given Markov process, how can we find a matrix which (i) represents another Markov process whose asymptotic state vector is a prescribed one and (ii) is 'near' to the first matrix? The distance condition is given an interpretation in terms of minimizing the cost of changing the structure generating the first Markov process into that generating the second. We apply this result to the problem of remodelling an adult educational programme to yield labour skills in desired proportions asymptotically.

7   FRIEDLANDER'S CONSTRAINED MATRIX PROBLEM

The next two sections are about alternatives to the biproportional formulation of the constrained matrix problem. In some, a functional relation is prescribed between a solution and an 'initial estimate'; in others, a solution minimizes a distance from the initial estimate or some other criterion function. We begin with a problem of the first class. Friedlander, in [32], wants to determine a matrix having prescribed row and column sums and of the form

$$A + \langle \xi \rangle A + A \langle \eta \rangle, \tag{9}$$

where A is a given matrix. He indicates that the solution of this problem, first posed by Deming and Stephan as a formalization of their contingency matrix estimation problem [23], is in general unique and is the limiting matrix of a certain iterative procedure suggested by the same authors.

At first sight the Friedlander problem looks like a useful alternative formulation of the problem of estimating an input–output matrix from marginal data, letting $L\langle q \rangle = A$. But examples can easily be found to show that the nonnegativity of A and of the marginals u, v do not ensure the nonnegativity of the unique solution of the Friedlander. They do, by contrast, guarantee a solution of the biproportional problem— definitionally nonnegative—in quite general circumstances that will be defined in Chapter 4. The biproportional model scores heavily here. Chapter 11 presents numerical calculations of both estimates which illustrate these and other properties.

On the other hand, from the Friedlander solution one easily obtains the first variation of the solution of a general biproportional problem with respect to changes in the marginals entering the latter. This is shown in Chapter 5; it is there used to obtain the approximate variance–covariance matrix of the r_i's and s_j's of the solution of a biproportional problem, in terms of the variance–covariance matrix of its marginals when these are considered to be subject to random errors of observation.

8   OTHER CONSTRAINED MATRIX MODELS

Some work has been done on a type of constrained matrix problem in which no 'initial estimate' explicitly appears. Upper and lower bounds (which may be infinite) are imposed on the elements of a matrix required to fit given marginals. Formally, the problem is the same as that [30] of finding a flow through a network when capacities on flows in arcs are differentiated by direction: the analogy will be enlarged on in a moment. Particularizing this approach one may answer questions such as: under what conditions does there exist *some* nonnegative matrix that preserves the zero elements of a given matrix while fitting prescribed marginals?—a point which is relevant to the problem of finding nonnegative solutions of more specific types of constrained matrix problem. Fréchet[31] has obtained results in this field; Thionet[69], Marin-Curtoud[52] and Paelinck[60] are among others who consider the network-theoretic aspects of the theory of transactions matrices.

This line of attack produces information about the existence of a feasible solution of a programming version of the constrained matrix problem; but none about the optimality of this solution. Matuszewski, Pitts and Sawyer, in a second study[54], adopt a full programming formulation. Their constraints are like Fréchet's—upper and lower bounds on each element as well as the usual marginal equalities. The criterion function is a sum of absolute deviations of elements of the solution matrix from corresponding elements of the initial estimate. Both in constraints and criterion Matuszewski, Pitts and Sawyer's problem much resembles Arrow and Hoffenberg's linear programme for estimating explanatory equations for coefficient changes.

Writing ϵ_{ij} for the deviation in the (i, j)th element of a solution if this deviation is positive, and $-\delta_{ij}$ if it is negative, the programme may be written

$$\min \sum_{i, j} c_{ij}(\epsilon_{ij} + \delta_{ij})$$

subject to

$$\sum_j (\epsilon_{ij} - \delta_{ij}) = u_i - l_i q, \tag{10}$$

$$\sum_i (\epsilon_{ij} - \delta_{ij}) = v_j - i l^j q_j, \tag{11}$$

$$\epsilon_{ij} \leqq l_{ij} q_j, \quad \delta_{ij} \leqq \tfrac{1}{2} l_{ij} q_j, \quad \epsilon_{ij}, \delta_{ij} \geqq 0, \tag{12}$$

where l_i, l^j denote the ith row and jth column of L. It can easily be shown that minimizing $\sum_{i, j} (\epsilon_{ij} + \delta_{ij})$ subject to $\epsilon_{ij}, \delta_{ij} \geqq 0$ is equivalent to minimizing the sum of absolute deviations[3, 54]. The c_{ij} are *ad lib.* weights. (12) is a specific version of constraints on individual elements that Matuszewski, Pitts and Sawyer use. It will be seen that the programme is exactly of transportation type, with oppositely directed gross flows between 'plant' i and 'market' j, (10) and (11) supply and demand restrictions, and (12) are capacity bounds differentiated by direction. This peculiarity, and a technique of Dantzig's[21] for introducing the upper bounds only when they are violated by provisional optima, yield an efficient method of solution. It is used by Matuszewski, Pitts and Sawyer to update the 1949 Canadian matrix to 1956. The updated matrix improves considerably on constant coefficients according to the usual kind of test by the conditional prediction of gross outputs. The test is done for 1957–9.

The equality in general, in a linear programming estimate, of the number of nonzero deviations with the number of effective non-sign constraints, has several important consequences which Schneider explores in [62]. For the typical medium-sized matrix only a minority of the initially nonzero elements will be revised at all. RAS, by contrast, changes them all. The methods are alike, however, in tending to change the largest elements most. Clearly, the *a priori* specification of maximum per cent changes is critical for the programming solution; it is inherent in the RAS method, on the other hand, that a maldistribution of the burden of changes is avoided. Setting all programming bounds stringently would, of course, tend to give a more RAS-like result.

The problems created by the limited number of changes in the linear programming solution are avoided if a quadratic criterion is used, and the virtue of flexibility in placing constraints on individual elements is kept. Omar [58] has argued for a quadratic programming solution, but to my knowledge there has been no application yet. Like the linear programme, the quadratic programme belongs to the family of constrained matrix problems defined under (iii) (*b*) in the first paragraph of this chapter (p. 17), that is to say, the determining principle in the programming versions is the minimization of some distance-type or other criterion function. In the quadratic programme the minimand may be simple Euclidean distance, and in this case the programme may be viewed as a least-squares approach to the problem of adjusting the initial estimate to the marginal data into which have been introduced both element constraints where these seem wise, and a restriction to nonnegativity of the final matrix. Simple least squares would fail to preserve zeros, and is liable to turn elements negative. The need to introduce inequality constraints has the effect that the solution in the programming versions does not bear a simple functional relation to the initial matrix; that is, not only are these versions not set up as models of the family defined under (iii) (*a*) on p. 17, but nor do they turn out to be of this family. We shall see later, in Chapter 6, that the converse statement is not true of either the RAS or the Friedlander methods.

Apart from this, there are computational drawbacks to the quadratic programme. Foremost, most computing centres of planning bodies do not have working quadratic programme routines, and the *a priori* net advantages of the quadratic model do not seem great enough to justify the work of setting them up. Secondly, most well-known algorithms take more computing time than algorithms for alternative models: Omar estimates, for example, a ratio of 20 : 1 for the computing time of solutions of a 30-order problem (i) by the Wolfe simplex algorithm for quadratic programmes [75], and (ii) by RAS. It should be noted, however, that Wolfe's methods does not exploit the positive-definiteness of the quadratic form in the present problem, and that it may, indeed, no longer be the fastest of the methods for the case of only nonnegative-definiteness [12]. The linear programming algorithm used by Matuszewski, Pitts and Sawyer proved to be about four times slower than RAS in Schneider's computations for a 24-order problem. There is more description of computational experience of the RAS and Friedlander problems in section 1 of Chapter 11.

Another variant of the approach to 'closing' the constrained matrix problem by minimizing a criterion function has been proposed recently by Uribe, de Leeuw and Theil [**68, 73**]. These writers take as their estimate the matrix B that minimizes the expression

$$\sum_{i,j} a_{ij} \log \frac{a_{ij}}{b_{ij}},$$

subject to marginal constraints—where A denotes some initial estimate of the unknown matrix. Information theory offers an interpretation of this sum as the amount of new 'information' contained in the message that the value A has 'happened', when the value B has been predicted. This idea will be described at more length in section 5 of Chapter 6, where we shall see that it may also be used as a way of rationalizing the biproportional estimate.

9   MATRIX ESTIMATES AND OUTPUT FORECASTS

This book is about the intersecting topics of input–output change and of biproportional methods of matrix estimation. It develops the case that, of all constrained matrix estimates of input–output flows, the biproportional one is the best because it has the widest spread of good properties. The claim begs the question of whether the updating and extrapolation of whole matrices is, in the first place, a good way of achieving practical aims. The point of projecting an input–output matrix is to transform projected final demands into figures for gross outputs. Perhaps, then, whatever resources there are should be concentrated more directly on the projection of this transformation, rather than applied diffusedly to a structural analysis that involves whole matrices. Arrow and Hoffenberg's study has already shown how, by so limiting the aims of estimation, one may gain efficiency through an increase in degrees of freedom and a fall in standard errors.

The background of the Arrow and Hoffenberg study is, however, very different from that against which the present chapter and the present book are set. The approach of constrained matrix estimation was justified in section 2 by drawing attention to a typical pattern of available data, consisting only of a past matrix and current marginals. In this situation, is there a way of making the most of the statistics to forecast gross outputs conditionally which does not entail the estimation of a whole matrix? Tilanus, in his many-faceted study of Netherlands data [**70**], suggests one way: naive (i.e. constant-coefficient) conditional gross output predictions are multiplied by corrective factors; the factors are those which, had they been applied in the year $t = 1$, would have given estimates exactly equalling observations. That is, Tilanus makes the prediction of intermediate demands at $t = 2$:

$$u^*(2) = \langle c \rangle [(I-L)^{-1} - I] f(2), \tag{13}$$

where the corrective multipliers c are given by

$$u = c[(1-L)^{-1} - I] f.$$

($f, f(2)$ are final demands less competitive imports at $t = 1$, $t = 2$.) Tilanus argues that this estimate of $u(2)$ may be as good as one calculated from the *true* matrix for $t = 1$ but not 'corrected' in the manner of (13). The criterion is the variance of the *logarithmic error* of the forecast, i.e. of the logarithm of the ratio of forecast to realization. The argument is based on simplifying stochastic assumptions: homoscedasticity of the logarithmic error in making 'one-year' naive conditional predictions of the ith intermediate output, etc.; and on the 'cumulation rule', which says that the logarithmic error in a t-year naive conditional prediction of the ith intermediate output is a sum of one-year ones. The cumulation rule is in turn based on strong assumptions: that the components of final demand move approximately proportionately, and that changes over time in the input–output inverse matrix are small. These assumptions of regularity in the temporal behaviour of the elements of the Leontief model are certainly a severe restriction on applications of the theory to medium-term macro-economic planning. But neither they nor the stochastic assumptions prevent Netherlands data from bearing out Tilanus's argument.

Tilanus's claim is not exaggerated. It says that—in the regularly moving system of interindustry relations he assumes—the information on the flow matrix of year $t = 1$ that is useful in supplementing the base year input–output matrix is contained in its marginals. Knowing details of changes within the flow table does not help. But Tilanus says nothing about the usefulness of information *inferred from* the year 1 matrix (or an estimate of it) about the matrix of year 2. He does not consider the question of whether predictions of $u(2)$ made by somehow extrapolating the series L, $L(1)$ to a prediction of $L(2)$ are better or worse than predictions made by somehow extrapolating the corrective factors c.

Tilanus's results are a warning against easy-going application of RAS—or any other—updates. Within the Tilanus assumptions, even if the RAS estimate were exactly right, it would not do better in a projective application than a simplistic alternative. The alternative is primitive not only in its non-structural character, its attention to marginal aggregates to the neglect of what is going on inside the matrix; but, more than that, in its failure to take any notice of one set of the marginals themselves—the intermediate *inputs* of industries. In effect, Tilanus makes a 'half-constrained' estimate of the square-bracketed matrix expression in (14). If there is practical advantage in the biproportional approach, in the greater refinement of its inferences about $t = 1$, it can only be realized in bold projection. If the RAS estimate is better than others of its class, it is so because it provides a better time series of matrices, a more accurate second point through which to sight the future.

10   SUMMARY OF RESULTS FOR BIPROPORTIONAL MATRIX MODELS

We round off this chapter by summarizing the main properties of the biproportional model and its applications that have either been discussed already or will be the subjects of later chapters. Taken together, these properties establish the theoretical and operational advantages of the biproportional model that Chapter 1 claimed for it.

We have already seen in section 3 that the model allows much differentiation between relative changes in various elements. At the same time, it preserves the general shape of the matrix. In particular all zero elements of the initial matrix stay zero.

In the next chapter we prove fundamental mathematical results concerning the solution of the biproportional constrained matrix problem, results which confirm the practical usefulness of this model as a formalization of input–output and other estimation problems. We begin by generalizing the statement of the problem by admitting as solutions limits of sequences of matrices of the form $\langle r \rangle A \langle s \rangle$ that are not themselves expressible in this form: here A represents the initially given matrix. We show that a solution is unique (section 3), and establish necessary and sufficient conditions for its existence. This is done (in section 4) by studying the properties of a certain matrix sequence which, if it converges, converges to a solution. The process generating this sequence is the method that has customarily been employed to obtain solutions in biproportional applications. Chapter 4 continues (section 5) by showing the conditions for the existence of a biproportional solution to be rather weak. Section 5 ends by determining circumstances in which an initially positive element is driven to zero in a biproportional solution.

Chapter 5 obtains (in sections 1 and 2) existence and uniqueness properties of the solution of the Friedlander model (see section 7 above) and uses them (section 4) to treat the (r, s) pair of a solution of the form $\langle r \rangle A \langle s \rangle$ as an implicit function of the marginal pair (u, v). The properties of this function are used (in section 5) to show the (approximate) correctness of a solution $L*$ of the input–output estimation problem when the true matrix $L(1)$ is (approximately) biproportional to L. Finally (section 7) the approximate distribution of deviations in the r, s is obtained in terms of the distribution of u, v considered as random observations.

Chapter 6 ties together the functional and distance-minimizing approaches to constrained matrix estimation by considering the question: how 'far' from the given matrix A are the matrices obtained by adjusting A to given u, v subject to alternative forms of functional relation between A and a solution? The two main forms of relation considered are those defining the Friedlander and the biproportional problem respectively. The approach is to seek distance-like functions that are minimized subject to the marginal constraints by matrices having the prescribed relations to A (sections 2 to 4). It is shown (in section 4) that a biproportional solution minimizes, on the class of non-negative matrices B satisfying the constraints, a function of matrix pairs (A, B) which, in the neighbourhood of (A, A), is a positive linear transform of the χ^2 function $\sum_{i,j} \dfrac{(b_{ij} - a_{ij})^2}{a_{ij}}$. This minimizing property is used to show that a biproportional solution is indeed a conservative estimate, as we have conjectured. We show, too (section 6), a distance-minimization property of the proportional-row (or proportional-column) solution of a 'half-constrained' matrix problem—one with only one set of marginal constraints.

Chapter 7 is concerned with the specific input–output application of the biproportional model. We consider the estimate $L*$ as a function of the vector q of outputs at time 1—on which depend the magnitudes of the marginals at given prices, and the price vector at time 1—which determines the units in which the marginals are expressed. We ask the question: if the true matrix $L(1)$ is invariant with respect to q and p, under what conditions is $L*$—as we would wish—also invariant with respect to these variables? It is shown (sections 2, 3) that $L*$ is invariant if and only if $L(1)$ is biproportional to L, and then $L* = L(1)$, but that, if $L(1)$ is nearly biproportional to L, then $L*$ is nearly invariant. More precisely, as $L(1)$ approaches a value $\langle r \rangle L \langle s \rangle$, $L*$ approaches $\langle r \rangle L \langle s \rangle$ uniformly on q, p. The chapter reveals an exact symmetry between the roles played by q and p in the model.

Chapter 8 takes up another aspect of the input–output application of the biproportional model. Instead of estimating a single set of substitution effects r_i between goods, it might pay to estimate, successively, substitutions between broad classes of inputs—say fuels, raw materials, services—and substitutions within such classes. It is shown that if the true matrix $L(1)$ is generated by a certain process that brings about this two-stage substitution, the two-stage estimation procedure gets $L(1)$

right and $L*$ in general errs. The alternate statement is, however, also true, so there is no clear case for ousting the fruitful 'one-stage' model in favour of its two-stage variant.

Chapter 9 considers the vital practical problem of how best to project a time series L, $L*$ of input–output to a future year. It is shown in section 1 that the projection $\langle r \rangle^t L \langle s \rangle^t$, $t > 1$, introduces an unacceptable upward bias in the column sums of the projected matrix, i.e. in the projected intermediate input ratios. In particular, this form of projection can give a projected column sum which exceeds that at time 0 when the estimated sum at time 1 falls short of that at time 0. More generally, it is shown (section 2) that there exists no continuous function $f(r_i, s_j)$ such that the projection $\{f(r_i, s_j) l_{ij}\}$ of L, $L*$ (i) is not merely identical with $L*$, (ii) is nonnegative, and (iii) gives monotonic column-sum sequences. Section 3 adopts a different approach: our subjective feelings on future intermediate input ratios, which we have begun by expressing as monotonicity constraints, are sharpened to exact predictions (section 4): we are then left with a 'half-constrained matrix problem'. The proportional-column solution of this problem has a desirable minimal-distance property that has already been shown in Chapter 6. Section 5 considers the specific problems of projecting a time series of 'make' matrices consisting of an observed one and a biproportional estimate for a later date and proposes a solution to these problems.

Chapter 10 deals with the application of the biproportional model to the problem of reprogramming a Markov structure that was sketched in section 6 above. A particular application is discussed, to the problem of recasting an adult training programme. Various grades of labour constitute the Markovian 'states', and the effect of the programme is expressed as the probability that a person in grade j in one year will find himself in grade i in the following year. The problem is to redesign the training programme (alter these probabilities) in such a way that, within each batch of adults undergoing training, the numbers in different grades will after some years approach prescribed proportions.

Chapter 11 describes computational experience with the biproportional model in various applications, and presents numerical examples to demonstrate its input–output and Markov uses. The input–output data are taken from the work of the Cambridge Growth Project on the British economy. The Markov example is a purely illustrative one for the training problem of Chapter 10.

Chapter 4

THE SOLUTION OF THE BIPROPORTIONAL CONSTRAINED MATRIX PROBLEM

1 Introduction

In this chapter we establish basic existence and uniqueness theorems for the solution of the biproportional constrained matrix problem and consider the convergence of the iterative procedure for solving it that is customarily used in practice and which is described in detail in section 2 below. We consider the following questions. (i) When does there exist a solution to the biproportional constrained matrix problem—that is, a matrix biproportional to a given nonnegative matrix and having prescribed nonnegative row and column sums? (ii) When does the standard iterative procedure described in section 2 converge to a solution? (iii) Is a solution unique?

No rigorous mathematical enquiry into the properties of the biproportional model seems to have been carried out before Stone's resurrection of the model in 1962[24]. Friedlander, referring in his 1961 survey[32] of constrained matrix methods to Deming and Stephan's proposal of the standard iterative procedure for the solution of the biproportional problem[23], states: 'The theory of this method is, however, intractable.'

Since interest in biproportional matrix applications was stimulated by Stone, Brown, Paelinck and Waelbroeck in 1962–3 Professor Gorman[36] has given answers to the theoretical questions (i) to (iii) based on regarding the constraining equations $\langle r \rangle As = u$, $rA\langle s \rangle = v$ as extremizing conditions on a differentiable function of $\log r$, $\log s$. Bingen[10] has simplified part of Gorman's proofs. This approach has nothing in common with the one pursued in sections 3 to 5 of this chapter; it is outlined in section 6. Thionet has also raised the existence and convergence questions. In [69] he conjectures a weak form of the existence result of section 4 of this chapter and illustrates the issues involved by numerical examples. Dr M. A. H. Dempster, in a private communication, uses a fixed point theorem to answer the question also raised by Fréchet and others (see section 8 of the last chapter): in what circumstances will there exist *some* nonnegative, zero-preserving matrix, satisfying the marginal constraints, but not necessarily biproportional to the initial matrix?

From now on, we shall consider a slightly wider set of matrices to be solutions that the set of nonnegative matrices fitting the constraints and of the form $\langle r \rangle A \langle s \rangle$. We shall allow as solutions limits of sequences of matrices of the form $\langle r \rangle A \langle s \rangle$ when these limits are not themselves expressible in this form. Loosely, our solution set will be the closure of the set

$$\{ B \mid B = \langle r \rangle A \langle s \rangle, B \geqq 0, Bi = u, iB = v \}. \tag{1}$$

We shall generalize the meaning of the term 'biproportional' accordingly. Henceforth, a matrix B will be called biproportional to A if it is nonnegative and the limit of a sequence $\{ \langle R^t \rangle A \langle S^s \rangle \}$ for some sequences $\{ R^t \}$, $\{ S^t \}$ of vectors. In this terminology, B will be admitted as a solution if it is biproportional to A and fits the marginal constraints. In the input–output application, we shall allow as an estimate of the transactions matrix in the updating year any appropriately constrained matrix of the form $\lim \langle R^t \rangle (L \langle q \rangle) \langle S^t \rangle$. Hence the estimate L^* of the input–output coefficient matrix $L(1)$ may be expressible as

$$L^* = \lim_{t \to \infty} \langle R^t \rangle L \langle S^t \rangle$$

but not as $\langle r \rangle L \langle s \rangle$.

The order of exposition we adopt is the reverse of the order in which the questions (i) to (iii) were put. We first consider uniqueness, next convergence. The presence of convergence is then used to establish existence. The proof of the convergence-existence result (Theorem 3) is rather intricate. It is therefore prefaced, at the start of section 4, with a fairly long description of its strategy.

A crucial concept in the theoretical parts of this book is that of matrix 'connectedness'. Loosely, a matrix is called *dis*connected if, after any necessary reordering of rows and columns, it has the form

$$\begin{bmatrix} A_{IJ} & 0 \\ 0 & A_{I'J'} \end{bmatrix},$$

and partially disconnected if it is of the form

$$\begin{bmatrix} A_{IJ} & A_{IJ'} \\ 0 & A_{I'J'} \end{bmatrix}.$$

Most of the complications of the analysis of this chapter—in particular, the elaborate nature of the proof of Theorem 3—are due to possible complete or partial disconnections of the matrix A; all the results can be proved much more rapidly in the strictly positive case.

2   THE PROBLEM (A, u, v) AND THE PROCESS (A, u, v)

In this section we define the biproportional matrix problem and the standard iterative solution method formally, and draw attention to one or two simple but useful facts about them.

We begin by giving a precise statement of the biproportional matrix problem.

DEFINITION. The *biproportional problem* (A, u, v) is to find A^B such that

$$A^B \geqq 0,$$

$$A^B i = u, \quad i A^B = v$$

$$A^B = \lim_{t \to \infty} \langle R^t \rangle A \langle S^t \rangle,$$

for some sequences $\{R^t\}$, $\{S^t\}$ of vectors with $R_1^t = 1$ for all t; where A is a given $m \times n$ matrix such that

$$a_i \geqslant 0, \quad a^j \geqslant 0 \quad \text{for all } i, j, \tag{2}$$

and u, v are given m- and n-vectors such that

$$u > 0, \quad v > 0. \mid \tag{3}$$

a_i, a^j denote the ith row and jth column of A. $\geqslant 0$ denotes semi-positivity, > 0 strict positivity. The superscript B in the notation A^B for a solution is the initial letter of 'biproportional'. The letter B is also used from time to time to denote a matrix, but no cases of ambiguity arise. In subsequent chapters, where we have occasion to consider A^B as a function of u, v, we shall sometimes write a solution of (A, u, v) as $A^B(u, v)$. A solution of the form $\langle r \rangle A \langle s \rangle$ will sometimes be called an 'interior' solution; a solution not expressible in this form a 'boundary' solution.

The normalization $R_1^t = 1$, which is convenient in proving a uniqueness result in section 3, involves no real loss of generality. The definition covers any matrix of the form $\langle r \rangle A \langle s \rangle$ which is nonnegative and fits the constraints. For the conditions $u > 0$, $v > 0$ ensure that for all $i, j, r_i \neq 0$, $s_j \neq 0$ in such a solution, whence there is a number λ such that $\langle \lambda r \rangle A \langle (1/\lambda) s \rangle$ is nonnegative and fits the constraints and $\lambda r_1 = 1$. The definition generalizes this notion of a solution by also admitting nonnegative, constraint-fitting limits of sequences of matrices of the form $\langle r \rangle A \langle s \rangle$, $r_1 = 1$.

The specification (2), (3) differs only trivially from the general case of nonnegative A, u, v. If some a_i vanishes a solution exists only if u_i vanishes too. If u_i vanishes then all questions concerning a solution reduce to questions about a solution of $(\bar{A}, \bar{u}, v)$, where bars denote the suppression of the ith row of A and the ith element of u. If there is no solution to the latter problem there is clearly none to the first. Conversely, if, in an obvious notation, a solution of $(\bar{A}, \bar{u}, v)$ is given by the sequences $\{\bar{R}^t\}$, $\{S^t\}$, then the original problem is solved by the sequences $\{R^t\}$, $\{S^t\}$ with $R_i^t = 0$ for all t. Similar remarks apply to the a^j's and v_j's.

We have defined the matrix A of any biproportional problem (A, u, v) to have semipositive rows and columns. Not only in this context but throughout this book the symbol A will denote such a matrix, unless the contrary is explicitly stated. In the same way, u, v are always to be understood to be strictly positive vectors.

We next define the process that provides the standard method of solution used in practice [7, 24, 26, 59, 62, 70, 74]. Starting with the given matrix A, one first multiplies each row by a scalar that will make the row sum equal the row constraint, next multiplies each column of the resulting matrix A^1 by a scalar that will make its sum equal its constraint. This gives a matrix A^2 that serves as starting point for the next iteration. The formal definition is as follows.

DEFINITION. The *biproportional process* (A, u, v) is:

$$A^{2t+1} = \langle r^{t+1} \rangle A^{2t}, \tag{4}$$

$$A^{2t+2} = A^{2t+1} \langle s^{t+1} \rangle = \langle r^{t+1} \rangle A^{2t} \langle s^{t+1} \rangle, \tag{5}$$

where
$$r_i^{t+1} = \frac{u_i}{\sum\limits_{j=1}^{n} a_{ij}^{2t}}, \tag{6}$$

$$s_j^{t+1} = \frac{v_j}{\sum\limits_{i=1}^{m} a_{ij}^{2t+1}}. \tag{7}$$

t takes the values $0, 1, 2, \ldots$. We start the process by setting $A^0 = A.$|

We shall frequently refer to the biproportional problem (A, u, v) as 'the problem (A, u, v)' or simply '(A, u, v)' and to the biproportional process (A, u, v) as 'the process (A, u, v)'.

The sequence of matrices A^t is so computed that, for all t,

$$A^{2t+1}i = u, \tag{8}$$

$$iA^{2t+2} = v. \tag{9}$$

We shall find convenient the notation $r^t(A, u, v)$ or, where there is no ambiguity, $r^t(A)$. Note that

$$r^{t+1}(A) = r^1(A^{2t}). \tag{10}$$

A few obvious properties of the sequences $\{A^{2t}\}$, $\{A^{2t+1}\}$, $\{r^t\}$, $\{s^t\}$ are worth pointing out. (2) and (3) ensure that r^1 is defined and is positive, whence by (4) A^1 has finite semipositive rows and columns, whence by (7) s^1 is defined and is positive. So $A^2 = \langle r^1 \rangle A \langle s^1 \rangle$ has finite semipositive rows and columns; by an easy induction

$$a_i^{2t}, a^{2t+1, j} \geqslant 0 \quad (t \geqq 0, 1, 2, \ldots), \tag{11}$$

$$r^t, s^t > 0 \quad (t = 0, 1, 2, \ldots), \tag{12}$$

where $a^{2t+1, j}$ denotes the jth column of A^{2t+1}; and (12) means that

$$a_i^{2t} = 0 \quad \text{or} \quad a_{ij}^{2t+1} = 0 \quad \text{implies} \quad a_{ij} = 0 \quad (t = 0, 1, 2, \ldots), \tag{13}$$

that is, a positive element of A can never vanish in the course of the process (A, u, v).

3 UNIQUENESS

A matrix A will be called *disconnected* if there are nonvacuous index sets I, I', J, J' such that $a_{ij} = 0$ for $i \in I, j \in J'$ and for $i \in I', j \in J$, where prime denotes complementarity. We shall also write this condition, in an obvious notation for partitions of A, as $A_{IJ'} = 0$, $A_{I'J} = 0$. The concept generalizes decomposability, as I may differ from J, and indeed the matrix need not be square. A matrix is called *connected* if it is not disconnected.

We first prove the following theorem on the uniqueness of an interior solution.

THEOREM 1. *If A is connected then a solution A^B of (A, u, v) expressible as $A^B = \langle r \rangle A \langle s \rangle$ is unique.*

PROOF. We first note that if A is connected then the provision that a solution be nonnegative means that the r, s of a solution of the form $\langle r \rangle A \langle s \rangle$ are either both positive or both negative. Clearly neither can contain zeros; suppose then that some r_i are positive and the rest negative, say $r_I > 0$, $r_{I'} < 0$. Then certainly s cannot be positive or negative, so say $s_J > 0$, $s_{J'} < 0$. Then $A_{IJ'}$, $A_{I'J}$ must be null if the solution is not to contain negative elements: thus A is disconnected.

Suppose that there are two solutions of the stated form. Then there exist ρ, σ such that

$$\langle \rho \rangle A^B \sigma = A^B i = u, \qquad (14)$$

$$\rho A^B \langle \sigma \rangle = i A^B = v, \qquad (15)$$

where A^B is the first solution of the problem, and ρ, σ are either both positive or both negative as A^B is clearly connected; first assume

$$\rho > 0, \quad \sigma > 0. \qquad (16)$$

Reorder the elements of ρ, σ so that

$$\rho_1 \geqq \rho_2 \geqq \cdots \geqq \rho_m, \qquad (17)$$

$$\sigma_1 \leqq \sigma_2 \leqq \cdots \leqq \sigma_n. \qquad (18)$$

To prove that the two solutions are the same it suffices to show that if $a_{ij}^B > 0$ then $\rho_i \sigma_j = 1$. Suppose the contrary, for instance, that for some (i_0, j_0)

$$a_{i_0 j_0}^B > 0, \quad \rho_{i_0} \sigma_{j_0} > 1.$$

We first show that this implies either $\rho_1 \sigma_1 < 1$ or $\rho_1 \sigma_1 > 1$. If $j_0 = 1$ then $\rho_1 \sigma_1 > 1$ by (17). If $j_0 > 1$ then there must be a $j_1 < j_0$ such that $a_{i_0 j_1}^B > 0$, $\rho_{i_0} \sigma_{j_1} < 1$, for otherwise $\sum_{j=1}^{n} \rho_{i_0} \sigma_j a_{i_0 j}^B > \sum_{j=1}^{n} a_{i_0 j}^B$ by (18), contrary to (14). Suppose that $j_1 > 1$. Then, similarly, there is an $i_1 < i_0$ such that $a_{i_1 j_1}^B > 0$, $\rho_{i_1} \sigma_{j_1} > 1$. In the sequence $j_0, i_0, j_1, i_1, \ldots$ there is a first member equal to 1. If this is an i_t we have $a_{1j_t}^B > 0$, $\rho_1 \sigma_{j_t} > 1$, whence $\rho_1 \sigma_1 < 1$ by (18) and (14). If it is a j_t, we have $a_{i_{t-1}1}^B > 0$, $\rho_{i_{t-1}} \sigma_1 < 1$, whence $\rho_1 \sigma_1 > 1$ by (17) and (15).

However, $\rho_1 \sigma_1 < 1$ implies $\rho_i \sigma_1 < 1$ for all i by (17), whence $\sum_{i=1}^{m} \rho_i \sigma_1 a_{i1}^B < \sum_{i=1}^{m} a_{i1}^B$, contradicting (15); and $\rho_1 \sigma_1 > 1$ is ruled out for a similar reason. An argument dual to the above applies in the case of the opposite inequality $\rho_{i_0} \sigma_{j_0} < 1$. If in place of (16) we had assumed $\rho < 0$, $\sigma < 0$ and $\langle \rho \rangle A^B \langle \sigma \rangle$ differed from A^B, so would $\langle -\rho \rangle A^B \langle -\sigma \rangle$, contrary to what we have just shown. This completes the proof.|

We next generalize Theorem 1 to cover boundary solutions as well as interior ones. We still restrict A to be connected.

THEOREM 2. If A is connected then a solution of (A, u, v) is unique.

PROOF. Let the sequence $\{R^t, S^t\}$ yield a solution A^B of (A, u, v). By definition,

$$\lim_{t \to \infty} \langle R^t \rangle A \langle S^t \rangle = A^B, \qquad (19)$$

$$R_1^t = 1 \quad \text{all } t. \qquad (20)$$

Let (r, s) be a limit point of $\{R^t, S^t\}$. Then

$$r_i s_j a_{ij} = a_{ij}^B \qquad (21)$$

for all (i, j) for which the left-hand side is defined. Now suppose the set of infinite elements of r, $\quad I = \{i | r_i = \pm \infty\}$

is not empty. For any i, $a_{ij} > 0$ for some j, by (2), hence the set $\{j | s_j = 0\}$, $= J'$ say, is also nonempty. But I' is nonempty by the normalization (20), hence so finally is J.

Then $A_{IJ} = 0$ (otherwise some $a_{ij}^B = \infty$), so that $A_{IJ}^B = 0$ by (19). But $A_{I'J'}^B = 0$ from (21) and the definitions of I', J'; thus the solution A^B is disconnected. Very similar arguments show that A^B is disconnected if we begin by supposing $\{j | s_j = \pm \infty\}$ to be nonempty, instead of I. Note that if both these sets are empty then the solution A^B is of the kind already dealt with in Theorem 1.

Theorem 1 can now be applied to show that any connected solution A^B is unique. But suppose that A^B is disconnected. Then we have, for some nonvacuous sets I, I', J, J'

$$A_{IJ'} = 0, \quad A_{I'J} \neq 0,$$

$$A_{IJ'}^B = 0, \quad A_{I'J}^B = 0, \quad A_{IJ}^B \text{ connected.} \qquad (22)$$

In this case, (22) must hold for any solution A^* say. For clearly $A_{IJ'}^* = 0$. Next, $A_{IJ'}^B = 0$, $A_{I'J}^B = 0$ imply that

$$U_I = V_J, \quad U_{I'} = V_{J'},$$

where $U_I = \sum_{i \in I} u_i$, etc., whence $A^*_{I'J} = 0$. Thirdly, A^*_{IJ} is connected. For suppose not: then we would have, similarly, $U_{I_1} = V_{J_2}$, $U_{I_2} = V_{J_1}$, where I_1, I_2 partition I and J_1, J_2 partition J, and A^B_{IJ} would also be disconnected, contrary to (22). But Theorem 1 now shows that A^B_{IJ} is the unique value for this partition of any nonnegative solution, being a connected solution of (A_{IJ}, u_I, v_J), in an obvious notation. We know that $A^B_{IJ'}, A^B_{I'J} = 0$ in any solution, so applying the above argument concerning A^B_{IJ} to each such connected partition of A^B in turn clinches the theorem.|

Finally, we relax the requirement that A be connected.

COROLLARY 1. A solution of (A, u, v) is unique.

PROOF. If A is disconnected then by suitable partitioning of A_{IJ}, $A_{I'J'}$ in the case that either of these is disconnected, and continuing in the same way, after a finite number of partitionings and by suitable permutations of rows and of columns, we will have got A in block-diagonal form with each diagonal partition connected. Then Theorem 2 can easily be applied to each diagonal partition considered as a matrix.|

4 CONVERGENCE OF THE PROCESS

In this section we establish, in Theorem 3, necessary and sufficient conditions for the convergence of the process (A, u, v) to a solution of the problem (A, u, v). These enable us easily to obtain necessary and sufficient conditions for the existence of such a solution. The strategy is as follows. We show first, in Lemma 1, that if A is connected $\min_i r_i^{t+m-1}(A)$ is strictly greater than $\min_i r_i^t(A)$ if the latter is less than $\max_i r_i^t(A)$. That is, if the row multipliers are not all equal at the tth iteration, the least of them will have increased by the $(t+m-1)$th. But the increase $[\min_i r_i^{t+m-1}(A) - \min_i r_i^t(A)]$ depends continuously on A. We consider (case (i)) a connected limit point A^B of $\{A^{2t}\}$ and suppose that $[\max_i r_i^1(A^B) - \min_i r_i^1(A^B)] > 0$, whence we know from the lemma that $[\min_i r_i^m(A^B) - \min_i r_i^1(A^B)] = h > 0$. Then on the one hand

$$[\min_i r_i^m(A^{2t'}) - \min_i r_i^1(A^{2t'})]$$

must be close to h for $A^{2t'}$ near A^B, whence

$$[\min_i r_i^1(A^{2t}) - \min_i r_i^1(A^{2t'})] > \tfrac{1}{2}h \quad \text{for all} \quad t \geq t' + m - 1.$$

On the other, the last difference must be near zero if $A^{2t'}$ and A^{2t} are late enough members of a subsequence which has A^B as limit. This shows that $r^1(A^B) = \lambda i$ and it is only left to show that the condition asserted in the theorem to be sufficient implies that $\lambda = 1$.

We now consider the more difficult case (case (ii)) of a disconnected limit point A^B. The reasoning for the connected case is applied to show that the partition of $r^1(A^B)$ corresponding to A^B's kth connected partition, $r^1_k(A^B)$ say, has the form $\lambda_k i$ for a positive scalar λ_k. It is easily shown that if $\min_i \lambda_k = 1$ then the condition of the theorem implies that A^B is the solution. The only possible alternative is that $\min_k \lambda_k < 1$. Letting I denote the set of rows i for which $r^1_i(A^B) = \min_k \lambda_k$ and J the set of columns j connected with I in A^B, it is easy to show that $s^1_j(A^B) = 1/\min_k \lambda_k$ for j in J and $A^B_{I'J} = 0$.

We now establish that, if $A_{I'J} \neq 0$, then $iA^{2t}_{I'J}i$ is increasing whenever it is near enough to zero. This is used to show that there can be no limit point in which the partition (I', J) is null; but we have obtained $A^B_{I'J} = 0$. The contradiction shows that $A_{I'J} = 0$. But $\min_k \lambda_k < 1$ implies $\sum_{i \in I} u_i / \sum_{i \in J} v_j < 1$, and together with $A_{I'J} = 0$ this constitutes a violation of the sufficient condition for convergence stated in Theorem 3.

LEMMA 1. *If A is connected and $\min_i r^{t'}_i < \max_i r^{t'}_i$, then $\min_i r^t_i > \min_i r^t_i$ and $\max_i r^t_i < \max_i r^{t'}_i$ for all $t \geq t' + m - 1$, for any t'.*

PROOF. The difficulty lies entirely in the possible nonuniqueness of the i for which $r^{t'}_i$ is a minimum. Consider for the time being a problem in which the initial matrix A satisfies one set of constraints, namely

$$iA = v.$$

Reorder if necessary so that

$$r^1_1 = \min_i r^1_i,$$

and suppose that

$$r^1_1 < \max_i r^1_i.$$

Define

$$\underline{I} = \{i | r^1_i = r^1_1\}.$$

Now (7), (4) give

$$s^{t+1}_j = v_j \Big/ \sum_{i=1}^m r^{t+1}_i a^{2t}_{ij} = 1 \Big/ \sum_{i=1}^m r^{t+1}_i (a^{2t}_{ij}/v_j),$$

which is the reciprocal of a convex combination of the r^{t+1}_i by (9) and (11). So

$$s^{t+1}_j \leq \frac{1}{\min_i r^{t+1}_i} \tag{23}$$

and in particular $s^1_j \leq 1/\min_i r^1_i = 1/r^1_1$.

Define $J = \{j | s^1_j = 1/r^1_1\}$, then

$$a_{ij} = 0 \quad \text{for} \quad i \in \underline{I}', j \in J. \tag{24}$$

But similarly (6), (5) give $r_i^{t+2} = 1 \Big/ \sum_{j=1}^{n} s_j^{t+1}(a_{ij}^{2t+1}/u_i)$; hence as before, this time by (8), (11),

$$r_i^{t+2} \geq \frac{1}{\max\limits_{j} s_j^{t+1}} \tag{25}$$

and in particular $r_i^2 \geq 1/\max\limits_{j} s_j^1 \geq r_1^1$. Define $\underline{I} = \{i \,|\, r_i^2 = r_1^1\}$, then $a_{ij}^1 = 0$— and therefore $a_{ij} = 0$ by (13)—for $i \in \underline{I}, j \in J'$. But A is connected, so this together with (24) implies that $\underline{I}$ is a proper subset of I. Continuing, it is clear that the tth set of the sequence $I, \underline{I}, \ldots$ must be null, for some $t \leq m$.

Thus for some $t \leq m$, $\min\limits_{i} r_i^t > \min\limits_{i} r_i^1$. But (23), (25) easily give $\min\limits_{i} r_i^t$ nondecreasing, hence $\min\limits_{i} r_i^t > \min\limits_{i} r_i^1$ for all $t \geq m$. We have assumed that the columns of A already sum to v. But if in a general problem (A, u, v) A is connected then so is A^{2t} by (13). Applying the above result to A^{2t} establishes the lemma. |

An alternative way of proving the lemma is suggested by its close analogy to a result in global stability theory (see e.g. [42], pp. 301–16). An analogous proof might be found if the successive row multipliers r_i^t, regarded as prices adjusted dynamically in proportion to excess demands, had a strict gross substitutability property, that is to say if $\partial(\Delta r_h^t)/\partial r_i > 0$ for $h \neq i$.

We are now in a position to prove the main theorem, on convergence of the iterative process.

THEOREM 3. The process (A, u, v) converges to the unique solution of the problem (A, u, v) if and only if

$$A_{I'J} = 0 \text{ implies} \begin{cases} U_{I'} \leq V_{J'}, & (26) \\ U_I \geq V_J, & (27) \end{cases}$$

where

$$U_I = \sum_{i \in I} u_i, \quad V_J = \sum_{j \in J} v_j, \quad \text{etc.}$$

Note that if we take $I' = \{1, \ldots, m\}$ then $A_{I'J} = 0$ only for $J = \{0\}$ by (2), and (26) gives $iu \leq iv$, and if we take $J = \{1, \ldots, n\}$ then $A_{I'J} = \{0\}$ only for $I' = \{0\}$ and (27) gives $iu \geq iv$. Thus one condition covered by the theorem is the important one

$$iu = iv. \tag{28}$$

PROOF. The a_{ij}^{2t} are nonnegative and bounded above by $\max\limits_{j} v_j$, from (9) and (11). Thus $\{A^{2t}\}$ has a finite limit point A^B say. We shall show first that if the conditions of the theorem are met, A^B is the solution.

A^B has semipositive rows, for clearly $a_{ij}^B \geq 0$, and if $a_i^B = 0$, some r_i^t would be forced arbitrarily large. This would contradict the fact that

$\max_i r_i^t$ is nonincreasing, easily established from (23), (25). Similarly, A^B has semipositive columns: for if its jth column $a^{B,j} = 0$ then for some t $a^{2t,j}$ and hence $a^{2t+1,j}$ are arbitrarily small, and so s_j^{t+1} is arbitrarily large.

Case (i). Suppose A^B is connected. We shall show first that

$$r^1(A^B, u, v) = r^1(A^B) = \lambda i$$

for some $\lambda > 0$, then that $\lambda = 1$. Suppose that on the contrary the elements of $r^1(A^B)$ are not all equal, then by Lemma 1

$$\min_i r_i^m(A^B) = \min_i r_i^1(A^B) + h \quad (\text{some } h > 0).$$

$r^1(B)$ is clearly a continuous function of B for a matrix with semipositive rows and columns. It follows that $\min_i r_i^1(B)$ is also continuous at B. (This is obvious if the minimum is unique. Let

$$\min_i r_i^1(B) = r_1^1(B) = \dots = r_k^1(B) < r_{k+1}^1(B).$$

Then each of $r_1^1(C), \dots, r_k^1(C)$ is within any e of its value at B for C near enough B, and the minimum at C is found among them if C is near to B.) Being obtained by a finite sequence of permissible algebraic operations on B, u, v, also $r^t(B)$, $t > 1$, is a continuous function of B. Thus $\min_i r_i^t(B)$ and finally $[\min_i r_i^t(B) - \min_i r_i^1(B)]$ are continuous functions of B.

Consider two points $A^{2t'}$, A^{2t} of a subsequence of $\{A^{2t}\}$ having A^B as a limit. By the above continuity property there exists $\epsilon > 0$ such that

$$|a_{ij}^{2t'} - a_{ij}^B| \leqq \epsilon \quad (\text{all } i,j), \tag{29}$$

implies that $[\min_i r_i^m(A^{2t'}) - \min_i r_i^1(A^{2t'})]$ is arbitrarily close to h, e.g.

$$\min_i r_i^m(A^{2t'}) - \min_i r_i^1(A^{2t'}) > \tfrac{1}{2}h. \tag{30}$$

Hence by the nondecreasing property of $\min_i r_i^t$ and (10)

$$\min_i r_i^1(A^{2t}) - \min_i r_i^1(A^{2t'}) > \tfrac{1}{2}h \quad (t \geqq t' + m - 1). \tag{31}$$

On the other hand, $\min_i r_i^1(A^{2t'})$ and hence $\min_i r_i^1(A^{2t})$ are both brought arbitrarily near to $\min_i r_i^1(A^B)$ and thus to each other for $A^{2t'}$ near enough A^B, and in particular there exists $\eta > 0$ such that

$$\min_i r_i^1(A^{2t}) - \min_i r_i^1(A^{2t'}) < \tfrac{1}{2}h \tag{32}$$

provided that $\quad\quad |a_{ij}^{2t'} - a_{ij}^B| \leqq \eta \quad (\text{all } i,j). \tag{33}$

But we can certainly find t' such that both (29) and (33) are satisfied. Then the contradiction (31), (32) shows that

$$r^1(A^B) = \lambda i \tag{34}$$

and $\lambda > 0$ since A^B has semipositive rows.

Now $iu = iv$ (28) implies $\lambda = 1$ easily. Thus A^B satisfies both sets of constraints, but it is certainly nonnegative and of the form

$$\lim_{t \to \infty} (\langle R^t \rangle A \langle S^t \rangle)$$

with $R_1^t = 1$ for all t, hence it is unique by Theorem 2. Thus $\{A^{2t}\}$ has as its sole limit point and hence as its limit the unique solution of (A, u, v).

Case (ii). Assume A^B is disconnected, and let $k = 1, \ldots, K$ denote the subsets of rows or columns appearing in its connected partitions; then in an obvious notation $A_{kk'}^B$, has semipositive rows and columns or is null according as $k = k'$ or $k \neq k'$. Consideration of the biproportional problem (A_{kk}^B, u_k, v_k), where u_k, v_k are the kth partitions of u and v confirms that the case (i) argument up to (34) goes through for each A_{kk}^{2t}, and we get $r_k^1(A^B) = \lambda_k i$, where $r_k^1(A^B)$ denotes the kth partition of $r^1(A^B)$ and λ_k a positive number. Order so that $\lambda_1 \leq \lambda_2 \leq \ldots \leq \lambda_K$. Then $iu = iv$ implies $\lambda_1 \leq 1$ and $\lambda_K \geq 1$, and

$$s_k^1(A^B) = \frac{1}{\lambda_k} i \tag{35}$$

since each element of $s_k^1(A^B)$ is the reciprocal of a convex combination of the elements of $r_k^1(A^B)$ by the disconnection assumption.

If $\lambda_1 = 1$, A^B is quickly shown to be the solution; if $\lambda_1 < 1$, we shall show that the condition of the theorem is violated. First let $\lambda_1 = 1$; then $iu = iv$ implies $\lambda_K = 1$ and we have $r^t \to i$ as in case (i). (This is what happens if, for instance, the initial matrix A is disconnected and each connected partition satisfies the condition of the theorem. Note the theorem does not restrict A to be connected.) Suppose, therefore, that $\lambda_1 < 1$.

Define $I = \{i | r_i^1(A^B) = \lambda_1\}$, $J = \{j | s_j^1(A^B) = 1/\lambda_1\}$.

A^B is a limit point whose partition (I', J) is null and whose first-round row multipliers are equal to λ_1 just for the rows of I. Clearly, then,

$$\lambda_1 = \frac{U_I}{V_J}. \tag{36}$$

The first consequence of (36) together with the assumption $\lambda_1 < 1$ is that if $A_{I'J} = 0$ then the condition of the theorem is violated. The only case that remains to be dealt with, then, is $\lambda_1 < 1$ together with

$$A_{I'J} \neq 0. \tag{37}$$

The next step is to show that the first-round row multipliers not only of A^B, but of *any* limit point whose (I', J) partition vanishes, are equal to λ_1 for just the rows that make up the set I. Let $A*$ be any such limit point, then $\sum_J s_j^1(A*)\, ia_{Ij}^{*1} = V_J$ (where a_{Ij}^{*1} denotes the jth column of A_{IJ}^{*1} and A^{*1} denotes the first matrix of the sequence generated by $(A*, u, v)$). Hence

$$\sum_{j \in J}\left[s_j^1(A*)\, \frac{ia_{Ij}^{*1}}{iA_{IJ}^{*1}i}\right] = \frac{V_J}{iA_{IJ}^{*1}i} = \frac{V_J}{U_I - iA_{IJ'}^{*1}i}.$$

But the left-hand side is a convex combination of $s_j^1(A*)$, none of which can exceed $1/\lambda_1$ (by the nondecreasing property of $\max_j s_j^t$ implied by (23), (25)); and the right-hand side is not less than $1/\lambda_1$ by the non-negativity of $A_{IJ'}^{*1}$ and (36). Therefore $s_j^1(A*) = 1/\lambda_1$ for all $j \in J$ and $A_{IJ'}^{*1} = 0$; thus A_{IJ}^{*1} is an isolated partition of $A*$ and by an application of (35) $r_i^1(A*) = \lambda_1$ for all $i \in I$. That is, if $\bar{I}$ denotes the set of i for which $r_i^1(A*) = \lambda_1$, then $\bar{I} \supseteq I$. Then $I' \subseteq I'$ and $A_{\bar{I}'J} = 0$, so we have $1/\lambda_1 = V_J/U_{\bar{I}}$. (36) now shows that $\bar{I}$ and I must be one and the same.

The following few steps complete the proof. For any A and any cell (i, j) of (I', J) that is initially 'full' (i.e. contains a nonzero entry), $a_{ij}^{2t+2}/a_{ij}^{2t}$ gets near a number λ_k/λ_1 that exceeds 1, as A^{2t} gets near $A*$: $(iA_{I'J}^{2t+2}i)/(iA_{I'J}^{2t}i)$ too, therefore, approaches a number greater than 1. But the set of $A*$'s is finite, so whenever $iA_{I'J}^{2t}i$ is sufficiently close to 0 it must be increasing. The last paragraph establishes a barrier through which $iA_{I'J}^{2t}i$ can never sink, and so achieves a contradiction of the assumption that $A_{I'J} \neq 0$. The details follow.

It follows from the continuity property of $r^1(B)$ that if A^{2t} is near enough to some $A*$ then for any $(i, j) \in (I', J)$ for which $a_{ij} > 0$, $a_{ij}^{2t+2}/a_{ij}^{2t}$ is arbitrarily near λ_k/λ_1 for some $\lambda_k > \lambda_1$. Since $A_{I'J} \neq 0$, $iA_{I'J}^{2t}i > 0$ for all t and there is a positive number $\epsilon*$, depending on $A*$, such that

$$|a_{ij}^{2t} - a_{ij}^*| \leq \epsilon* \text{ for all } i, j \text{ implies } iA_{I'J}^{2t+2}i > iA_{I'J}^{2t}i. \tag{38}$$

The set of limit points of $\{A^{2t}\}$ is finite. For let A^B, A^{BB} be any two that are disconnected in the same way. Then $r_i^1(A^{BB}) = \lambda_k$ for $i \in k$ and A_{kk}^B, A_{kk}^{BB} are both solutions of $\left(A_{kk}, \dfrac{1}{\lambda_k} u_k, v_k\right)$ and so are one and the same. But the number of distinct disconnections of a matrix is finite.

$\min_{A*} \epsilon*$ exists as the set of $A*$'s is finite, and it is positive. But then there is a positive number $\epsilon \leq \min \epsilon*$ such that, if $a_{ij}^{2t} \leq \epsilon$ for all $(i, j) \in (I', J)$ then, for some $A*$, $|a_{ij}^{2t} - a_{ij}^*| < \min \epsilon*$ for all (i, j). For otherwise there is a subsequence of $\{A^{2t}\}$ whose partition $(I'J)$ tends to zero but none of whose limit points is an $A*$, contrary to the definition of the set of $A*$'s. It follows by (38) that

$$a_{ij}^{2t} \leq \epsilon \text{ for all } (i, j) \in (I', J) \text{ implies } iA_{I'J}^{2t+2}i > iA_{I'J}^{2t}i, \tag{39}$$

i.e. that if every element of $A^{2t}_{I'J}$ is near enough to zero, then the sum of the elements of $A^{2t}_{I'J}$ is increasing.

Let us write $\min_i r^1_i = r^-$, $\min_j s^1_j = s^-$. By (37), $iA^{2t}_{I'J}i > r^-s^-\eta$ for $t = 0$ and for some positive number $\eta \leq \epsilon$. Assume that for arbitrary t $iA^{2t}_{I'J}i > r^-s^-\eta$. If, on the one hand, $iA^{2t}_{I'J}i > \eta$, then $iA^{2t+2}_{I'J}i > r^-s^-\eta$ by the fact that $a^{2t+2}_{ij} = r^t_i s^t_j a^{2t}_{ij}$ and the monotone properties of $\min_i r^t_i$, $\min_j s^t_j$. If, on the other hand, $iA^{2t}_{I'J}i \leq \eta$, then $iA^{2t+2}_{I'J}i > iA^{2t}_{I'J}i > r^-s^-\eta$ by (39) and the fact that $\eta \leq \epsilon$. We have shown that $iA^{2t}_{I'J}i > r^-s^-\eta$ for all t and so that no limit point $A*$ exists, contrary to the assumption that A^B is such a limit point. The assumption (37) that $A_{I'J} \neq 0$ is therefore false.

This proves the sufficiency of (26)–(27). Necessity is easily shown. If $A_{I'J} = 0$ then in any solution A^B

$$V_{J'} = \sum_{i=1}^{m} \sum_{j \in J'} a^B_{ij} \geq \sum_{i \in I'} \sum_{j \in J'} a^B_{ij},$$

and the last summation $= U_{I'}$, by hypothesis. This is (26), and (27) follows from a similar argument. $\mid$

COROLLARY 2. A solution of (A, u, v) exists if and only if (26)–(27) holds.

PROOF. Necessity was shown in proving the necessity of Theorem 3. Sufficiency follows from the sufficiency part of Theorem 3. $\mid$

It may be worth while to summarize the outcomes of the process (A, u, v) that have emerged as possible ones if conditions (26), (27) are fulfilled, and at the same time to clarify the logical role played by these conditions in the proof of the theorem. One *possible* case is that $\{A^{2t}\}$ has a connected limit point. If it does, $iu = iv$ is enough by itself to establish solution. The only other possible case is that $\{A^{2t}\}$ has no connected limit point but one or more disconnected ones. We showed that, on this assumption, if in addition (a) $\lambda_1 = 1$ then $iu = iv$ is again sufficient. We ended up by showing that indeed λ_1 must equal 1: this may create the impression that $iu = iv$ is an all-case sufficient condition for the theorem, but that is not so. For stronger conditions were needed precisely to establish that $\lambda_1 = 1$. We showed that, on the same case (ii) assumption, if in addition (b) $\lambda_1 < 1$ then (26), (27) were violated (but not necessarily the weaker condition $iu = iv$). The negative converse is that the full conditions (26), (27) imply that $\lambda_1 = 1$. In short, if any limit point is disconnected, then (26), (27) are needed to show λ_1 is such that the limit point is also a solution.

5   SOME COROLLARIES

In this section we present various corollaries of the fundamental unique-ness and convergence-existence theorems of the last two sections. The first of these connects our conditions for the existence of a matrix A^B obeying the row and column constraints and *biproportional* to a given matrix A, with those for the existence of a nonnegative matrix B obeying the same constraints but otherwise constrained only to preserve zero elements of a given matrix A. The two sets of conditions are one and the same.

COROLLARY 3. There exists a matrix B satisfying

$$B \geq 0,$$

$$Bi = u, \quad iB = v,$$

$$a_{ij} = 0 \quad \text{implies} \quad b_{ij} = 0$$

if and only if conditions (26), (27) are fulfilled.

PROOF. Sufficiency is obvious. Necessity is proved by an immediate generalization of the proof of the necessity part of Theorem 3.|

Corollary 3 establishes that the conditions for the existence of a biproportional solution are not very stringent. In input–output terms, it shows that a biproportional estimate fails to exist only in circumstances in which there exists no transactions matrix estimate that fulfils the marginal constraints and the minimal further conditions that we would wish to impose. The biproportional input–output estimation model, then, is not handicapped by the condition of biproportionality itself: relaxing this condition would not make available any other 'minimally restricted' marginally constrained estimate.

Dr M. A. H. Dempster, in a private communication, suggests proving sufficiency in Corollary 3 by considering the zero-preserving function, f say, which maps A^{2t} into A^{2t+2} for given u and v. A fixed point theorem shows that $iu = iv$ (one implication of (26)–(27)) implies that among non-negative matrices that satisfy the column constraints there exists one, B say, such that $f(B) = B$, i.e. $B^2(u, v) = B$. There remains the difficulty of establishing the conditions under which $B^2(u, v) = B$ implies that $Bi = u$. The question of conditions for the existence of nonnegative, zero-preserving matrices subject to more general constraints than the marginal equalities of Corollary 3 has been considered by Fréchet [31] and by others referred to in [69].

The next corollary specifies the circumstances in which a positive element of A is driven to zero in a solution A^B.

COROLLARY 4. Let $a_{ij} > 0$. Then $a_{ij}^B = 0$ if and only if (26), (27) hold as equations for some nonempty I', J and $i \in I$, $j \in J'$.

PROOF. Sufficiency is obvious. Necessity may be shown by going through the proof of Theorem 2 using the normalization $R_i^t = 1$.|

We have the following further result relating the vanishing of a positive element of A to A^B's being a boundary solution.

COROLLARY 5. $a_{ij} > 0$ and $a_{ij}^B = 0$ for some (i,j) if and only if A^B is a boundary solution.

PROOF. Necessity follows easily from the definition of an interior solution. Conversely, suppose A^B is a boundary solution. Then for some connected partition A_{kk} of A the corresponding partition A_{kk}^B of A^B cannot be expressed in the form $\langle r_k \rangle A_{kk} \langle s_k \rangle$. Applying the method of proof of Theorem 2 to A_{kk} shows that A_{kk}^B is disconnected, proving the sufficiency statement.|

We next show that a solution A^B of a problem (A, u, v) may always be expressed in the form $\langle r \rangle \overset{0}{A} \langle s \rangle$ for a matrix $\overset{0}{A}$ whose nonzero partition is the same as the corresponding partition of A. By permutations of rows and columns we may always express a solution A^B of (A, u, v) in the form

$$
A^B = \begin{bmatrix} A_{11}^B & 0 & \cdots & 0 \\ 0 & A_{22}^B & \cdots & 0 \\ \vdots & \vdots & & \vdots \\ 0 & 0 & \cdots & A_{KK}^B \end{bmatrix},
$$

where each diagonal partition A_{kk}^B is connected, $k = 1, \ldots, K$. Suppose this to have been done. Then we have

COROLLARY 6. The solution A^B of (A, u, v) has the form

$$
A^B = \begin{bmatrix} \langle r_1 \rangle & \cdots & 0 \\ \vdots & & \vdots \\ 0 & \cdots & \langle r_K \rangle \end{bmatrix} \begin{bmatrix} A_{11} & \cdots & 0 \\ \vdots & & \vdots \\ 0 & \cdots & A_{KK} \end{bmatrix} \begin{bmatrix} \langle s_1 \rangle & \cdots & 0 \\ \vdots & & \vdots \\ 0 & \cdots & \langle s_K \rangle \end{bmatrix}
$$

where A_{kk} is the partition of A corresponding to the partition A_{kk}^B of A^B, and the vector-pair (r_k, s_k) is unique up to the transformation

$$
\left(\lambda_k r_k, \frac{1}{\lambda_k} s_k \right),
$$

where λ_k is a nonzero real number, $k = 1, \ldots, K$.

PROOF. The partition A_{kk}^B is a connected solution of the problem (A_{kk}, u_k, v_k), in an obvious notation. Hence by the proof of Theorem 2, $A_{kk}^B = \langle r_k \rangle A_{kk} \langle s_k \rangle$ for some vectors r_k, s_k unique up to multiplication by reciprocal real numbers.|

Let us write

$$
\begin{pmatrix} r_1 \\ \vdots \\ r_K \end{pmatrix} = r, \qquad \begin{pmatrix} s_1 \\ \vdots \\ s_K \end{pmatrix} = s,
$$

$$
\begin{bmatrix} A_{11} & \cdots & 0 \\ \vdots & & \vdots \\ 0 & \cdots & A_{KK} \end{bmatrix} = \overset{0}{A}. \tag{40}
$$

We note the obvious fact that $\overset{0}{A} = A$ is equivalent to A^B's being an interior solution. The expression of any solution A^B in the form $\langle r \rangle \overset{0}{A} \langle s \rangle$ which Corollary 6 provides will come in useful in certain applications in Chapters 6, 7 and 9.

Finally, Corollary 7 relates the connectedness of A^B to the equality of $\overset{0}{A}$ with A — and hence to A^B's status as an interior solution.

COROLLARY 7. Let A be connected. A^B is connected if and only if $\overset{0}{A} = A$.

PROOF. Sufficiency is obvious. If A^B is connected then $K = 1$ in the expression (40) for $\overset{0}{A}$ and $\overset{0}{A} = A_{11}$ is an $(m \times n)$-order partition of A and therefore equal to A. |

We may also prove Corollary 7 by a different route. If A is connected then we know from the proof of Theorem 2 that A^B is connected only if it is an interior solution, and the sufficiency of this condition is clear. The result then follows from the observation above that $\overset{0}{A} = A$ if and only if A^B is interior.

6 ANOTHER APPROACH

Gorman[36] has tackled the central questions (i)–(iii) put in the first paragraph of this chapter by considering the function

$$f(\alpha, \beta) = \sum_{i,j} a_{ij} e^{\alpha_i + \beta_j} - \sum_i u_i \alpha_i - \sum_j v_j \beta_j,$$

which has a stationary value only if $\sum_j a_{ij} e^{\alpha_i + \beta_j} = u_i$ and an analogous equation for v_j hold, i.e. only if $\langle r \rangle A \langle s \rangle$ satisfies the marginal constraints, where $r_i = e^{\alpha_i}$, $s_j = e^{\beta_j}$.

The existence result that is proved by this route is, in our terms, that an *interior* solution exists if and only if some connected, zero-preserving, constraint-satisfying matrix does (a result that follows from combining Theorem 3 and Corollary 3). We shall sketch the proof.

Since f is convex, it does have a minimum if it tends to infinity in every direction (other than the 'exceptional direction' represented by adding ki to α, $-ki$ to β). Taking an arbitrary origin (α^0, β^0), consider the direction $(d, -e)$ of the vector $(\alpha, \beta) = (\alpha^0 + kd, \beta^0 - ke)$. If, for some full cell (i, j), $d_i > e_j$, f does indeed tend to infinity. If on the other hand $d_i \leqq e_j$ for all such cells, f still tends to ∞ if its linear part does so, and its linear part does so as long as $\Sigma u_i d_i - \Sigma v_j e_j < 0$. The final part of the existence proof consists of showing that, on the conditions of the theorem, the last inequality indeed holds except for the case $d = ki$, $e = -ki$. Bingen's simplification[10] of Gorman's original proof comes in this part. It is easily shown that $\Sigma u_i d_i - \Sigma v_j e_j = \Sigma b_{ij}(d_i - e_j)$ for the non-negative, connected matrix B posited in the theorem, so the supposition $d_i \leq e_j$ implies the nonpositivity of $\Sigma u_i d_i - \Sigma v_j e_j$. The only worrying case is equality of $\Sigma u_i d_i$ and $\Sigma v_j e_j$. If this *is* the case, an inductive argument on rows and columns of the zero-preserving matrix B, much like the argument in the proof of Theorem 1, shows that either (impossibly) B is disconnected, or else all the d_i's and e_j's are equal, that is (α, β) lies in the 'exceptional direction'.

Uniqueness of an interior solution follows immediately from the convexity of f. Finally, convergence of the process (A, u, v) to this solution is shown by the following consideration. Defining $\alpha^t = \log r^t$, $\beta^t = \log s^t$, β^t minimizes $f(\alpha^t, \beta)$ given α^t, and α^t minimizes $f(\alpha, \beta^{t-1})$ given β^{t-1}, whence the sequence $f^t = f(\alpha^t, \beta^t)$ is monotonically decreasing. But f^t is bounded below by, and now can easily be shown to approach, the minimum value of f attained at the solution (α, β) whose existence has already been established.

The elegant indirect demonstrations of Gorman and Bingen are a little more limited in their objectives than the constructive but long-winded arguments of sections 3 to 5. Theorem 3 was really two theorems in one: the first is the Gorman–Bingen existence result, the second a statement of concrete conditions (26), (27) for the more abstract conditions of Gorman–Bingen. (26), (27) are directly verifiable, at least for small matrices. In the second place, sections 3 to 5 tried to give an account of the conditions and character of boundary solutions as well as of interior solutions of the biproportional problem.

CHAPTER 5

FRIEDLANDER'S PROBLEM AND THE DISTURBED BIPROPORTIONAL PROBLEM

1 INTRODUCTION

In the first part of this chapter we turn our attention to the constrained matrix problem raised by Friedlander[32] which was introduced in section 7 of Chapter 3. We begin with a formal statement of the problem.

DEFINITION. The *Friedlander problem* (A, u, v) is to find a matrix A^F such that
$$A^F = A + \langle \xi \rangle A + A \langle \eta \rangle, \quad (1)$$

$$A^F i = u, \quad i A^F = v, \quad (2)$$

for some vectors ξ, η; where u, v are given vectors and A is a given matrix such that
$$a_i \geqslant 0, \quad a^j \geqslant 0 \quad (i = 1, ..., m; j = 1, ..., n).$$

It is important to notice that, unlike in the biproportional problem (A, u, v), neither the marginal vectors nor the solution are restricted to being non-negative.

The main reason for studying Friedlander's problem is to throw additional light on the biproportional problem. We first (section 2) establish exact conditions for the existence and uniqueness of Friedlander solutions, as Friedlander himself did not do in [32]. In sections 4 and 6 we use these conditions in showing and exploring the implications of the fact that a Friedlander solution yields first variations of the r, s solving a general biproportional problem. In sections 5 and 7 we examine the effects on a biproportional estimate of errors in the assumption of biproportionality for the matrix to be estimated and of errors of observation in the marginal constraints. Assuming errors of these kinds to be small allows us to make use of our results on the differential behaviour of the (r, s) of a biproportional solution.

2 THE SOLUTION OF THE FRIEDLANDER PROBLEM

As a preliminary to proving the basic existence-uniqueness result for the Friedlander problem (Theorem 4), we need to prove two lemmas. These lemmas relate the connectedness of a matrix A with the primitivity of the matrix AA' and of a certain other matrix. Here and henceforth a prime attached to a matrix denotes transposition.

LEMMA 2. Let A be a matrix with semipositive rows and columns. If A is connected then AA' is neither decomposable nor cyclic.

PROOF. Suppose AA' decomposable. Then there is an index set I such that $I \neq \{0\}$, $I' \neq \{0\}$, $(AA')_{II'} = 0$. I.e. for all $i \in I$, $i' \in I'$, $a_i a_{i'} = 0$. Letting

$$J' = \{j \mid a_{ij} > 0 \text{ for some } i \in I\} \tag{3}$$

this implies that $\quad a_{ij} = 0 \quad$ for all $i \in I'$, for each $j \in J'$. $\tag{4}$

J' is non-empty by the semipositivity of A's rows together with (3), and J is non-empty by the semipositivity of A's rows together with (4). We have shown that there exist non-empty I, I', J, J' such that $A_{IJ} = 0$, $A_{I'J'} = 0$, i.e. that A is disconnected.

Suppose AA' cyclic. Then there exists a non-empty index-set I such that $(AA')_{II} = 0$. Then $a_i a_i = 0$ for a non-empty set of i, contrary to the assumption of semipositive rows.

Conversely, it is easily shown that disconnection of A implies decomposability of AA.|

Let the operators $\mathscr{R}$ ('form coefficients by rows') and $\mathscr{C}$ ('form coefficients by columns') be defined as follows, for a matrix A with semipositive rows and columns:

$$\mathscr{R}A = \langle Ai \rangle^{-1} A,$$
$$\mathscr{C}A = A \langle iA \rangle^{-1}.$$

We have the following corollary of Lemma 2.

LEMMA 3. Let A be a matrix with semipositive rows and columns. If A is connected then $(\mathscr{R}A)(\mathscr{C}A)'$ is neither decomposable nor cyclic.

PROOF. By the semipositivity assumption, if the (i,j)th element of $(\mathscr{R}A)(\mathscr{C}A)'$ is zero then so is the (i,j)th element of AA'. Thus the decomposability or cyclicity of $(\mathscr{R}A)(\mathscr{C}A)'$ implies that of AA'.|

THEOREM 4. Suppose A is connected; then a solution to the Friedlander problem (A, u, v) exists if and only if $iu = iv$, and this solution is unique.

PROOF. (1), (2) may be written

$$Ai + \langle \xi \rangle Ai + A\eta = u,$$
$$iA + \xi A + iA \langle \eta \rangle = v,$$

which, by the semipositivity of the rows and columns of A, may be written as

$$\begin{aligned} i + \langle \xi \rangle i + (\mathscr{R}A)\eta &= \langle Ai \rangle^{-1} u, \\ i + \xi(\mathscr{C}A) + i\langle \eta \rangle &= v \langle iA \rangle^{-1}, \end{aligned} \tag{5}$$

or, transposing the second equation, as

$$\xi + (\mathscr{R}A)\eta = \langle Ai \rangle^{-1} u - i,$$
$$(\mathscr{C}A)'\xi + \eta = \langle iA \rangle^{-1} v - i.$$

But these equations are equivalent to

$$[I - (\mathscr{R}A)(\mathscr{C}A)']\,\xi = \langle Ai \rangle^{-1}u - (\mathscr{R}A)\langle Ai \rangle^{-1}v = c \text{ say,} \tag{6}$$

$$\eta = -(\mathscr{C}A)'\,\xi + \langle iA \rangle^{-1}v - i. \tag{7}$$

$(\mathscr{R}A)(\mathscr{C}A)'$ is a nonnegative square matrix whose rows sum to i, i.e. its transpose is a Markov matrix (on the convention of writing the state probability vector of a Markov process as a column). Further, since A is connected $(\mathscr{R}A)(\mathscr{C}A)'$ is indecomposable and acyclic by Lemma 3, and so therefore is its transpose. Hence by a well-known theorem on Markov matrices (see e.g. [22]) there is a uniquely proportioned vector w such that

$$\{I - [(\mathscr{R}A)(\mathscr{C}A)']'\}\,w = 0, \tag{8}$$

i.e. such that $w[I - (\mathscr{R}A)(\mathscr{C}A)'] = 0$. It follows by a basic result of linear algebra (see e.g. [63]) that (6) has a solution if $wc = 0$. But it is easily seen that

$$(iA')[I - (\mathscr{R}A)(\mathscr{C}A)'] = 0 \tag{9}$$

and that

$$(iA')\,c = iA'[\langle iA' \rangle^{-1}u - (\mathscr{R}A)\langle iA \rangle^{-1}v] \tag{10}$$

$$= iu - iv = 0$$

by the condition of the theorem. Thus (6) has a solution ξ; taken together with η given by (7), this provides a solution of the Friedlander problem.

It follows from (8) by a standard theorem on eigenvectors that there is also a uniquely proportioned vector, ζ say, such that

$$[I - (\mathscr{R}A)(\mathscr{C}A)']\,\zeta = 0,$$

and by another basic theorem of linear algebra (see e.g. [63]) that every solution of (6) is of the form $\xi + \lambda\zeta$, where λ is a real number. But

$$[I - (\mathscr{R}A)(\mathscr{C}A)']\,i = 0,$$

so every solution of (6) is of the form $\xi + \lambda i$. (7) then gives

$$-(\mathscr{C}A)'\,(\xi + \lambda i) + \langle iA \rangle^{-1}v - i = -(\mathscr{C}A)'\,\xi + \langle iA \rangle^{-1}v - i - \lambda i$$

$$= \eta - \lambda i.$$

But $A + \langle \xi + \lambda i \rangle A + A\langle \eta - \lambda i \rangle = A + \langle \xi \rangle A + A\langle \eta \rangle$; thus the solution of the Friedlander is unique.

The condition $iu = iv$ is obviously necessary for a solution to exist. |

3   The explicit solution of the Friedlander problem

In section 5 we shall find that the Friedlander solution describes the differential behaviour of a biproportional solution with respect to its marginals. An explicit mapping of (u, v) into the (ξ, η) of a Friedlander solution would enable us, then, to trace the implications for the biproportional solution of a specific pattern of local random variation in (u, v). In this section, accordingly, we derive such an explicit mapping. We display a matrix transformation of (u, v) into a normalized pair (ξ, η) solving the Friedlander for given connected A. We shall assume throughout this section that $m, n \geq 2$. The case of m or $n = 1$ is trivial and its inclusion would complicate the analysis pointlessly.

We first rewrite (6) as

$$B\xi = \begin{bmatrix} b_{11} & \tilde{b}_1 \\ \bar{b}^1 & \bar{\bar{B}} \end{bmatrix} \begin{pmatrix} \xi_1 \\ \bar{\xi} \end{pmatrix} = \begin{pmatrix} c_1 \\ \bar{c} \end{pmatrix}.$$

Here and henceforth a super-bar denotes the deletion of the first row (element) of a matrix (vector), a super-tilde the deletion of the first column (element) of a matrix (vector), and two super-bars the deletion of the first row and column of a matrix. We have

$$b_{11}\xi_1 + \tilde{b}_1\bar{\xi} = c_1, \quad \bar{b}^1\xi_1 + \bar{\bar{B}}\bar{\xi} = \bar{c}. \tag{11}$$

It follows from (11) and the fact, shown in the proof of Theorem 4, that $\bar{\xi}$ is uniquely determined by setting ξ_1, that $\bar{\bar{B}}$ is invertible. Let us normalize ξ by setting

$$\xi_1 = 0. \tag{12}$$

Then we have

$$\bar{\xi} = \bar{\bar{B}}^{-1}\bar{c}. \tag{13}$$

(Satisfaction of the consistency requirement that $\tilde{b}_1\bar{\xi} = c_1$ is checked as follows.

$$iA' \begin{bmatrix} \tilde{b}_1 \\ \bar{\bar{B}} \end{bmatrix} = ia_1 b_1 + i\widetilde{A'}\bar{B} = 0 \quad \text{from (9),}$$

$$iA' \begin{pmatrix} c_1 \\ \bar{c} \end{pmatrix} = ia_1 c_1 + i\widetilde{A'}\bar{c} = 0 \quad \text{from (10).}$$

Hence $\bar{\bar{B}}\bar{\xi} = \bar{c}$ implies $ia_1 b_1 \bar{\xi} = ia_1 c_1$.)

In terms of A, u, v, (13) may be written

$$\bar{\xi} = [\overline{I - (\mathscr{R}A)\,(\mathscr{C}A)'}]^{-1} (\langle \overline{Ai} \rangle^{-1}\bar{u} - \overline{\mathscr{R}A}\langle iA \rangle^{-1}v), \tag{14}$$

and finally, we have from (7), (12), (14)

$$\eta = -[(\mathscr{C}A)']^1 \xi_1 - \widetilde{(\mathscr{C}A)}'\bar{\xi} + \langle iA \rangle^{-1}v - i$$

$$= -\widetilde{(\mathscr{C}A)}'[\overline{I - (\mathscr{R}A)\,(\mathscr{C}A)'}]^{-1}\langle \overline{Ai} \rangle^{-1}\bar{u}$$

$$+ \{\widetilde{(\mathscr{C}A)}'\,[\overline{I - (\mathscr{R}A)\,(\mathscr{C}A)'}]i^{-1}\,\overline{\mathscr{R}A} + I\}\langle iA \rangle^{-1}v - i, \tag{15}$$

where $[(\mathscr{C}A)']^1$ denotes the first column of $(\mathscr{C}A)'$. (14), (15) together with (12) give the following explicit expression for the normalized (ξ, η)

of the Friedlander solution as a linear transformation of (u, v):

$$\binom{\xi}{\eta} = \begin{bmatrix} 0 & 0 \\ \bar{B}^{-1}\langle \overline{Ai}\rangle^{-1} & -\bar{B}^{-1}\overline{\mathscr{R}A}\langle iA\rangle^{-1} \\ -(\widetilde{\mathscr{C}A})'\bar{B}^{-1}\langle \overline{Ai}\rangle^{-1} & [(\widetilde{\mathscr{C}A})'\bar{B}^{-1}\overline{\mathscr{R}A}+I]\langle \overline{iA}\rangle^{-1} \end{bmatrix} \binom{\bar{u}}{v} - \binom{0}{0}$$

$$= C\binom{\bar{u}}{v} - \binom{0}{i}, \quad \text{say.} \tag{16}$$

Rather surprisingly, $\bar{C}$ is symmetric: the effect of variation in the kth element of $(\bar{u}, v)$ on the hth of $(\bar{\xi}, \eta)$, $h, k = 1, ..., m+n-1$, and of the hth element of $(\bar{u}, v)$ on the kth of $(\bar{\xi}, \eta)$ are the same. Thus

$$\frac{\partial \xi_i}{\partial u_{i'}} = \frac{\partial \xi_{i'}}{\partial u_i}, \quad \frac{\partial \xi_i}{\partial v_j} = \frac{\partial \eta_j}{\partial u_i}, \quad \text{etc.}$$

In economic terms this means, in particular, that an increase in the intermediate input of an industry increases the Friedlander measure of the substitution effect for its product exactly as much as the same increase in its intermediate output increases the Friedlander measure of its fabrication effect.

First, the partition $\bar{B}^{-1}\langle \overline{Ai}\rangle^{-1}$ of $\bar{C}$ is symmetric if its inverse $\langle \overline{Ai}\rangle \bar{B}$ is, and this is so if $\langle Ai\rangle B$ is. But

$$\langle Ai\rangle B = \langle Ai\rangle[I - (\mathscr{R}A)(\mathscr{C}A)'] = \langle Ai\rangle - A\langle iA\rangle^{-1}A'.$$

Secondly, we must show that the transpose of $\bar{B}^{-1}\overline{\mathscr{R}A}\langle iA\rangle^{-1}$ is $(\widetilde{\mathscr{C}A})'\bar{B}^{-1}\langle \overline{Ai}\rangle^{-1}$. Now $\bar{B}^{-1}\overline{\mathscr{R}A}\langle iA\rangle^{-1} = \bar{B}^{-1}\langle \overline{Ai}\rangle^{-1}\bar{A}\langle iA\rangle^{-1}$, whose transpose is $(\bar{A}\langle iA\rangle^{-1})'(\bar{B}^{-1}\langle \overline{Ai}\rangle^{-1})$, by what was shown in the last paragraph. But $\bar{A}\langle iA\rangle^{-1} = \widetilde{\mathscr{C}A}$, the transpose of which is indeed $(\widetilde{\mathscr{C}A})'$.

Finally, consider the bottom right-hand partition of $\bar{C}$. Its second term is diagonal and therefore symmetric; its first is symmetric too since it equals

$$(\bar{A}\langle iA\rangle^{-1})'\bar{B}^{-1}(\langle \overline{Ai}\rangle^{-1}\bar{A})\langle iA\rangle^{-1} = (\bar{A}\langle iA\rangle^{-1})'(\bar{B}^{-1}\langle \overline{Ai}\rangle^{-1})(\bar{A}\langle iA\rangle^{-1}).$$

4　DIFFERENTIABILITY OF (r, s) AS A FUNCTION OF (u, v)

We now come to the point: to the problem, that is, of determining variations of a normalized (r, s) pair solving the biproportionality problem (A, u, v) with respect to small disturbances of the marginal vectors u, v. We already know that under certain conditions on A, u, v this (r, s) is given as a single-valued function of (u, v). In order to proceed we next need to make sure of the differentiability properties of this function. Its continuity will enable us, in section 5, to make a statement about the behaviour of the estimate A^B of $A(1)$ as $A(1)$ approaches a value biproportional to the initial matrix A. This statement will be generalized in

Chapter 7, where we shall discuss its significance in the light of the evidence of the Belgian tests on the intertemporal biproportionality of input–output matrices. In the course of investigating the differentiability properties of the function, facts will be established about a certain Jacobian which later on (section 6) will prove helpful in evaluating the partial derivatives $\partial r_i/\partial u_{i'}$, etc. These partials, in turn, are employed in section 7 to express the joint distribution of (r, s) in terms of that of (u, v).

It will be convenient to define the vector-valued function of u, v, r, s

$$f(u, v, r, s) = \begin{pmatrix} \langle r \rangle As - u \\ \langle s \rangle A'r - v \end{pmatrix},$$

where, we recall, A' denotes the transpose of A. We are now ready to prove the differentiability of (r, s) as a function of (u, v).

THEOREM 5. Suppose that A is connected and suppose that

$$f(u^0, v^0, r^0, s^0) = 0. \tag{17}$$

Then there exists a function $\phi(u, v)$ defined on pairs (u, v) lying in a neighbourhood of (u^0, v^0) and satisfying $iu = iv$ (i) such that $(r, s) = \phi(u, v)$ provides the unique solution of $f(u, v, r, s) = 0$ and (ii) having continuous partial derivatives with respect to the u, v.

PROOF. Consider the Jacobian

$$J = \frac{\partial f}{\partial (r, s)} = \begin{bmatrix} a_1 s & \cdots & 0 & r_1 a_1 \\ \vdots & & \vdots & \vdots \\ 0 & \cdots & a_m s & r_m a_m \\ & & & \\ s_1 a^1 & & a^1 r & \cdots & 0 \\ \vdots & & \vdots & & \vdots \\ s_n a^n & & 0 & \cdots & a^n r \end{bmatrix}.$$

Evaluating this at (u^0, v^0, r^0, s^0) we have

$$J(u^0, v^0, r^0, s^0) = \begin{bmatrix} \langle u^0 \rangle \langle r^0 \rangle^{-1} & \langle r^0 \rangle A \\ \langle s^0 \rangle A' & \langle v^0 \rangle \langle s^0 \rangle^{-1} \end{bmatrix}$$

$$= \begin{bmatrix} \langle u^0 \rangle \langle r^0 \rangle^{-1} & \langle u^0 \rangle (\mathscr{R}A^{B0}) \langle s^0 \rangle^{-1} \\ \langle v^0 \rangle (\mathscr{C}A^{B0})' \langle r^0 \rangle^{-1} & \langle v^0 \rangle \langle s^0 \rangle^{-1} \end{bmatrix}$$

$$= \begin{bmatrix} \langle u^0 \rangle & 0 \\ 0 & \langle v^0 \rangle \end{bmatrix} \begin{bmatrix} I & \mathscr{R}A^{B0} \\ (\mathscr{C}A^{B0})' & I \end{bmatrix} \begin{bmatrix} \langle r^0 \rangle^{-1} & 0 \\ 0 & \langle s^0 \rangle^{-1} \end{bmatrix}, \tag{18}$$

where $A^{B0} = A^B(u^0, v^0) = \langle r^0 \rangle A \langle s^0 \rangle.$

But the second factor of the right-hand side of (18) with its first row and column deleted is nonsingular if A^{B0} is connected by virtue of Theorem 4, and A^{B0} is indeed connected since A is. Thus the matrix of the partials of all the elements of f but the first with respect to all the r, s but r_1 is nonsingular. I.e.

$$\left|\frac{\partial \bar{f}}{\partial(\bar{r}, s)}\right| \neq 0, \quad \text{where } f = \binom{f_1}{\bar{f}}, \quad r = \binom{r_1}{\bar{r}}.$$

But setting $r_1 = r_1^0$ we have $\bar{f}(u^0, v^0, \bar{r}^0, s^0) = 0$. Hence by a standard implicit function theorem (see e.g. [37]) there exists a function $\bar{\phi}(u, v)$ on (u, v) in a neighbourhood N_1 of (u^0, v^0) (i) such that $(\bar{r}, s) = \bar{\phi}(u, v)$ gives the unique solution of $\bar{f}(u, v, \bar{r}, s) = 0$ and (ii) having continuous partial derivatives. Now consider the function ϕ defined by

$$\phi(u, v) = \binom{r_1^0}{\bar{\phi}(u, v)}.$$

As (A, u^0, v^0) has an interior solution it is clear from Theorem 3 and Corollaries 4 and 5 that for any (u, v) in some neighbourhood N_2 of (u^0, v^0) and such that $iu = iv$, there is a vector (r, s) with $r_1 = r_1^0$ that solves (A, u, v). Hence the partition $(\bar{r}, s)$ of this vector equals $\bar{\phi}(u, v)$ if $(u, v) \in N_1 \cap N_2$. Finally, the differentiability of $\bar{\phi}(u, v)$ implies that of $\phi(u, v)$. |

5   ERROR IN THE ASSUMPTION OF BIPROPORTIONALITY

We can make use of the continuity result we have just proved (Theorem 5) to investigate how the biproportional estimation model behaves when the true value, $A(1)$ say, of the matrix to be estimated approximates a biproportional transform of the initial matrix A. In other words, we consider the effect upon the estimate of specification error in a hypothesis of the biproportionality of A and $A(1)$. What we learn now will be generalized in Chapter 7, and used to shed further light on the question of the economic appropriateness of biproportional estimates of input–output matrices.

Suppose first that the true matrix $A(1)$ is exactly biproportional to A and that its row and column sums are observed without error. That is,

$$A(1) \text{ biproportional to } A, \tag{19}$$

$$A(1) i = u, \quad iA(1) = v. \tag{20}$$

Then it is clear from the uniqueness result for the biproportional problem (Corollary 1) that $A(1)$ is correctly estimated as $A^B(u, v)$, i.e. that $A^B(u, v) = A(1)$. Conversely, it is obvious that (19), (20) are necessary conditions for the correct estimation of $A(1)$.

Let us now make $A(1)$ approach a value biproportional to A. We shall suppose that this value is expressible as $\langle r^0 \rangle A \langle s^0 \rangle$. Instead of (19) we now have

$$A(1) \to \langle r^0 \rangle A \langle s^0 \rangle \geqq 0. \tag{21}$$

Then
$$u = A(1)\, i \to \langle r^0 \rangle A s^0 = u^0 \text{ say,}$$

$$v = iA(1) \to r^0 A \langle s^0 \rangle = v^0 \text{ say.}$$

By Theorem 5, as $(u, v) \to (u^0, v^0)$ the normalized pair (r, s) solving the biproportional problem (A, u, v) approaches (r^0, s^0); we have therefore shown that A^B tends to $\langle r^0 \rangle A \langle s^0 \rangle$ with $A(1)$.

Conversely, if $A(1)$ tends to a limit A_{lim} say, then A^B tends to the same limit A_{lim} only if A_{lim} is biproportional to A. We have the following theorem.

THEOREM 6. Let $A(1) \to A_{\text{lim}}$. Then $A^B(A(1)\, i,\, iA(1)) \to A_{\text{lim}}$ if A_{lim} is nonnegative and of the form $\langle r^0 \rangle A \langle s^0 \rangle$ and only if A_{lim} is biproportional to A.

The case discussed above in which $A(1)$ is equal to $\langle r^0 \rangle A \langle s^0 \rangle$ may of course be read as a special case of the theorem.

6 PARTIAL DERIVATIVES OF a_{ij}^B WITH RESPECT TO u, v

We showed in the previous section but one that there is a function $\phi(u, v)$ with continuous partial derivatives which gives the normalized (r, s) solving the biproportional problem (A, u, v) for (u, v) satisfying $iu = iv$ and in the neighbourhood of a point yielding an initial interior solution. It follows that the proportionate changes from their initial values in the normalized (r, s) of the solution are also a continuously differentiable function on this domain of (u, v) space. We shall now identify the partial derivatives of this function, evaluated at the initial solution, as the elements of the matrix C of (16), appropriately evaluated.

We have
$$f_i(u^0, v^0, r^0, s^0) = 0,$$
$$\left. f_i[u^0 + \delta u, v^0 + \delta v, \phi(u^0 + \delta u, v^0 + \delta v)] = 0. \right\} \quad (i = 1, \dots, m+n).$$

Since f_i is differentiable in a neighbourhood of (u^0, v^0, r^0, s^0) the mean value theorem implies that for $i = 1, \dots, m+n$

$$\left(\frac{\partial f_i}{\partial u_1} + \epsilon_{i1} \right) \delta u_1 + \dots + \left(\frac{\partial f_i}{\partial v_n} + \epsilon_{i,\, m+n} \right) \delta v_n$$

$$+ \left(\frac{\partial f_i}{\partial r_i} + \eta_{i1} \right) \delta r_1 + \dots + \left(\frac{\partial f_i}{\partial s_n} + \eta_{i,\, m+n} \right) \delta s_n = 0,$$

where it is understood that the partial derivatives are evaluated at (u^0, v^0, r^0, s^0); and where

$$(\delta u, \delta v) = (u, v) - (u^0, v^0),$$

$$(\delta r, \delta s) = \phi(u^0 + \delta u, v^0 + \delta v) - \phi(u^0, v^0);$$

and the ϵ_{ij}, η_{ij} tend to zero with δu, δv. We may write

$$\left[\frac{\partial f}{\partial(u,v)}+\mathrm{E}\right]\binom{\delta u}{\delta v}+\left[\frac{\partial f}{\partial(r,s)}+\mathrm{H}\right]\binom{\delta r}{\delta s}=0,$$

where $\mathrm{E}=\{\epsilon_{ij}\}$, $\mathrm{H}=\{\eta_{ij}\}$, $i,j=1,\ldots,m+n$, and where E, H $\to 0$ with δu, δv. But from (18) this is just

$$\left\{\begin{bmatrix}\langle u^0\rangle & 0 \\ 0 & \langle v^0\rangle\end{bmatrix}\begin{bmatrix}I & \mathscr{R}A^{B0} \\ (\mathscr{C}A^{B0})' & I\end{bmatrix}\begin{bmatrix}\langle r^0\rangle^{-1} & 0 \\ 0 & \langle s^0\rangle^{-1}\end{bmatrix}+\mathrm{H}\right\}\binom{\delta r}{\delta s}$$

$$=[I-\mathrm{E}]\binom{u-u^0}{v-v^0}$$

or　$$\left\{\begin{bmatrix}I & \mathscr{R}A^{B0} \\ (\mathscr{C}A^{B0})' & I\end{bmatrix}+\mathrm{H}_1\right\}\binom{x}{y}=[I-\mathrm{E}_1]\binom{\langle A^{B0}i\rangle^{-1}u-i}{\langle iA^{B0}\rangle^{-1}v-i},$$

where x, y are proportionate deviations from r^0, s^0, and the matrices E_1, $\mathrm{H}_1 \to 0$ with δu, δv. It can be seen from (5) that, loosely speaking, (x,y) approximately solves the Friedlander (A^{B0},u,v). For small enough δu, δv the left-hand side matrix with its first row and column deleted is nonsingular. Since the inverse of a matrix B is continuous at a non-singular B, (x,y) normalized by $x_1=0$ is given by

$$\binom{x}{y}=(C^{B0}+\mathrm{E}_2)\binom{\bar{u}}{v}-\binom{0}{i}+\delta,$$

where E_2, $\delta \to 0$ with δu, δv, and C^{B0} is C of (16) evaluated at A^{B0}. From this we easily get

$$\frac{\partial X_i}{\partial U_k}=c_{ik}^{B0}\qquad (i=1,\ldots,m+n;\ k=2,\ldots,m+n),\qquad(22)$$

where $X=(x,y)$, $U=(u,v)$, or alternatively

$$\frac{\partial R_i}{\partial U_k}=R_1^0 c_{ik}^{B0},$$

where $R=(r,s)$. The elements of C^{B0} are the 'growth rates', or relative rates of change, at (u^0,v^0), of the R_i's with respect to the U_k's. Finally we have

$$\frac{\partial a_{ij}^B}{\partial U_k}=\frac{\partial}{\partial U_k}(r_i s_j a_{ij})=(r_i^0 s_j c_{ik}^{B0}+r_i s_j^0 c_{m+j,k}^{B0})a_{ij}$$

$$=(c_{ik}^{B0}+c_{m+j,k}^{B0})a_{ij}.$$

When the deviations of the u, v from the u^0, v^0, are small—in the circumstances, that is, in which the above formulae apply—the x's and y's, which have been defined as proportionate errors in the r's and s's, become also approximations for the logarithms of the ratios of calculated to true values of the r's and s's; for example,

$$x_i \approx \log\frac{r_i}{r_i^0}.$$

The x's and y's are then known as (approximate) *logarithmic errors* in the r's and s's.

7 THE DISTRIBUTION OF THE ESTIMATES u, v AND THE DISTRIBUTION OF r, s

In this section we make use of the above analysis of the differential behaviour of the biproportional solution to examine the random variation in this solution generated by small random variations in the row and column sums u, v. We refer to the input–output application of the biproportionality problem, so that u, v are intermediate output and input totals. For convenience, we shall take $m = n$.

The following model is an approximate representation of the stochastic process that generated the estimates of marginals that were used in the Cambridge Growth Project calculations described in [26]. We begin by assuming that observations of gross outputs, net outputs and final demands are independent: in particular, the sum of observed net outputs does not necessarily equal the sum of observed final demands. This is not true of any net output and final demand figures that were available to the Cambridge Growth Project: but it is true of the raw figures first reported to official statisticians. Thus the model is to be thought of as depicting not the work of the Cambridge group itself, but background statistical work carried out by the Central Statistical Office and other official bodies and applied by the Growth Project to the estimation of a 1960 input–output table. Its approximate nature comes partly from its rigid formalization of what was probably a loose, intuitive procedure; and partly from the fact that secondary errors were introduced in adjusting official figures to the Cambridge industrial classification. The model does not attempt to describe this secondary process. We shall have more to say on it in the context of the numerical example of Chapter 11.

In the rest of this section superscripts 0 will denote true values and asterisks observed values. The letters q, y, u, v will be used to denote gross outputs, net outputs, intermediate outputs and intermediate inputs respectively. It will be recalled from section 3 of Chapter 3 that the input–output matrix L includes absorptions of competitive imports but gross outputs q measure domestic production alone. So in the balance equation $q = Lq + f$, f stands for the difference between final demands and competitive imports. The elements of f are referred to for short as 'net final demands'.

A single observation is made on the vectors of net final demands, net outputs, and gross outputs, and is subject to error. Specifically, we assume that

$$f_i^* = f_i^0 + e_i \quad (i = 1, \ldots, m), \tag{23}$$

$$y_j^* = y_j^0 + e_{m+j} \quad (j = 1, \ldots, m), \tag{24}$$

$$q_k^* = q_k^0 + e_{2m+k} \quad (k = 1, \ldots, m), \tag{25}$$

where e_i is a normal $(0, \sigma_i)$ variate, $i = 1, ..., 3m$,

$$E(e_h, e_i) = 0 \quad \text{for} \quad h \neq i \quad (h, i = 1, ..., 3m), \tag{26}$$

and the standard deviations σ_i are known numbers. It might seem more appropriate to distinguish, in our stochastic assumptions, between the final demand and competitive import components of f. But the present model is intended to describe the generation of a particular set of estimates—the Cambridge ones—and observation errors in the import data entering these estimates were probably negligible by comparison with those in final demands. So we would gain nothing by generalizing our statement of the problem.

The log-likelihood function of the observed vectors f^*, y^*, q^* given that true intermediate output totals, intermediate input totals and gross outputs are respectively (resp.) u^0, v^0, q^0 is, from (23), (24), (25), (26),

$$L[(f^*, y^*, q^*) \mid (u^0, v^0, q^0)] = -3m \log \sqrt{(2\pi)} - \log \sum_{i=1}^{3m} \sigma_i$$

$$- \sum_{i=1}^{m} \frac{(f_i^* - q_i^0 + u_i^0)^2}{2\sigma_i^2} - \sum_{j=1}^{m} \frac{(y_j^* - q_j^0 + v_j^0)^2}{2\sigma_{m+j}^2} - \sum_{k=1}^{m} \frac{(q_k^* - q_k^0)^2}{2\sigma_{2m+k}^2}.$$

To maximize $L[(f^*, y^*, q^*) \mid (u^0, v^0, q^0)]$ subject to the requirement that

$$iu^0 - iv^0 = 0, \tag{27}$$

we partially differentiate with respect to the u_i^0, v_j^0, and $q_k^0 (i, j, k = 1, ..., m)$, the Lagrangian $L[(f^*, y^*, q^*) \mid (u^0, v^0, q^0)] + \lambda \left(\sum_{i=1}^{m} u_i^0 - \sum_{j=1}^{m} v_j^0 \right)$. We get the necessary conditions (easily seen to be also sufficient)

$$-\frac{(f_i^* - q_i^0 + u_i^0)}{\sigma_i^2} + \lambda = 0 \quad (i = 1, ..., m), \tag{28}$$

$$-\frac{(y_j^* - q_j^0 + v_j^0)}{\sigma_{m+j}^2} - \lambda = 0 \quad (j = 1, ..., m), \tag{29}$$

$$\frac{(f_k^* - q_k^0 + u_k^0)}{\sigma_k^2} + \frac{(y_k^* - q_k^0 + v_k^0)}{\sigma_{m+k}^2} + \frac{(q_k^* - q_k^0)}{\sigma_{2m+k}^2} = 0 \quad (k = 1, ..., m). \tag{30}$$

Substituting (28), (29) into (30) we obtain $q_k^0 = q_k^*$. Then denoting a maximum likelihood estimate of (u^0, v^0) by (u, v) we have from (28), (29):

$$u_i = q_i^* - f_i^* + \lambda \sigma_i^2, \quad v_j = q_j^* - y_j^* - \lambda \sigma_{m+j}^2.$$

(27) then implies $\quad \lambda = \left[\sum_{j=1}^{m} (f_j^* - y_j^*) \right] \Big/ \sum_{j=1}^{2m} \sigma_j^2.$

Hence for $i = 1, ..., m$,

$$u_i = q_i^* - f_i^* + \frac{\sigma_i^2}{\sum_{j=1}^{2m} \sigma_j^2} \sum_{j} (f_j^* - y_j^*) \tag{31}$$

$$= u_i^0 + e_{2m+i} - e_i + \beta_i \sum_{j} (e_j - e_{m+j}), \tag{32}$$

from (23), (24), (25), where

$$\beta_i = \frac{\sigma_i^2}{\sum\limits_{j=1}^{2m} \sigma_j^2} \qquad (i = 1, \ldots, m).$$

Similarly, for $j = 1, \ldots, m$,

$$v_j = q_j^* - y_j^* - \frac{\sigma_{m+j}^2}{\sum\limits_{i=1}^{2m} \sigma_i^2} \sum_i (f_i^* - y_i^*) \tag{33}$$

$$= v_j^0 + e_{2m+j} - e_{m+j} - \beta_{m+j} \sum_i (e_i - e_{m+i}), \tag{34}$$

where the definition of β_i is extended to indices $i = m+1, \ldots, 2m$. The estimate of u_i (resp. v_j) is seen from (31) (resp. (33)) to be its 'observed' value $(q_i^* - f_i^*)$ (resp. $(q_j^* - y_j^*)$) plus (resp. minus) a part of the excess of total 'observed' intermediate input over total 'observed' intermediate output, the part being proportional to e_i's (resp. e_{m+j}'s) contribution to the sum of the variances of the e_i's $(i = 1, \ldots, 2m)$.

It will be convenient to write $(u, v) = U$, as before, so that

$$u_i = U_i \qquad (i = 1, \ldots, m),$$

$$v_j = U_{m+j} \qquad (j = 1, \ldots, m),$$

to introduce the errors and standard deviations $e_{3m+k}, \sigma_{3m+k}, k = 1, \ldots, m$, defined by

$$e_{2m+k} = e_{3m+k}, \qquad \sigma_{2m+k} = \sigma_{3m+k} \qquad (k = 1, \ldots, m),$$

and lastly to introduce the sign function defined on indices $h = 1, \ldots, 2m$

$$S(h) = \begin{cases} 1 & \text{for} \quad 1 \le h \le m, \\ -1 & \text{for} \quad m+1 \le h \le 2m. \end{cases}$$

With these conventions (32), (34) may be combined into

$$U_h = U_h^0 + e_{2m+h} - e_h + S(h)\,\beta_h \sum_{i=1}^m (e_i - e_{m+i}) \qquad (h = 1, \ldots, 2m).$$

For the variance of U_h, $h = 1, \ldots, 2m$, we get

$$\operatorname{var} U_h = \sigma_{2m+h}^2 - 2\beta_h \sigma_h^2 + \sigma_h^2 + \beta_h^2 \sum_{i=1}^m \sigma_i^2$$

$$= \sigma_{2m+h}^2 - \frac{2\sigma_h^2}{\sum\limits_{i=1}^{2m} \sigma_i^2} \sigma_h^2 + \sigma_h^2 + \frac{\sigma_h^4}{\left(\sum\limits_{i=1}^{2m} \sigma_i^2\right)^2} \sum_{i=1}^{2m} \sigma_i^2$$

$$= \sigma_{2m+h}^2 + \sigma_h^2 \left(1 - \frac{\sigma_h^2}{\sum\limits_{i=1}^{2m} \sigma_i^2}\right).$$

For the covariance of U_h, U_k $(h, k = 1, \ldots, 2m; h \neq k)$ we have

$$\text{covar} (U_h, U_k) = E(U_h, U_k) - U_h^0 U_k^0$$

$$= E\left\{ e_{2m+h} e_{2m+k} - \beta_k S(k) \sum_{i=1}^{m} (e_i - e_{m+i}) \right.$$
$$\left. - \beta_h S(h) e_k \sum_{i=1}^{m} (e_i - e_{m+i}) + \beta_h \beta_k S(h) S(k) \left[\sum_{i=1}^{m} (e_i - e_{m+i}) \right]^2 \right\}$$

$$= E(e_{2m+h} e_{2m+k}) - \beta_k S(k) S(h) \sigma_h^2 - \beta_h S(h) S(k) \sigma_k^2$$
$$+ \beta_h \beta_k S(h) S(k) \sum_{i=1}^{2m} \sigma_i^2$$

$$= E(e_{2m+h} e_{2m+k}) - \frac{S(h) S(k) \sigma_h^2 \sigma_k^2}{\sum\limits_{i=1}^{2m} \sigma_i^2},$$

and $E(e_{2m+h} e_{2m+k}) = \sigma_{2m+h}^2$ if $|h-k| = m$ and 0 otherwise.

We are now in a position to describe the effect on a biproportional input–output estimate L^* of random error in the figures for intermediate outputs and inputs used in making it. As before, let

$$A^B(u^0, v^0) = \langle r^0 \rangle A \langle s^0 \rangle,$$

and let us write $A^B(u^0, v^0) = A^{B0}$. Equation (22) gives the partial derivatives of x, y, the proportional deviations from (r^0, s^0) of the (r, s) of the biproportional solution $A^B(u, v)$, with respect to the marginals $(\bar{u}, v)$; C^{B0} being C of (16) evaluated at A^{B0}. The proportional deviations of the r, s from (r^0, s^0) are, of course, the normalized row and column multipliers giving the solution of (A^{B0}, u, v), minus ones.

Equation (22), then, gives partial derivatives of the proportional deviations of r, s from their true values, with respect to the random estimate $(\bar{u}, v)$ of $(\bar{u}^0, v^0)$. Let us denote the covariance matrix of $(\bar{u}, v)$ by Ω, and suppose that $\Omega \to 0$. Let us assume, further, that as $\Omega \to 0$ the distribution of (u, v) becomes confined in the neighbourhood defined in the statement of Theorem 5. Then by a well-known theorem on functions of random variables (see e.g. [35, 45]) the covariance matrix of the x, y approaches

$$C^{B0} \Omega (C^{B0})'. \tag{35}$$

In other words, for small values of the variances σ_i^2 of observation errors we have this approximation for the covariance matrix of the x, y. Similarly, for the covariance matrix of the r, s we have the approximation

$$\begin{bmatrix} \langle r^0 \rangle & 0 \\ 0 & \langle s^0 \rangle \end{bmatrix} C^{B0} \Omega (CB^0)' \begin{bmatrix} \langle r^0 \rangle & 0 \\ 0 & \langle s^0 \rangle \end{bmatrix}. \tag{36}$$

(36) together with our formulae for the variances and covariances of the u, v enables us to obtain the covariance matrix of the r's and s's from the standard deviations of observation errors in the f's, y's and q's.

In practice we can only estimate (35) and (36) from sample observations on the parameters (u^0, v^0), (r^0, s^0) which enter them. In the present problem our sample consists of a single observation, namely the (r, s) solving the problem (A, u, v) defined by the single adjusted observation (u, v)—the maximum likelihood estimate of (u^0, v^0) derived from the raw observation (u^*, v^*). Evaluating (35), (36) at (r, s) we obtain estimates of the approximate covariance matrices of (x, y), (r, s) respectively. These estimates are consistent, as $(\bar{u}, v)$ has probability limit $(\bar{u}^0, v^0)$ and the matrices (35), (36) are continuous functions of $(\bar{u}, v)$ for small enough Ω (see [34]). (They are not, however, unbiased: the nonlinearity of C^{B0} as a function of (u, v) means that its second partial derivatives, which multiply the variances and covariances of the u's and v's in the expression for bias, do not vanish. For the same reason, the expectation of the multipliers (r, s) themselves differs from the value of them that would be calculated from observing the expectation of (u, v): that is, $E(r, s) \neq (r^0, s^0)$.)

The estimates of the variances and covariances of the x's and y's (or of the r's and s's) give us, in turn, estimates of the variances of the coefficient estimates l_{ij}^* themselves. (Here, of course, the asterisk does not indicate a raw observation.) For we have

$$\operatorname{var} l_{ij}^* = (l_{ij}^{*0})^2 [\operatorname{var} x_i + \operatorname{var} y_j + 2 \operatorname{covar} (x_i, y_j)],$$

where l_{ij}^{*0} denotes the estimate that would follow from observing (u^0, v^0). It is these estimates of the variances of coefficient updates that are our proper concern. Our inability to interpret the row and column multipliers convincingly even in the determinate model should warn against reading too much into measures of their stability under changes in the u and v—or, therefore, into measures of their statistical variability. In particular, arbitrariness in the normalization created difficulty before, and it does so now. To realize how, it has only to be noticed that if we change the normalization rule to, say, $r_h = 1$, then not only does the variance of the hth row multiplier (or its proportionate error) automatically vanish, but any multiplier positively correlated with r_h (under the original normalization) will undergo a corresponding decline in variance. Not only may we only speak of a 'high r_i' relatively to some normalization, but to speak of r_i's or x_i's having a high variance demands the same qualification.

Let r_i, s_j, as before, denote multipliers whose values are determined by the rule $r_1 = 1$. Let x_i, y_j, too, be defined as before, so that for example x_i satisfies

$$r_i = (1 + x_i) r_i^0.$$

Now let the accent $^\vee$ denote the values assumed by corresponding variables under the normalization rule

$$\check{r}_h = 1.$$

(The development is analogous for the rule $\breve{s}_k = 1$.) Then we have

$$\breve{r}_i = r_i/r_h, \quad \breve{s}_j = s_j r_h$$

and their consequence $\quad \breve{r}_i \breve{s}_j = r_i s_j.$

The relations between the x's and y's and their accented counterparts are

$$\breve{x}_i = \frac{x_i - x_h}{1 + x_h}, \quad \breve{y}_j = (1 + y_j)(1 + x_h) - 1.$$

Recall the assumption that errors in the u's and v's are small, so that the x's and y's are too, and approximate logarithmic errors in the r's and s's. Then

$$\breve{x}_i \approx x_i - x_h, \quad \breve{y}_j \approx y_j + x_h,$$

and for the variances and covariances of x's and y's there follow the approximations

$$\operatorname{var} \breve{x}_i \approx \operatorname{var} x_i + \operatorname{var} x_h - 2 \operatorname{covar}(x_i, x_h),$$

$$\operatorname{var} \breve{y}_j \approx \operatorname{var} y_j + \operatorname{var} x_h + 2 \operatorname{covar}(y_j, x_h),$$

$$\operatorname{covar}(\breve{x}_i, \breve{x}_{i'}) \approx \operatorname{covar}(x_i, x_{i'}) - \operatorname{covar}(x_h, x_i) - \operatorname{covar}(x_h, x_{j'}) + \operatorname{var} x_h,$$

$$\operatorname{covar}(\breve{x}_i, \breve{y}_j) \approx \operatorname{covar}(x_i, y_j) + \operatorname{covar}(x_h, x_i) - \operatorname{covar}(x_h, y_j) - \operatorname{var} x_h,$$

$$\operatorname{covar}(\breve{y}_j, \breve{y}_{j'}) \approx \operatorname{covar}(y_j, y_{j'}) + \operatorname{covar}(x_h, y_j) + \operatorname{covar}(x_h, y_{j'}) + \operatorname{var} x_h.$$

It may be confirmed from these formulae that the approximate values of $\operatorname{var}(\breve{r}_i \breve{s}_j / \breve{r}_i^0 \breve{s}_j^0)$ and of $\operatorname{var}(r_i s_j / r_i^0 s_j^0)$ are the same, as they should be since each expression equals the variance of (a_{ij}^B / a_{ij}^{B0}).

The estimated approximations in (35) and (36), and those for the variances of the l_{ij}^* which can be derived from them, are of some practical importance in assessing the quality of, for instance, the Cambridge Growth Project's biproportional estimate of an input–output matrix for Britain in 1960[26]. Estimates of the reliability of the various data entering the calculation of the biproportional input–output estimate $L^* = [(L\langle q \rangle)^B (u, v)] \langle q \rangle^{-1}$ can only be subjective. They must be based on the judgment of their compilers on the reliability of the raw data from which they are derived, and on the possible sizes of errors introduced in the course of manipulating these data into the required industrial categories. In the report on the Cambridge Growth Project's study most doubt was cast on the estimates of the u, v. Part of this doubt sprang from the fact that the u, v were obtained as residuals, so that in cases in which final demand (net output) was a large part of gross output, the proportional error in u_i (v_j) was likely to be particularly great. The importance of proportional errors in the u's and v's can be seen from formula (35), the definition of C^{B0}, and the part played by the matrices $\langle \overline{Ai} \rangle^{-1}$ and $\langle iA \rangle^{-1}$ in (16).

In Chapter 11 we shall use subjective estimates of the observation variances of net final demands, net outputs and gross outputs to compute a numerical estimate of the covariance matrix of the r, s given by (36).

CHAPTER 6

DISTANCE PROPERTIES OF MARGINALLY CONSTRAINED MATRICES

1 INTRODUCTION

We shall on several occasions be interested to know how 'far' from some given nonnegative matrix is a second matrix determined in one way or another so as to fit given nonnegative marginal vectors. More particularly we may seek a matrix that, among those which fit the given marginals, is 'nearest' to the given matrix. We would be faced with such a problem if, for instance, we wished to maintain the hypothesis of constant input–output coefficients as nearly as was consistent with observed intermediate output and intermediate input totals. Another problem of the same kind arises when, in Chapter 9, we attempt to project the time series L, $L*$ consisting of an observed input–output matrix for one year and a biproportional estimate of that for a second year by extropolating the 'trends' represented by (r, s) in the expression $L* = \langle r \rangle L \langle s \rangle$. The extrapolated matrix may not conform with marginal information about the projection year, and it is then natural to look for the 'nearest' matrix to the extrapolation that does so. A third such problem occurs in the application of the biproportional model to reprogramming a Markov structure (Chapter 10): here we seek to alter the existing structure as little as is necessary to obtain a desired dominant characteristic vector.

In order to be prepared to deal with these problems as they arise we now investigate the problem of minimizing the 'distance' from a given matrix of a matrix subjected to various types of marginal constraints, using alternative distance-like functions of matrix-pairs. These functions are not all true distance functions; not all of them satisfy all three of the defining properties of such functions (6) to (8). They may be regarded, formally, as negative potential functions: then their minimization (subject to the marginal constraints) yields positions of stable equilibrium of a (constrained) particle in the associated fields of force. Finally, they may be thought of as cost functions: but this interpretation, though suggestive, is no less formal than the last until we can say why the cost of changing matrices should increase with 'distance'.

In any interpretation, their employment recalls the dichotomy in the approach to constrained matrix problems that was set out at the start of Chapter 3. It was suggested there that constrained matrix problems may be made determinate *either* by specifying a form of functional relationship between some initial estimate and a solution, *or* by choosing as solution a matrix in some sense 'nearest' to an initial estimate. We have already seen that linear and quadratic programming solutions, defined as members of the second class of solutions, fail to qualify for the first. In this chapter we shall see that there are solutions of the first class which incidentally belong to the second. These include RAS.

Throughout, it will be assumed that

$$iu = iv.$$

2   EUCLIDEAN DISTANCE

A natural formulation of the problem uses the square root of the sum of squared deviations of elements as distance and has the usual marginal constraints. Given A, u, v we equivalently

$$\min \tfrac{1}{2} \sum_{i,j} (b_{ij} - a_{ij})^2 \quad \text{subject to} \quad Bi = u, \; iB = v.$$

The Lagrangian is

$$L_1 = \tfrac{1}{2} \sum_{i,j} (b_{ij} - a_{ij})^2 + \sum_i \lambda_i (u_i - \sum_j b_{ij}) + \sum_j \mu_j (v_j - \sum_j b_{ij}).$$

$$\frac{\partial L_i}{\partial b_{ij}} = b_{ij} - a_{ij} - \lambda_i - \mu_j$$

vanishes for
$$b_{ij} = a_{ij} + \lambda_i + \mu_j,$$

and then
$$\frac{\partial^2 L_1}{\partial (b_{ij})^2} = 1.$$

Thus the least-squares solution is given by any solution B of

$$B = A + \langle \lambda \rangle H + H \langle \mu \rangle, \tag{1}$$

$$Bi = u, \quad iB = v, \tag{2}$$

where H is a $(m \times n)$-order matrix of ones. We record this as

THEOREM 1. $[\sum_{i,j} (b_{ij} - a_{ij})^2]^{\frac{1}{2}}$ is minimized subject to $Bi = u$, $iB = v$ by $B = A + \langle \lambda \rangle H + H \langle \mu \rangle$.

The matrix equation (1), in which the deviation $b_{ij} - a_{ij}$ is expressed as the sum of a row effect λ_i and a column effect μ_j, is reminiscent of the two-way classification model in the analysis of variance (see e.g. [43]). If A is an input–output matrix, λ_i, like r_i in the biproportional model and ξ_i in the Friedlander model, is interpretable as a substitution effect and μ_j, like s_j and η_j in those models, as a fabrication effect. In the present case the interpretations have less appeal, however, as the amount of commodity i that is substituted in industry j is, in (1), independent of j's existing usage of i. In particular, this amount is the same even if j uses no i at all.

We digress briefly to show the existence and uniqueness of a solution of (1), (2). We have

$$n\lambda + H\mu = u - Ai, \quad H'\lambda + m\mu = v - A'i. \tag{3}$$

Let $i\lambda = l$. Then from (1)

$$\mu = \frac{1}{m}(v - A'i - li). \tag{4}$$

Hence (3) gives $\quad \lambda = \frac{1}{n}(u - Ai) - \frac{1}{mn}H(v - A'i - li). \tag{5}$

Thus (4), (5) uniquely solve the system (1), (2) for $i\lambda = l$. But it is clear that we may add ki to λ, $-ki$ to μ and leave B unaltered, for any real number k. Hence (4), (5) give the unique solution B of (1), (2).

Writing $l = 0$ it is easily seen that

$$b_{ij} = a_{ij} + \frac{1}{n}(u_i - a_i i) + \frac{1}{m}(v_j - a^j i) - \frac{1}{mn}(iv - iA'i).$$

Hence we may have $A \geq 0$, $u, v > 0$ but for large enough iv, $b_{ij} < 0$. The least-squares solution is therefore unacceptable when the constrained matrix is *a priori* nonnegative. Moreover, as we have seen, B in general fails to preserve the zero elements of A.

3 χ^2

The minimizer of χ^2 defined on proportionate deviations from the positive elements of A of the corresponding elements of B, subject to the general constraints $Bi = u$, $iB = v$, is easily shown (cf. e.g. [32]) to be the Friedlander matrix $A^F(u, v)$. We define

$$\chi^2(A, B) = \sum_{(i, j) \in S} \frac{(b_{ij} - a_{ij})^2}{a_{ij}},$$

where A, B are $(m \times n)$-order matrices, A has semipositive rows and columns, and

$$S = \{(i, j) \mid a_{ij} > 0\}.$$

The notation χ^2 is suggested by the well-known result which is the basis for the Karl Pearson χ^2 test of goodness of fit: if b_{ij} is the frequency with which the jth industry spends a 'random dollar' on commodity i and a_{ij} is its expected value, then it can be shown that the quantity $\sum_i (b_{ij} - a_{ij})^2/a_{ij}$ is, for large samples, χ^2-distributed with $m - 1$ degrees of freedom (assuming for simplicity that all m a_{ij}'s > 0) [20]. In this way the Friedlander estimate may be interpreted as a χ^2-minimum estimate with the meaning of statistical theory—that estimate which imposes least pressure to throw over the no-change hypothesis that inputs into industry j are governed by the same stochastic law as ruled in the base year.

χ^2 is not a true distance function even when restricted to pairs (A, B) of strictly positive matrices. χ^2 then satisfies the requirement

$$d(A, B) \begin{cases} \geq 0, \\ = 0 & \text{if and only if} \quad A = B, \end{cases} \tag{6}$$

but fails to satisfy the requirements

$$\left. \begin{array}{l} d(A, B) = d(B, A), \\ d(A, C) + d(C, B) \geq d(A, B), \end{array} \right\} \text{ all } A, B \qquad \begin{array}{l} (7) \\ (8) \end{array}$$

for d to be a distance function on the matrix space. However, the weighting of squared deviations carried out in it makes it in many applications intuitively preferable as a minimand to the genuine distance function $[\Sigma(b_{ij} - a_{ij})^2]^{\frac{1}{2}}$.

Consider the Lagrangian

$$L_2 = \tfrac{1}{2} \sum_{(i,j) \in S} \frac{1}{a_{ij}} (b_{ij} - a_{ij})^2 + \sum_i \xi_i (u_i - \sum_j b_{ij}) + \sum_j \eta_j (v_j - \sum_i b_{ij}).$$

$$\frac{\partial L_2}{\partial b_{ij}} = \frac{b_{ij} - a_{ij}}{a_{ij}} - \xi_i - \eta_j \quad ((i, j) \in S)$$

vanishes when

$$b_{ij} = a_{ij}(1 + \xi_i + \eta_j),$$

and then

$$\frac{\partial^2 L_2}{\partial (b_{ij})^2} = 1/a_{ij} > 0.$$

Hence a Friedlander solution $A^F(u, v)$ minimizes $\chi^2(A, B)$. We cannot yet be satisfied, however. We must first make sure that elements of B corresponding to zero elements of A are not sent far from zero in the Friedlander solution. In fact, B preserves zero elements of A. Thus $A^F(u, v)$ minimizes, subject to $Bi = u$, $iB = v$, any function of A, B of the form

$$\chi^2(A, B) + \psi(A, B),$$

where

$$\psi(A, B) = \sum_{(i,j) \in S'} \psi(a_{ij}, b_{ij}),$$

$$\psi(a, b) \begin{cases} \geq 0 & \text{for all real numbers } a, b, \\ = 0 & \text{when} \quad a = b. \end{cases} \tag{9}$$

S' denotes the complement of S.

We may express this more compactly as follows. Let $\tilde{\chi}^2$ be the function of pairs (a, b) of real numbers defined as follows:

$$\tilde{\chi}^2(a, b) = \begin{cases} \chi^2(a, b) & \text{if} \quad a > 0, \\ \psi(a, b) & \text{otherwise.} \end{cases} \tag{10}$$

Then we have

THEOREM 8. Subject to (2), $A^F(u, v)$ minimizes $\sum_{i,j} \tilde{\chi}^2(a_{ij}, b_{ij})$. We shall find it convenient to write $\sum_{i,j} \tilde{\chi}^2(a_{ij}, b_{ij}) = \tilde{\chi}^2(A, B)$.

Like Euclidean distance, $\tilde{\chi}^2$ cannot be accepted wholeheartedly as a minimand when B's nonnegativity is demanded *a priori*. It can easily be shown by example, and is in Chapter 11, that the nonnegativity of A and the positivity of (u, v) are not enough to guarantee that $A^F(u, v) \geqq 0$. On the other hand, these conditions do imply that $A^F(u, v)$ is nonnegative for all (u, v) close enough in direction to (Ai, iA): for (16) of the last chapter shows that $A^F(u, v)$ is continuous on (u, v) such that $iu = iv$; but $A^F(kAi, kiA) = kA \geqq 0$ for any number $k > 0$, and its zero elements are the zero elements of A and so remain zero in any solution $A^F(u, v)$. When the condition that (u, v) be near some (kAi, kiA) appears to be met, therefore, it may be worthwhile to set up the constrained matrix estimation problem as a Friedlander one. But we shall see in the next section that in these circumstances the biproportional method shares much of the interpretative virtue of minimizing χ^2, while it enjoys the advantage of assured nonnegativity when (u, v) is remote in direction from (Ai, iA).

It is true that the failure of the least-squares and Friedlander approaches to assure nonnegativity and of the least-squares approach to preserve zeros might be put right by introducing these conditions as extra restrictions. There would result quadratic programming problems of the kind discussed in section 8 of Chapter 3. Likewise, we have seen that a linear programme results from minimizing, under the same restrictions, the potential-type function $\sum_{i,j} |b_{ij} - a_{ij}|$. However, the solutions of such programmes cannot in general be expressed as explicit functions of the given matrix. In particular, once we introduce side-restrictions on sign we can no longer hope to reduce the 'potential' approach to the 'functional' approach in the formulation of determinate constrained matrix problems.

4 A FUNCTION WITH CONSTRAINED MINIMIZER $A^B(u, v)$

We now invert the procedure of the last two sections, and ask: can we find a function of pairs (A, B) of $(m \times n)$-order matrices that, given A, is minimized with respect to B subject to $Bi = u$, $iB = v$ by a matrix biproportional to A, i.e. by $B = A^B(u, v)$? Our procedure will also differ from the earlier one in that we shall introduce nonnegativity conditions at the beginning, rather than considering, at the end, the nonnegativity properties of a solution obtained without sign restrictions. Thus we require of B that

$$B \geqq 0 \tag{11}$$

in addition to (2). As usual, we also have

$$a_i \geqslant 0, \quad a^j \geqslant 0 \quad (i = 1, ..., m; j = 1, ..., n), \tag{12}$$

$$u, v > 0. \tag{13}$$

In order that there should exist any matrix at all that satisfies both the marginal constraints and (11), we must also have, by Corollary 3,

$$A_{I'J} = 0 \quad \text{implies} \quad U_{I'} \leqq V_{J'}, \quad U_I \geqq V_J. \tag{14}$$

Consider the Lagrangian

$$L_3 = f(A, B) + \sum_i \alpha_i(u_i - \sum_j b_{ij}) + \sum_j \beta_j(v_j - \sum_i b_{ij}).$$

Since
$$\frac{\partial L_3}{\partial b_{ij}} = \frac{\partial f}{\partial b_{ij}} - \alpha_i - \beta_j, \tag{15}$$

it is enough for $\partial L_3/\partial b_{ij} = 0$ to imply the biproportionality of A and B, that $\partial f/\partial b_{ij} = \log b_{ij}/a_{ij} + \text{const}$. A function that has this partial derivative is $\sum \phi(a_{ij}, b_{ij})$, where

$$\phi(a_{ij}, b_{ij}) = b_{ij} \log \frac{b_{ij}}{ca_{ij}},$$

c is a constant, and the summation is taken over the set of (i, j) for which $a_{ij}, b_{ij} > 0$. As a matter of convenience, we set $c = e$.

Let S_1 be the subset of S (the set of 'full cells' of A) for which $a_{ij}, a_{ij}^B(u, v) > 0$. We know from Theorem 3 that (12), (13), (14) imply the existence of a biproportional solution $B = A^B(u, v)$. Let us try this B as a nonnegative, marginally constrained minimizer of $\phi(a_{ij}, b_{ij})$ summed over $(i, j) \in S_1$, i.e. of

$$\sum_{(i,j) \in S_1} \phi(a_{ij}, b_{ij}) = \phi(A, B) \quad \text{say.}$$

We know from Corollary 6 that there exist vectors $r, s > 0$ such that for all $(i, j) \in S_1$,
$$\log b_{ij} = \log a_{ij}^B = \log a_{ij} + \log r_i + \log s_j,$$

and (15) shows that $\partial L_3/\partial b_{ij}$ vanishes writing $\alpha = \log r$, $\beta = \log s$. Further

$$\frac{\partial^2 L_3}{\partial (b_{ij})^2} = \frac{1}{b_{ij}} > 0 \quad \text{when} \quad B = A^B.$$

Hence $B = A^B(u, v)$ minimizes $\phi(A, B)$ subject to $Bi = u$, $iB = v$, $B \geqq 0$.

We have now to consider the two questions: (i) is ϕ a good minimand on b_{ij} for (i, j) in S_1? (ii) is a_{ij}^B a desirable value for b_{ij} for (i, j) not in S_1? We first take up question (ii), which breaks up into the questions: (a) is a_{ij}^B a desirable value for b_{ij} when $a_{ij} = 0$, (b) is zero a desirable value for b_{ij} when $a_{ij} > 0$, $a_{ij}^B = 0$? It is not hard to show that the answer to both these questions is yes.

(a) When $a_{ij} = 0$, $a_{ij}^B = 0$, so writing S' for the set of (i, j) for which $a_{ij} = 0$, A^B minimizes $\phi(A, B) + \sum_{(i,j) \in S'} \psi(a_{ij}, b_{ij})$ subject to all the constraints, where ψ is defined as in the previous section.

(b) Let S_2 be the subset of S for which $a_{ij} > 0$, $b_{ij} = 0$. Then S_1, S_2, S' partition the set of all (i, j). When $a_{ij} > 0$, $a_{ij}^B = 0$, we know from Corollary 4 that zero is the only possible value of b_{ij} in a matrix B satisfying all the constraints. Hence we have shown that, subject to (2), (11) $A^B(u, v)$ minimizes

$$\phi(A, B) + \sum_{(i,j) \in S_1'} \psi(a_{ij}, b_{ij}).$$

We may re-express this result more compactly as follows. Let $\tilde{\phi}$ be the function of pairs (a, b) of nonnegative numbers defined as follows:

$$\tilde{\phi}(a, b) = \begin{cases} \phi(a, b) & \text{if } a > 0, b > 0, \\ \psi(a, b) & \text{otherwise.} \end{cases}$$

Then we have

THEOREM 9. Subject to (2), (11) $A^B(u, v)$ minimizes $\sum\limits_{(i, j)} \tilde{\phi}(a_{ij}, b_{ij})$. We shall for convenience write $\sum\limits_{i, j} \tilde{\phi}(a_{ij}, b_{ij}) = \tilde{\phi}(A, B)$.

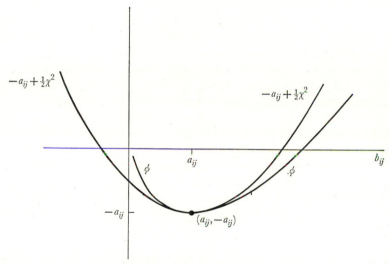

Fig. 1

We now turn to the question (i) posed above. We note first that the function ϕ has the good property that its only local unconstrained minimizer with respect to B is A, since

$$\frac{\partial \phi}{\partial b_{ij}} = \log \frac{b_{ij}}{a_{ij}} = 0 \quad \text{only when} \quad b_{ij} = a_{ij},$$

and

$$\frac{\partial^2 \phi}{\partial (b_{ij})^2} = \frac{1}{b_{ij}} > 0 \quad \text{when} \quad b_{ij} = a_{ij}.$$

The function has the appearance of the asymmetric curve in figure 1.

The weighting of changes in elements that ϕ effects has some virtue. As b_{ij} grows large the marginal 'cost' that ϕ attributes to a (further) increment in b_{ij} increases, but at a decreasing rate. For small deviations of the b_{ij} from the a_{ij}, $\phi(A, B)$ approximates a linear function of $\chi^2(A, B)$ restricted to the same set of (a_{ij}, b_{ij}), namely it approximates

$$\frac{1}{2} \sum_{(i, j) \in S_1} \frac{(b_{ij} - a_{ij})^2}{a_{ij}} + \text{constant.}$$

The additivity of each of ϕ, χ^2 allows us to show this by considering a single element. Writing $b_{ij} = a_{ij} + \epsilon_{ij}$, we have

$$\phi(a_{ij}, b_{ij}) = b_{ij} \log \frac{b_{ij}}{ea_{ij}} = (a_{ij} + \epsilon_{ij}) \left(\log \frac{a_{ij} + \epsilon_{ij}}{a_{ij}} - 1 \right)$$

$$= (a_{ij} + \epsilon_{ij}) \left[-1 + \frac{\epsilon_{ij}}{a_{ij}} - \frac{\epsilon_{ij}^2}{2a_{ij}^2} + O(\epsilon_{ij}^3) \right]$$

$$= -a_{ij} + \frac{\epsilon_{ij}^2}{2a_{ij}} + O(\epsilon_{ij}^3)$$

$$= -a_{ij} + \tfrac{1}{2}\chi^2(a_{ij}, b_{ij}) + O(\epsilon_{ij}^3). \qquad (16)$$

The symmetric curve in figure 1 represents $-a_{ij} + \tfrac{1}{2}\chi^2(a_{ij}, b_{ij})$.

Now we know from the continuity result Theorem 5 that A^B approaches A as (u, v) approaches (Ai, iA). In view of (16) this suggests the approximate equivalence, in some sense, of minimizing $\phi(A, B)$ subject to marginal and nonnegativity constraints and minimizing $\chi^2(A, B)$ (restricted to the same set of a_{ij}, b_{ij}) subject to marginal constraints alone, when (u, v) approximates (Ai, iA).

We shall make this precise in a somewhat more general form. As (u, v) approaches (Ai, iA) in *direction*, the minimizer of $\tilde{\phi}(A, B)$ subject to (2), (11) approaches the minimizer of $\tilde{\chi}^2(A, B)$ subject to (2). ((14) is understood to hold.) For let $(u, v) = (kAi, kiA)$ for some $k > 0$; then it is easily seen that

$$A^B(u, v) = A^F(u, v) = kA.$$

$A^F(u, v)$ is a continuous function of (u, v) from (16) of the last chapter and $A^B(u, v)$ is continuous at (kAi, kiA) from Theorem 5, hence as $(u, v) \to (kAi, kiA)$,

$$A^B(u, v) - A^F(u, v) \to 0.$$

But $A^B(u, v)$, $A^F(u, v)$ are the constrained minimizers defined above.

We note that, for (u, v) near enough (kAi, kiA), $A^B(u, v)$ is arbitrarily near a scalar multiple of A and S_2 is therefore empty. Then the domain of ϕ coincides with the domain of χ^2 defined in section 3, viz. the entire set of (a_{ij}, b_{ij}) for which $a_{ij} > 0$.

We have seen that $A^B(u, v)$ approximates the constrained minimizer of $\tilde{\chi}^2$ found in section 3 when (u, v) is near to (Ai, iA) in direction. But this was the only circumstance in which we could be sure of the nonnegativity of the latter minimizer, $A^F(u, v)$. In it, then, $A^B(u, v)$ shares the χ^2-minimizer interpretation of $A^F(u, v)$. Outside it, we have already shown that $A^B(u, v)$ is to be preferred in numerous applications by virtue of its assured nonnegativity for all (u, v) such that some nonnegative matrix exists satisfying the marginal constraints and preserving A's zeros.

5 CRITERIA FROM INFORMATION THEORY

So far we have pursued the simple idea of finding constraint-satisfying matrices that are 'near' to an initial estimate. This search may be justified by a conservative attitude to estimation or the wish to hold down a cost that happens to increase with distance. We have seen that the nearest constraint-satisfying matrices may lack other important properties, and that a constraint-satisfying matrix that has them—the biproportional— is only 'near' in a qualified sense.

The method of solution of constrained matrix problems that Uribe, de Leeuw and Theil propose in [**73**] is a 'potential' method but not one that sets out to find a matrix 'near' to the initial estimate. Instead it seeks one with the property that, taking it as our final estimate, we are likely to be minimally 'surprised' by the matrix that eventualizes. The word 'surprise' serves to dramatize the concept of 'amount of information' that is at the centre of information theory [**68**]. If warm dry weather was forecast yesterday and forecasts tend to be correct, the news that today has turned out sunny is less 'informative' that it would otherwise have been. Generalizing this notion, one might say, too, that if we are in July and July days are *a priori* likely to be sunny, then yesterday's 24-hour forecast that today will be sunny has so much the less information content. Concretely, if such a forecast, or any message, changes the prior probabilities x_i of exhaustive and mutually exclusive events E_i to posterior probabilities y_i, the *expected information value* of the message is measured as

$$I(y:x) = \sum_i y_i \log \frac{y_i}{x_i}.$$

I is our expectation, now, of the information content $\log (y_{i'}/x_{i'})$ of that single forecast—with at present unknown identity i'—which will turn out to be correct.

Now let E_i stand for the event that a 'random guilder' of the out-goings of an industry is spent on commodity i; then the ith element of that industry's vector of intermediate and primary input coefficients is a measure of the probability of E_i. In the same way, if c_{ij} is the (i,j)th flow in an input–output, or international trading matrix, divided by the sum of all flows, C is a matrix of measures of contingency probabilities. If b_{ij} is an estimate of c_{ij}—a prior probability of the contingency (i,j)— the quantity

$$I(C:B) = \sum_{i,j} c_{ij} \log \frac{c_{ij}}{b_{ij}}$$

may be viewed as the expected information value of the message that the value of the probability matrix is C. Uribe, de Leeuw and Theil's proposed solution of the usual constrained matrix problem is to minimize $I(C:B)$ over B subject to $Bi = u$, $iB = v$ (where u, v have, like C, been normalized to have unit sums). But C is unknown, and must be estimated, before this minimization problem can be solved. An initial estimate A (normalized in the same way), has to be used in its place. The normalization of A, B, u, v is obviously irrelevant except in interpretation, and the procedure amounts to

$$\min_{B} \sum_{i,j} a_{ij} \log \frac{a_{ij}}{b_{ij}},$$

subject to marginal constraints, where the symbols now revert to their unnormalized denotations. The Lagrangian derivative vanishes when

$$b_{ij} = a_{ij}/(\lambda_i + \mu_j),$$

which leads to awkward equations in the Lagrange multipliers λ, μ. However, the usual Taylor approximation is available if we only explore a neighbourhood of A for the optimizer B. The minimand becomes $\frac{1}{2} \sum_{(i,j) \in S} [(b_{ij} - a_{ij})^2/a_{ij}]$ and, as in the approximate minimization of $\phi(A, B)$, we are back with Friedlander.

There is something back-to-front about the Uribe–de Leeuw–Theil attack. For what is being minimized is, in essence, our probable surprise at learning that the probability matrix has turned out equal to the estimate we started out with, an outcome whose very *impossibility* is the origin of our problem. Another approach by means of the same concepts casts the final estimate which we seek as the posterior message instead of as the prior. One estimates the unknown matrix as that value which, if realized, would occasion least 'surprise' in view of the prior message A. Here, then, the impossible, constraint-violating value A is seen as an estimate (which is conceivable), not as a realization (which is not). If there were no marginal constraints, this least surprising posterior estimate B would coincide with the initial estimate A. As there are, we must look for the least surprising posterior of those posteriors that satisfy them. This means we should minimize $I(B:A)$, i.e.

$$\min_{B} \sum_{(i,j) \in S} b_{ij} \log \frac{b_{ij}}{a_{ij}} \quad \text{subject to} \quad Bi = u, \quad iB = v.$$

The minimizer is the biproportional estimate.

Uribe, de Leeuw and Theil have already appealed to information concepts in determining their *initial* estimate A. Here, too, RAS turns out to be subtly present. If, as before, we normalize the observed marginal vectors u, v to have unit sums then u_i, for instance, may be read as the marginal probability that a random guilder of interindustry transactions is a payment to industry i. If the probabilities of the i-value and j-value of a randomly spent guilder were independent then the joint probability $z_{ij}(1)$ that a guilder be both a payment to i and an expense of j would equal $u_i v_j$: input structures would be the same for all industries. The ratio $z_{ij}(1)/(u_i v_j)$ is thus a measure of deviation from stochastic independence and from input homogeneity. In the language of information theory this ratio is the *mutual information* between the 'message' that the guilder was paid to i and the 'message' that it was paid by j. A way of using the marginal information u, v that, it seems plain, improves on the hypothesis of stochastic independence (input homogeneity) is by the hypothesis that for each (i,j) mutual information is the same as in the base year. That is,

$$\frac{z_{ij}(1)}{u_i v_j} = \frac{z_{ij}(0)}{u_i(0)\, v_j(0)},$$

or

$$z_{ij}(1) = [u_i/u_i(0)]\, z_{ij}(0)\, [v_j/v_j(0)],$$

where $z_{ij}(1)$ is the (i,j)th transaction in year 1. This value (normalized to be a contingency matrix) is taken as initial estimate in the method of Uribe, de Leeuw and Theil. It will be recognized as a biproportional adjustment of $z_{ij}(0)$ (that which results from applying simultaneously a single row-adjustment and a single column-adjustment in the RAS problem in which $Z(0)$ is taken as initial estimate). If, therefore, in Uribe, de Leeuw and Theil's 'two-stage information forecast' of a constrained matrix, one minimizes $I(B:A)$ at the second stage instead of minimizing $I(A:B)$, the first stage is rendered superfluous.

6 DISTANCE MINIMIZATION WITH ONE SET OF MARGINAL CONSTRAINTS

The central problem we have been concerned with so far is that of minimizing with respect to B one or another distance, potential or other function of (A, B) when B has preassigned row and column sums. Occasionally B has been required in advance also to be nonnegative. We now relax one set of marginal constraints. That is, we now seek B minimizing a distance-like function of (A, B) subject only to, say, $Bi = u$. (We shall also consider the nonnegativity of B.) We shall find that this problem has the same solution for either of the distance-like functions $\tilde{\chi}^2$, $\tilde{\phi}$. First let us take the Lagrangian

$$L_4 = \tfrac{1}{2} \sum_{(i,j)\in S} \frac{(b_{ij} - a_{ij})^2}{a_{ij}} + \sum_i \xi_i \Big(u_i - \sum_j b_{ij}\Big).$$

Then

$$\frac{\partial L_4}{\partial b_{ij}} = \frac{(b_{ij} - a_{ij})}{a_{ij}} - \xi_i,$$

which vanishes when

$$b_{ij} = (1 + \xi_i)\, a_{ij},$$

and then

$$\frac{\partial^2 L_4}{\partial (b_{ij})^2} = \frac{1}{a_{ij}} > 0.$$

Or, take

$$L_5 = \sum_{(i,j)\in S} b_{ij} \log \frac{b_{ij}}{e a_{ij}} + \sum_i \alpha_i \Big(u_i - \sum_j b_{ij}\Big).$$

Then
$$\frac{\partial L_5}{\partial b_{ij}} = \log \frac{b_{ij}}{a_{ij}} - \alpha_i,$$

which vanishes when $b_{ij} = \log a_{ij} + \alpha_i$, i.e. when $b_{ij} = (\text{antilog } \alpha_i) \, a_{ij}$, and then
$$\frac{\partial^2 L_5}{\partial (b_{ij})^2} = \frac{1}{b_{ij}} > 0.$$

It is clear that (12) and (13) ensure that there is a unique vector r such that $b_{ij} = r_i a_{ij}$ and the marginal constraints $\sum_i b_{ij} = u_i, i = 1, \ldots, m$, are satisfied, i.e. such that
$$B = \langle r \rangle A, \quad Bi = u. \tag{17}$$

Zero elements of A are clearly preserved. $r > 0$, which implies that $B \geq 0$, and also that S_2 is empty. Hence the unique solution of (17) minimizes either of the functions
$$\tilde{\chi}^2(A, B) = \chi^2(A, B) + \Sigma \psi(a_{ij}, b_{ij}),$$
$$\tilde{\phi}(A, B) = \phi(A, B) + \Sigma \psi(a_{ij}, b_{ij})$$

subject to $Bi = u$, $B \geq 0$, where the domains of χ^2, ϕ coincide and ψ is summed over the complementary set of (i,j).

Similarly, the unique solution of
$$B = A \langle s \rangle, \quad iB = v$$

minimizes either of $\tilde{\chi}^2(A, B)$, $\tilde{\phi}(A, B)$ subject to $iB = v$, $B \geq 0$, and the domains of χ^2, ϕ are the same.

These results on distance-minimization with one set of marginal constraints will have their use when, in Chapter 9, we come to consider the problem of projecting the time series of input–output matrices L, L^*.

CHAPTER 7

THE BIPROPORTIONAL INPUT–OUTPUT ESTIMATE AS A FUNCTION OF GROSS OUTPUTS AND PRICES

1 INTRODUCTION

This chapter, the next, and part of Chapter 9 are specifically concerned with input–output applications of results on biproportional matrices. Some of the results of these chapters are quite general, and might be useful in other applications. But it is the input–output one that we shall have in mind, and this will be expressed in the notation. The present chapter investigates the variation of a biproportional estimate L^* of an input–output coefficient matrix with respect to two economic variables. These are: the gross output vector and price vector at $t = 1$, the date for which the estimate L^* is made. It will be convenient to adopt a notation which differs slightly from the one we used in Chapter 3 in introducing the biproportional input–output model. It may be recalled that we there understood all magnitudes, input–output coefficients included, to be expressed in the prices of $t = 1$, which we regarded as fixed. But in this chapter we shall be concerned with virtual variations in those prices. Matters will be clearer if input–output coefficients and gross outputs—in particular the matrix L for $t = 0$, the matrix $L(1)$ for $t = 1$ and its estimate L^*, and the gross outputs q at $t = 1$—are from now on understood to be measured in physical terms. p will denote the vector of absolute prices at $t = 1$. Throughout this chapter we shall assume that

$$p > 0, \quad q > 0.$$

In this notation, the transactions matrix at $t = 1$, expressed in the values of that date, may be written

$$\langle p \rangle L(1) \langle q \rangle = Z(1) \quad \text{say,}$$

if we take for granted an assumption of constancy of the price of the ith product with respect to purchasing industry. We may also write this as

$$Z(1) = [\langle p \rangle L(1) \langle p \rangle^{-1}] (\langle p \rangle \langle q \rangle),$$

in which $Z(1)$ appears as the product of a matrix of input–output value coefficients and a diagonal matrix of gross output values. Intermediate outputs and inputs at $t = 1$ are

$$(u, v) = [Z(1) i, i Z(1)] = [\langle p \rangle L(1) q, p L(1) \langle q \rangle].$$

If (u, v) is correctly observed the biproportional estimation procedure is to make a biproportional adjustment to (u, v) of the 'constant-coefficients' transactions matrix $\langle p \rangle L \langle q \rangle$. We obtain $[\langle p \rangle L \langle q \rangle]^B (u, v)$. This is however the same as $[\langle p(0) \rangle L \langle p(0) \rangle^{-1}]^B (u, v)$, where $p(0)$ is the price vector at $t = 0$, so we may use $\langle p(0) \rangle L \langle p(0) \rangle^{-1}$ as the initial matrix A of the biproportional routine and do not need to form the constant-coefficients transactions matrix. The estimate is also equal to $L^B(u, v)$, a still more concise expression which we shall usually use. From $L^B(u, v)$ we obtain as our estimate of $L(1)$

$$L^* = \langle p \rangle^{-1} L^B(u, v) \langle q \rangle^{-1} = \langle p \rangle^{-1} L^B[\langle p \rangle L(1)\, q,\, pL(1) \langle q \rangle] \langle q \rangle^{-1}. \quad (1)$$

Equation (1) shows L^* explicitly as a function of p and q. The symmetry of the roles played by p and q is evident.

Let us suppose, with Leontief, that the true matrix $L(1)$ is invariant with respect to q, for values of q in a certain domain. Then we should certainly want L^* too to remain constant as q travels over this domain. If it did, we could look elsewhere than at the value of q for causes of any error in L^*. Similarly, if we believe that $L(1)$ is not dependent on p as long as p lies in a certain domain, we would wish L^* too to be independent of such p. The assumption that $L(1)$ is independent of p, i.e. that intermediate inputs have zero elasticities of substitution, is not likely to be endorsed by economists except in a very qualified sense. But such an assumption might be sensible if virtual variations of p are narrowly confined in p-space, or if one is considering virtual variations the response to which must take place in a short-term temporal context: in this case input–output ratios may be fixed because they are associated with specific items of capital equipment. There is another possible reason for wishing for the invariance of L^* with respect to changes in p. It might be that marginal data on $Z(1)$ become available only in the prices of some date other than $t = 1$, i.e. deflated values are reported to the statistical office. That is, instead of learning $(u, v) = [Z(1)\, i,\, iZ(1)]$ we learn

$$[\langle p' \rangle L(1) \langle q \rangle i,\, i \langle p' \rangle L(1) \langle q \rangle],$$

where $p' \neq p$. Our estimate is then

$$\langle p' \rangle^{-1} L^B[\langle p' \rangle L(1)\, q,\, p'L(1) \langle q \rangle] \langle q \rangle^{-1},$$

and we would certainly like this to be the same as the estimate we would have got had marginals been reported in current values.

We shall find an interesting quantity-price symmetry in our results on how L^* varies in response to q and in response to p—assuming the constancy of $L(1)$ under these variations. The extent of the variation in L^* will turn out to depend on the closeness with which $L(1)$ approximates a value biproportional to L. We first take up the question of how L^* behaves as a function of q.

2 THE BIPROPORTIONAL INPUT–OUTPUT ESTIMATE AND GROSS OUTPUTS

We begin with a formal statement of our Leontief-like assumption on the constancy of $L(1)$ with respect to virtual variations in q.

ASSUMPTION 1. The true value $L(1)$ of the input–output coefficient matrix at $t = 1$ is invariant with respect to gross outputs q at $t = 1$, $q \in Q$.

Of Q we make only the innocuous requirement that

$$Q \text{ has rank } m \qquad (2)$$

in addition to our previous assumption that $q > 0$ for $q \in Q$.

For the time being we shall regard p as fixed and L^* as a function of q. Accordingly we write $L^* = L^*(q)$. We shall first show that

THEOREM 10. $L^*(q)$ is invariant with respect to $q \in Q$ if and only if $L(1)$ is biproportional to L.

PROOF. (i) Sufficiency. Let $L(1)$ be biproportional to L. Then $\langle p \rangle L(1) \langle q \rangle$ is biproportional to $\langle p \rangle L^* \langle q \rangle$. It also has the same row and columns sums as $\langle p \rangle L^* \langle q \rangle$ by its definition (1) and hence is equal to $\langle p \rangle L^* \langle q \rangle$ by Corollary 1. Thus for all $q \in Q$, $L^*(q) = L(1) =$ constant by Assumption 1.

(ii) Necessity. (1) is equivalent to

$$\langle p \rangle L^*(q) \langle q \rangle = \langle r \rangle \overset{0}{L} \langle s \rangle, \qquad (3)$$

$$\langle r \rangle \overset{0}{L} s = \langle p \rangle L(1) q, \quad r \overset{0}{L} \langle s \rangle = p L(1) \langle q \rangle, \qquad (4)$$

where the overhead 0 has the meaning defined in the discussion of Corollary 6 in section 5 of Chapter 4. (3), (4) imply

$$\langle p \rangle L^*(q) q = \langle p \rangle L(1) q.$$

If $L^*(q)$ is to be constant $= L^*$ say, for all q in Q, then all such q must satisfy

$$[L^* - L(1)] q = 0. \qquad (5)$$

Q has rank m(2), but the solution set of (5) has rank m only if $L^* = L(1)$, and in this case $L(1)$ must be biproportional to L.|

Thus the estimate L^* is invariant with respect to q only in the case of biproportionality, and in this case its constant value is the true one.

We next investigate the way in which L^* depends upon q when $L(1)$ only approximates a value biproportional to L. We shall assume this value to be of the form $\langle r \rangle L \langle s \rangle$. Application of Theorem 6 to the matrix $Z(1)$ shows that as $L(1) \to \langle r \rangle L \langle s \rangle$ and thus $Z(1) \to \langle p \rangle \langle r \rangle L \langle s \rangle \langle q \rangle$, so does $L^B \to \langle p \rangle \langle r \rangle L \langle s \rangle \langle q \rangle$, i.e. $L^* \to \langle r \rangle L \langle s \rangle$. In other words, for any particular q, when $L(1)$ is close to $\langle r \rangle L \langle s \rangle$, L^* is also close to $\langle r \rangle L \langle s \rangle$ and hence is close to $L(1)$. This means that if we have reason to believe that

$L(1)$ approximates a matrix expressible as $\langle r \rangle L \langle s \rangle$, we may regard L^* as an approximation to the true value $L(1)$. This result owes its importance to the evidence of the Belgian tests [59], which showed that, save for a few of its elements, $L(1)$ was indeed near to a matrix of the form $\langle r \rangle L \langle s \rangle$. In principle one could, for given q, compute a neighbourhood of some $\langle r \rangle L \langle s \rangle$ such that if $L(1)$ lies in it L^* will lie within a prescribed distance of $L(1)$. This result would, however, lose much of its apparent usefulness unless one could find such a neighbourhood independently of q. We shall now show that one can always do so. To this end we first show that L^* converges to $\langle r \rangle L \langle s \rangle$ uniformly on q in Q.

THEOREM 11. As $L(1)$ approaches $\langle r \rangle L \langle s \rangle$, L^* approaches $\langle r \rangle L \langle s \rangle$ uniformly on q in Q.

PROOF. It is easily seen that $L^*(kq) = L^*(q)$ for any real number $k > 0$. Hence it is enough to show that $L^*(q) \to \langle r \rangle L \langle s \rangle$ uniformly on q in Q', where

$$Q' = \left\{ q' \middle| q' = \frac{1}{iq} q, \ q \in Q \right\}.$$

That is, we have to show that for any $\epsilon > 0$ there is a neighbourhood N of $\langle r \rangle L \langle s \rangle$ such that if $L(1)$ lies in N

$$|[L^*(q) - \langle r \rangle L \langle s \rangle]_{ij}| < \epsilon \tag{6}$$

for all q in Q', where the left-hand side denotes the absolute value of the (i,j)th element of $[L^*(q) - \langle r \rangle L \langle s \rangle]$ and $i,j = 1, \ldots, m$. From Theorem 5, (6) holds if $[\langle p \rangle L(1) q, p L(1) \langle q \rangle]$ is in a certain neighbourhood of $[\langle p \rangle (\langle r \rangle L \langle s \rangle) q, p (\langle r \rangle L \langle s \rangle) \langle q \rangle]$. By the boundedness of Q' the latter is true for all q in Q' if $L(1)$ is in a certain neighbourhood N of $\langle r \rangle L \langle s \rangle$. |

It now follows from Theorem 11 that as $L(1)$ approaches $\langle r \rangle L \langle s \rangle$, $L^* - L(1) \to 0$ uniformly on q in Q. Let the neighbourhood N introduced in the above proof be defined by

$$|[L(1) - \langle r \rangle L \langle s \rangle]_{ij}| < \eta \quad \text{(all } i,j).$$

We want to show that for any $\delta > 0$,

$$|[L(1) - L^*]_{ij}| < \delta \quad \text{(all } i,j), \tag{7}$$

for all q in Q, provided that $L(1) \in N(\eta)$ for some η. From Theorem 11,

$$|[L^* - \langle r \rangle L \langle s \rangle]_{ij}| < \tfrac{1}{2}\delta \quad \text{(all } i,j), \tag{8}$$

for all q in Q if $L(1) \in N(\eta_0)$, for some η_0. If this $\eta_0 \leq \tfrac{1}{2}\delta$ then adding $|[L^* - \langle r \rangle L \langle s \rangle]_{ij}|$ and $|[L(1) - \langle r \rangle L \langle s \rangle]_{ij}|$ shows that (7) holds for all q in Q if $L(1) \in N(\eta_0)$ and the result follows. And if $\eta_0 > \tfrac{1}{2}\delta$ then (8) certainly holds for $\eta \leq \tfrac{1}{2}\delta$ and so then does (7), for all q in Q.

3 THE BIPROPORTIONAL INPUT–OUTPUT ESTIMATE AND PRICES

As in the previous section, we begin by formally stating our assumption on the constancy of $L(1)$, this time with respect to p.

ASSUMPTION 2. The true value $L(1)$ of the input–output coefficient matrix at $t = 1$ is invariant with respect to prices p at $t = 1$, $p \in P$.

We recall that variation in p may be interpreted either as virtual variation in prices at $t = 1$, or as variation in the prices in which marginal transactions statistics are made available. We also assume that

$$P \text{ has rank } m,$$

and of course that $p > 0$ for p in P.

Regarding q as fixed and writing $L^*(p)$ for L^* considered as a function of p we may state the theorem, analogous to Theorem 10

THEOREM 12. $L^*(p)$ is invariant with respect to p if and only if $L(1)$ is biproportional to L.

PROOF. The proof is entirely analogous to that of Theorem 10, with the roles of p and q appropriately interchanged. From it, we may conclude that the estimate L^* is invariant with respect to p only in the case that $L(1)$ is biproportional to L, and that in this case its constant value is the true one. |

We may also show by methods analogous to those used in the proof of Theorem 11 that

THEOREM 13. As $L(1)$ approaches $\langle r \rangle L \langle s \rangle$, L^* approaches $\langle r \rangle L \langle s \rangle$ uniformly on p in P,

and deduce from this theorem that, as $L(1)$ approaches $\langle r \rangle L \langle s \rangle$, $L^* - L(1) \to 0$ uniformly on p in P.

Finally, we note a point concerning the relationship between the estimate L^* of the input–output coefficient matrix and the associated estimates of Paasche price indices for industries' intermediate input bundles. The true Paasche index of prices at $t = 1$ relative to prices at $t = 0$ for secondary inputs into industry j may be written

$$\pi_j(1) = \frac{p l^j(1) q_j}{p(0) l^j(1) q_j}, \tag{9}$$

and the estimate of this index derived from the estimate L^* of $L(1)$ as

$$\pi_j^* = \frac{p l^{*j} q_j}{p(0) l^{*j} q_j}. \tag{10}$$

It is obvious that correct estimation of $L(1)$ is sufficient for the correct estimation of $\pi_j(1)$, $j = 1, ..., m$. But (1) shows that the numerator in (10) is constrained to equal the numerator in (9), viz. the true value v_j of total secondary inputs into industry j at $t = 1$ expressed in the prices p of $t = 1$. Hence $\pi_j^* = \pi_j(1)$ only if the denominators in (9) and (10) are equal, i.e. only if $p(0) \, l^{*j} = p(0) \, l^j(1)$. If $p(0)$ varies over a set of rank m, it follows that $\pi_j^* = \pi_j(1)$ for all $p(0)$ only if l^{*j} is equal to $l^j(1)$. Thus correct estimation of $L(1)$ is also necessary to guarantee the correct estimation of Paasche price indices for industries' secondary inputs for all possible values of $p(0)$.

CHAPTER 8

TWO-STAGE BIPROPORTIONAL
INPUT–OUTPUT ESTIMATES

1 INTRODUCTION

We shall not again be concerned with price variations or their consequences. To stick to the convention of the last chapter, by which input–output ratios and certain commodity magnitudes were understood to be expressed in physical units, would, therefore, encumber us with superfluous notation. It will be best to revert to our original understanding: henceforth, our notation will express all commodity magnitudes and input–output coefficients in the prices of time $t = 1$.

We have seen in Chapter 3 that a value $L(1)$ of an input–output coefficient matrix at $t = 1$ biproportional to its value L at $t = 0$, may be interpreted as having arisen in part through the substitution of commodity inputs one for another. A more refined account of input substitution would first group commodity inputs into broad 'input classes', then separately consider inter-class and intra-class substitutions. It is certainly plausible that, for instance, the increase during the interval 1954–60 in the use of mineral oil refining products per unit output in the British economy came from the substitution of these products for rival fuels rather than for non-fuel inputs. On the other hand, an increase in the per unit use of, say, advertising services might arise from an increase in the use of services in general at the expense of material inputs rather than from a substitution of advertising for other services. An investigation of secondary input substitution should try to capture these distinctions whenever they occur, for the sake both of descriptive accuracy and of surer prediction.

In the next section we put forward a two-stage method of estimating an input–output matrix for $t = 1$ (given, as usual, its value at $t = 0$ and gross outputs and marginals for the transactions table at $t = 1$) that yields factors interpretable as measures of inter-class and intra-class substitutions. At each stage a certain biproportional problem is solved.

First we formalize the idea of an input class. Let us denote the set of commodities, m in number, by

$$I = \{1, ..., i, ..., m\}.$$

We partition this set, considered as inputs, into a set of *input classes*, n in number:

$$I = I_1 \cup ... \cup I_j \cup ... \cup I_n,$$
$$I_j \cap I_{j'} = \{0\} \quad \text{if} \quad j \neq j'.$$

Throughout this chapter the letter j will be used only to index input classes and will accordingly run from 1 to n.

We shall need the following $n \times m$ grouping or *aggregation matrix G*, which aggregates inputs into input classes:

$$G = \begin{bmatrix} i_1 & 0 & \ldots & 0 \\ 0 & i_2 & \ldots & 0 \\ \vdots & & & \vdots \\ 0 & 0 & \ldots & i_n \end{bmatrix},$$

where the (row) vector i_j consists of $m(j)$ ones.

If input classes are thought of as broad categories such as fuels, raw materials, current account equipment items, it is reasonable to assume that each industry uses a positive amount of each input class. In the present notation this may be written

$$GZ(t) > 0, \tag{1}$$

an assumption we make from now on.

2   THE TWO-STAGE ESTIMATION METHOD

Let us denote the 'constant coefficients' estimate of the transactions matrix at $t = 1$, $Z(1)$, by Z, i.e. let us write

$$L\langle q \rangle = Z.$$

Then GZ is a ('long') $n \times m$ matrix showing the constant-coefficients absorptions by industries of classes of inputs. The partition of Z corresponding to the jth input class will be denoted by Z_j. In accordance with our convention on the index j, u_j will denote the *partition* of u corresponding to the jth input class, $j = 1, \ldots, n$, and will not denote the jth element of u, $j = 1, \ldots, m$.

The two-stage biproportional estimation method is as follows:

Stage (i). Find an $n \times m$ matrix $Z^{\oplus}$ such that

$$\left. \begin{aligned} & Z^{\oplus} \text{ is biproportional to } GZ, \\ & Z^{\oplus} i = Gu, \quad i Z^{\oplus} = v. \end{aligned} \right\} \tag{2}$$

That is, solve the biproportional problem (GZ, Gu, v) and denote the solution $(GZ)^B (Gu, v)$ by $Z^{\oplus}$. Following our usual notation for matrix rows, we shall then write

$$Z^{\oplus} = \begin{bmatrix} z_1^{\oplus} \\ \vdots \\ z_n^{\oplus} \end{bmatrix}.$$

Stage (ii). For each j, $j = 1, \ldots, n$, find $Z_j^{\circledtwo}$ such that

$$\left. \begin{aligned} & Z_j^{\circledtwo} \text{ is biproportional to } Z_j, \\ & Z_j^{\circledtwo} i = u_j, \quad i Z_j^{\circledtwo} = z_j^{\oplus}. \end{aligned} \right\} \tag{3}$$

I.e. $Z_j^{\circledtwo} = (Z_j)^B (u_j, z_j^{\circledone})$. Then the two-stage estimate of the transactions matrix at $t = 1$ is

$$Z^{\circledtwo} = \begin{bmatrix} Z_1^{\circledtwo} \\ \vdots \\ Z_n^{\circledtwo} \end{bmatrix},$$

where the $Z_j^{\circledtwo}$ are $m(j) \times m$ partitions of $Z^{\circledtwo}$. We shall also write $Z^{\circledtwo}$ as $Z^{\circledtwo}(u, v)$.

At the first stage we have estimated substitution effects between input classes by fitting the aggregated matrix GZ to appropriately aggregated marginal data; at the second we have estimated substitution effects within each input class by fitting the corresponding partition of Z to marginal quantities, part of which—the partition's column sums—have been estimated at the first stage.

3 INEQUIVALENCE OF ONE-STAGE AND TWO-STAGE ESTIMATION METHODS

In this section we show that in general $Z^B(u, v) \neq Z^{\circledtwo}(u, v)$, from which it follows that the corresponding coefficient matrices L^*, $Z^{\circledtwo}\langle q \rangle^{-1}$ are also different. It is enough to show that the asserted inequality holds in general when

$$Z^B = \langle r \rangle Z \langle s \rangle, \tag{4}$$

—the standard input–output case.

We first note that the jth partition of Z^B, Z_j^B say, and the jth partition of $Z^{\circledtwo}$, $Z_j^{\circledtwo}$, are respectively biproportional adjustments of Z_j to fit (u_j, iZ_j^B) and (u_j, z_j), so $Z_j^B = Z_j^{\circledtwo}$ only if, for $j = 1, \ldots, n$,

$$iZ_j^B = z_j^{\circledone}, \tag{5}$$

i.e. forming the direct sum of each side over the j, only if

$$G \langle r \rangle Z \langle s \rangle = Z^{\circledone}. \tag{6}$$

From Corollaries 4 and 5 and the assumption (1) that $GZ > 0$ it follows that $Z^{\circledone}$ is an interior solution of (GZ, Gu, v), i.e. is as expressible as

$$Z^{\circledone} = \langle a \rangle GZ \langle b \rangle.$$

Then the necessary condition (6) for $Z^{\circledtwo} = Z^B$ may be written

$$G \langle r \rangle Z \langle s \rangle = \langle a \rangle GZ \langle b \rangle \tag{7}$$

and its jth partition (5) becomes

$$i_j \langle r_j \rangle Z_j \langle s \rangle = a_j i_j Z_j \langle b \rangle,$$

where r_j denotes the jth partition of r; i.e.

$$\frac{1}{a_j} r_j Z_j = i_j Z_j \langle b \rangle \langle s \rangle^{-1},$$

i.e.
$$\frac{1}{a_j} r_j \begin{bmatrix} z_{j_1 k} \\ \vdots \\ z_{j_{m(j)} k} \end{bmatrix} = (z_{j_1 k} + \dots + z_{j_{m(j)} k}) \frac{b_k}{s_k} \quad (k = 1, \dots, m). \tag{8}$$

Let us write
$$\frac{1}{a_j} r_j = \rho_j, \tag{9}$$

$$\frac{z_{j_i k}}{z_{j_1 k} + \dots + z_{j_{m(j)} k}} = \zeta_{j_i k} \quad (i = 1, \dots, m(j)), \tag{10}$$

$$\{\zeta_{j_i k}\} = \mathscr{Z},$$

$\zeta_{jk} = j$th partition of kth column of $\mathscr{Z}$.

We note that (1) ensures that ζ_{j_i} is always defined. (8) must hold for $j = 1, \dots, n$. But this involves that

$$\rho_j \zeta_{jk} = \rho_{j'} \zeta_{j'k} = \frac{b_k}{s_k} \quad (j, j' = 1, \dots, n),$$

$$(0 \dots 0 \; \rho_j \; 0 \dots 0 \; -\rho_{j'} \; 0 \dots 0) \, \mathscr{Z} = 0 \quad \text{for} \quad j < j', \tag{11}$$

where the symbols 0 in the vector in (11) denote null partitions, corresponding to input classes other than j, j'.

It may be helpful to give a verbal description of the matrix $\mathscr{Z}$ defined in (10). An element of $\mathscr{Z}$ is an element of the transactions matrix Z, divided by the partial column sum of Z to which it contributes (the partial sums being the sums of elements belonging to particular input classes or partitions). Thus in the notation of Chapter 5 the partition $\mathscr{Z}_j = \mathscr{C}Z_j$. Clearly

$$(0 \dots 0 \; i_j \; 0 \dots 0 \; -i_{j'} \; 0 \dots 0) \, \mathscr{Z} = 0, \tag{12}$$

whence a sufficient condition for (11) is that

$$\rho_{j_i} = \text{constant for } j_i = 1, \dots, m. \tag{13}$$

The free scalar multiple in the expression (4) may be chosen so that this constant $= 1$, and then, using (9), (13) may be written

$$r_{j_i} = a_j \quad (i = 1, \dots, m(j); j = 1, \dots, n). \tag{14}$$

A sufficient condition for (14) is that the rows of the jth partition of $(Z \; u)$ should be proportional to each other, $j = 1, \dots, n$. But as one might guess, this condition is not necessary for (14). For example if $r_{j_i} = 1$, $j_i = 1, \dots, m$, these rows need not be proportional. We have $Zs = u$, $iZ\langle s \rangle = v$, whence $Z\langle iZ \rangle^{-1} v = u$. One may choose Z, u quite freely, subject only to the existence of Z^{-1}, and then $v = \langle iZ \rangle Z^{-1} u > 0$ is sufficient for $r_{j_i} = 1, j_i = 1, \dots, m$.

It would be interesting to see whether, for some definitions of inputs and input classes, the data show any tendency to proportionality of the rows of a partition of $(Z \; u)$. In a consumer demand analogy, would one expect every geographical group of consumers to buy oil-, gas- and solid fuel-fired types of central heating equipment in roughly the same proportions? Compared with the 'same cost structure' condition for aggregating several using sectors in the Leontief model (see e.g. [51]) this condition is more restrictive in applying to all users, but less so in demanding only proportionality rather than equality of columns and indeed in demanding this proportionality only *within* input classes.

Suppose that (13) is not true. This is the general case, since for given Z, r and s can be any positive vectors without $\langle r \rangle Z \langle s \rangle$ violating any *a priori* restriction on transactions matrices. We shall show that a certain condition that is in this case necessary for $Z^B = Z^\otimes$ is in general unfulfilled. There are clearly at least $n-1$ linearly independent vectors of the form of the vector in (12): take $j = 1, j' = 2, ..., n$. So

$$\text{rank } \mathcal{L} \leq m-n+1.$$

But on the other hand (i) the $m(1)$ rows of Z_1 are 'in general' linearly independent (i.e. in the absence of a theory saying why linear dependence is to be expected we appeal to the principle of insufficient reason and assign to each row-vector of Z_1 a conditional probability distribution given the others having continuity properties that make the joint probability measure of a linearly dependent set of vectors zero). But $\mathcal{L}_1 = \mathcal{C}Z_1 = Z_1 \langle i_1 Z_1 \rangle^{-1}$ and the nonsingularity of $\langle i_1 Z_1 \rangle^{-1}$ means that $\mathcal{L}_1$ has the rank of Z_1, i.e. the $m(1)$ vectors of $\mathcal{L}_1$ are in general linearly independent. (ii) The first $m(2) - 1$ vectors of $\mathcal{L}_2$ are in general independent of the vectors of $\mathcal{L}_1$ and of each other; the first $m(3) - 1$ of $\mathcal{L}_3$ independent of those of $\mathcal{L}_1$, $\mathcal{L}_2$ and of each other; and so on. Thus $\mathcal{L}$ in general contains at least

$$m(1) + \sum_{j=2}^{n} [m(j) - 1] = m - n + 1$$

independent vectors, i.e.

$$\text{rank } \mathcal{L} \geq m-n+1.$$

The rank of $\mathcal{L}$ is therefore in general $m-n+1$ and the set of linear combinations of vectors of the form appearing in (12) is the entire solution set of the equation $x\mathcal{L} = 0$. But it is easily seen that

$$(0 \dots 0 \ \rho_j \ 0 \dots 0 \ -\rho_{j'} \ 0 \dots 0)$$

can be a linear combination of vectors of the form

$$(0 \dots 0 \ i_k \ 0 \dots 0 \ -i_{k'} \ 0 \dots 0)$$

for all j, j' such that $j < j'$ only if (13) holds, a possibility we have excluded.

4 COMPARATIVE PROPERTIES OF THE TWO METHODS

The two estimation methods in general lead to different estimates of the transactions matrix. We must therefore try to evaluate them comparatively. Any assessment of the 1-stage method must answer the question: how well does it do if the true matrix at $t = 1$ is of the same form as the estimate (and if it is not), i.e. if it is generated from the matrix at $t = 0$ by a (1-stage) biproportional process? Similarly, we can define a natural 2-stage biproportional generating process and ask how well the 2-stage estimation method performs if the matrix at $t = 1$ is so generated (and if not). We have seen already in section 5 of Chapter 5 that (i) a 1-stage estimate is correct if and only if the true matrix at $t = 1$ is 1-stage generated; we shall show now that (ii) a 2-stage estimate is correct if and only if the true matrix is 2-stage generated. The result of the last section then implies that (iii) each estimation method in general falsely estimates a matrix generated by the non-corresponding process.

(ii) Let the true matrix at $t = 1$ be $Z^{(2)}$ and let it be generated from Z by the following 2-stage biproportional process:

$$Z^{(1)} = \langle \alpha \rangle GZ \langle \beta \rangle, \tag{15}$$

$$\left. \begin{array}{l} Z_j^{(2)} \text{ is biproportional to } Z_j \quad (j = 1, ..., n), \\ GZ^{(2)} = Z^{(1)}. \end{array} \right\} \tag{16}$$

The partial sums of columns of $Z^{(2)}$ are, in (15), determined by a (1-stage) biproportional process on GZ generating $Z^{(1)}$. A second, intra-class biproportional process on partition Z_j of Z preserves these sums, determining only the disaggregation of $z_j^{(1)}$ into individual inputs $(j = 1, ..., n)$.

(It is readily seen that (15)–(16) is equivalent to assuming that the true coefficient matrix at $t = 1$, $L^{(2)}$ say, is given by: $L^{(1)} = \langle \alpha \rangle GL \langle \beta \rangle$, $L_j^{(2)}$ biproportional to L_j, $GL^{(2)} = L^{(1)}$.)

At the first stage of estimation, (2), we seek vectors a, b such that

$$\langle a \rangle GZ \langle b \rangle = Z^{\text{\textcircled{1}}}, \quad Z^{\text{\textcircled{1}}} i = Gu, \quad iZ^{\text{\textcircled{1}}} = v.$$

But $\langle \alpha \rangle GZ \langle \beta \rangle = Z^{(1)}, \quad Z^{(1)}i = GZ^{(2)}i = Gu, \quad iZ^{(1)} = iGZ^{(2)} = v.$

By uniqueness (Corollary 1), $Z^{\text{\textcircled{1}}} = Z^{(1)}$. At the second stage of estimation, (3), we seek, for each $j, j = 1, ..., n$, a matrix $Z_j^{\text{\textcircled{2}}}$ biproportional to Z_j and such that $Z_j^{\text{\textcircled{2}}}i = u_j$, $iZ_j^{\text{\textcircled{2}}} = z_j^{\text{\textcircled{1}}}$. But $Z_j^{\text{\textcircled{2}}}$ is biproportional to Z_j, $Z_j^{\text{\textcircled{2}}}i = u_j$, $iZ_j^{\text{\textcircled{2}}} = z_j^{(1)} = z_j^{\text{\textcircled{1}}}$. By Corollary 1, $Z^{\text{\textcircled{2}}} = Z^{(2)}$.

Conversely, it is fairly obvious that (15)–(16) is necessary for correct estimation. Suppose that the 2-stage estimate is correct, i.e. $Z^{\text{\textcircled{2}}} = $ true matrix $= Z^{(2)}$. Then its first stage correctly estimates $GZ^{(2)}$, for the first-stage estimate $Z^{\text{\textcircled{1}}} = GZ^{\text{\textcircled{2}}} = GZ^{(2)}$. Therefore $GZ^{(2)}$ is biproportional to GZ (in fact $GZ^{(2)} = \langle a \rangle GZ \langle b \rangle$). Writing $GZ^{(2)} = Z^{(1)}$ we see that (15) is satisfied. The second stage, (3), correctly estimates $Z_j^{(2)} = Z^{\text{\textcircled{2}}}$ for each j. Thus $Z_j^{(2)}$ is biproportional to Z_j.

(iii) If the transactions matrix for $t = 1$ is 1-stage generated, its 1-stage estimate is correct, hence by the result of section 3, the 2-stage estimation method in general estimates it incorrectly; and conversely.

It is even possible that the 2-stage method provides no solution at all if the true matrix has been 1-stage generated. This is because the partitions Z_j which the second stage tries to adjust by biproportional transformations may have partial disconnections not present in the matrix Z itself (for these partial disconnections may disappear in direct addition); and there is no guarantee that the necessary conditions for a solution given in Theorem 3, applicable if the initial matrix of a biproportional problem has partial disconnections, be fulfilled. This possibility is illustrated in a numerical example presented in Chapter 11. A further drawback of the 2-stage method is that, in general, it fails to provide column-multipliers interpretable as uniform fabrication effects: the various partitions of a column are typically multiplied by different column-factors in a 2-stage estimate. It would be hard to interpret these convincingly as fabrication effects operating uniformly over the inputs of each input class but differentially between classes.

We have seen that neither estimation method dominates the other—i.e. neither is in general good against both generation processes with the other in general good against one only. In particular, we have found no compelling reason to jettison the established virtues of the one-stage model in favour of a less tractable two-stage model.

CHAPTER 9

PROJECTIONS OF BIPROPORTIONAL ESTIMATES

1 PROJECTIONS OF BIPROPORTIONAL INPUT–OUTPUT MATRICES

A central aim of the Cambridge Growth Project was to predict gross outputs from given projections of final demands. Several considerations ruled out an application of Arrow and Hoffenberg's successful method, described in Chapter 3, based on regressions on a set of predetermined variables of 'constant-coefficient residuals'—the deviations of actual intermediate outputs from those implied by an assumption of constant input–output coefficients. First, one would have to begin by predicting the values of the predetermined variables for the years in question. Secondly, the validity of forecasts from a 'reduced form' depends on its stability under changes in the underlying structure. But the Cambridge Growth Project's predictions were conditional on a change in the growth rate of British G.N.P. from a $2\frac{1}{2}$ % average in the 1950s to a rate of 4 % by the prediction year. One could be sure that such a change would impinge heavily on elements of the reduced form, but one could not specify which elements or how much. Thirdly, there was a chance [26] of bringing to bear the specialized knowledge of industrial engineers and marketers. An input–output matrix prediction, however unreliable, would stimulate the flow of information from these sources in a way which could not be expected from predictions of gross outputs from given final demands. The problem of predicting the matrix itself could not be escaped.

We have at our disposal the two-term time series L, L^* consisting of an observed input–output coefficient matrix for $t = 0$ and a biproportional estimate of the matrix at $t = 1$. Is there a way of projecting this series that is both natural and consistent with *a priori* economic requirements? In particular, can we meet these requirements: (i) the projected matrix, L^P say, should not merely be identical with L; (ii) it should be nonnegative; (iii) the column sums of the matrix sequence L, L^*, L^P should obey certain *a priori* constraints? These sums are estimates of the ratios of industries' intermediate to total inputs at the three dates, and in the absence of information to the contrary we should expect these ratios to move in some regular way through time.

The constraints coming under (iii) should certainly, for instance, rule out any 'bias' in the projected column sums in the sense of a tendency for the projected sums to reverse the directions of movement between the corresponding sums in L and $L*$. One way of ensuring against such tendencies is to insist that corresponding column sums of L, $L*$ and the projected matrix L^P should in all cases form monotonic sequences. This is a fairly severe version of the constraint, as we could tolerate a few countervailing nonmonotonicities, but it has the merits of simplicity and tractability. This form of monotonicity constraint will, therefore, constitute our formal version of requirement (iii).

Were we working in current prices we might well wish, in addition, to impose upper bounds of unity on the column sums of privately owned industries and of a little more on publicly owned ones. In constant prices analogous bounds operate for the same reason—the non-viability of loss-making industries—but in this case the bounds are functions of bounds on product prices on whose magnitudes economic theory has little to say. We shall return a little later to the question of bounding from above the column sums of input–output matrices. Meanwhile, there is no need to pursue it, for it will turn out (Theorem 13) that the requirements we have made so far are already too stringent for a method of projection satisfying them all to exist. We note that the nonnegativity condition (ii) on the projected matrix L^P ensures that any upper bound on a column sum would imply the same upper bound on each element of the column.

We note, too, that the row sums of an input–output coefficient matrix are devoid of economic meaning, so that no *a priori* restraints apply to them directly. It may be that some estimate is available of the gross outputs of commodities in the projection year, q^P say. In this case it might be sensible to impose some constraints, say monotonicity ones, on the row sums of the transactions matrix $L^P\langle q^P\rangle$, as the ratios of intermediate to total demands for commodities are economically meaningful magnitudes which we might expect to move in some regular fashion through time. Indeed, it may be recalled from section 2 of Chapter 2 that an assumption of constancy in these ratios formed the basis of the 'final demand blowup' method of predicting gross outputs from final demands that Leontief [49], Selma Arrow [4], Hoffenberg (see [16]) and Barnett [5] used. But for the reason given at the end of the last paragraph, there is no point in imposing these extra restrictions.

The same may be said of monotonicity restrictions on the individual coefficients. In any case, the requirement seems too strong a one. It would be daring to assert, *a priori*, that turning points in particular input–output ratios occur infrequently enough to warrant it, even for a shortish period of less than ten years. The restriction seems more reasonable for the sums of these ratios that figure in (iii). (iii) also ensures that individual coefficients move monotonically 'on the average'.

For the same reason again, there is no need to consider the general case $L^* = \lim_{t \to \infty} \langle R^t \rangle L \langle S^t \rangle$, but only the 'interior' case

$$L^* = \langle r \rangle L \langle s \rangle. \tag{1}$$

To illustrate the projection problem, let us consider the most natural projection of L, L^* to a time with date $t > 1$, the exponential projection suggested in [26]:
$$L^P = \langle r \rangle^t L \langle s \rangle^t \quad (t > 1).$$

This projection has the intuitively desirable property of being mapped from L^* by a transformation which also maps L into L^*, viz. pre-multiplication by (some positive power of) $\langle r \rangle$ and postmultiplication by (the same positive power of) $\langle s \rangle$. We certainly have $L^P \geq 0$, and $r_i^t l_{ij} s_j^t$ may certainly differ from $r_i l_{ij} s_j$. But suppose that

$$il^j = il^{*j} = rl^j s_j.$$

We may write this as
$$\sum_{i=1}^m \lambda_{ij} r_i s_j = 1,$$

where
$$\lambda_{ij} = l_{ij} \bigg/ \sum_{i=1}^m l_{ij}.$$

Hence by Cauchy's inequality $\sum_i \lambda_{ij} r_i^t s_j^t > 1$, i.e. $il^{Pj} > il^j$, unless $r_1 = \ldots = r_m$, where l^{Pj} denotes the jth column of L^P. Thus if

$$r_i \neq r_1, \quad \text{some } i,$$
$$il^j = il^{*j}, \quad \text{some } j,$$

then
$$il^j < il^{Pj}.$$

We have not yet displayed a nonmonotonicity, but continuity considerations now readily reveal one. Any decrease however small in, say, r_1, depresses il^{*j} below il^j. But if such a decrease is small enough il^{Pj} certainly remains greater than il^j.

The question put in the first paragraph may be formalized thus: does there exist a continuous function f defined on pairs of positive real numbers such that for all $r_i, s_j > 0$

$$f(r_i, s_j) \geq 0, \tag{2}$$

$$\sum_i \lambda_{ij} f(r_i, s_j) \gtreqless \sum_i \lambda_{ij} r_i s_j \quad \text{according as} \quad \sum_i \lambda_{ij} r_i s_j \gtreqless 1,$$

for all probability vectors $(\lambda_{1j}, \ldots, \lambda_{mj})$, (3)

and such that for some r_i, s_j,

$$f(r_i, s_j) \neq r_i s_j? \tag{4}$$

We note in passing that there is a natural way of extending this formulation of the problem to the case in which L^* is not expressible as in (1) which does not involve limiting processes. By Corollary 6 L^* is always expressible as

$$L^* = \begin{bmatrix} \langle r_1 \rangle & \cdots & 0 \\ \vdots & & \vdots \\ 0 & \cdots & \langle r_K \rangle \end{bmatrix} \begin{bmatrix} L_{11} & \cdots & 0 \\ \vdots & & \vdots \\ 0 & \cdots & L_{KK} \end{bmatrix} \begin{bmatrix} \langle s_1 \rangle & \cdots & 0 \\ \vdots & & \vdots \\ 0 & \cdots & \langle s_K \rangle \end{bmatrix} = \langle r \rangle \overset{0}{L} \langle s \rangle,$$

$\overset{0}{L}$ reducing to L only when (1) is satisfied. Let $i \in k$, $j \in k'$, where k, k' are any two of the index sets defining the above partitioning. If $k = k'$ then $\overset{0}{l}_{ij} = l_{ij}$, $l_{ij}^* = r_i s_j l_{ij}$, and $f(r_i, s_j) l_{ij} = f(r_i, s_j) \overset{0}{l}_{ij}$ for any f. If $k \neq k'$ and (ρ_i, σ_j) is any pair of scalar multipliers such that $l_{ij}^* = \rho_i \sigma_j l_{ij}$ then $f(\rho_i, \sigma_j) l_{ij} = f(r_i, s_j) \overset{0}{l}_{ij} = 0$ as long as f is finite-valued and vanishes with either of its arguments. Condition (3) needs only to be rewritten as

$$\sum_i \overset{0}{l}_{ij} f(r_i, s_j) \gtreqless \sum_i \overset{0}{l}_{ij} r_i s_j \quad \text{according as} \quad \sum_i \overset{0}{l}_{ij} r_i s_j \gtreqless \sum l_{ij},$$

to allow for the fact that $\sum_i \left(\dfrac{\overset{0}{l}_i}{\sum l_i} \right)$ is no longer necessarily equal to one, and the generalization is accomplished. We shall not, however, have to investigate this wider case.

As we are interested only in projecting to a single time beyond the time of L^* there is no need to write a time variable t as an argument of f. Such a variable is of course implicit in the above formulation: L and L^* are dated by $t = 0, 1$ and the function f in (3) is evaluated at some $t > 1$, i.e. the inequality implications in (3) are required to hold only for extrapolations on the time-pair $(0, 1)$. The variable t would have to be made explicit if we wanted to take account of corresponding sets of conditions for interpolations on $(0, 1)$ or for time-triples neither of the form $(0, 1, t)$, $t > 1$ nor of the form $(0, t, 1)$, $0 < t < 1$, e.g. for the triple $(1, t, t')$, $1 < t < t'$. But our finding will be that no function exists satisfying even the limited conditions (2) to (4); a fortiori it will, once again, be needless to pose the question in a more general and more stringent form.

2 NON-EXISTENCE OF AN ACCEPTABLE $f(r_i, s_j)$

Set $s_j = s_j^0$, then the equality implication in (3) may be written

$$\sum_i \lambda_{ij} f(r_i, s_j^0) = 1 \quad \text{if} \quad \sum \lambda_{ij} r_i = 1/s_j^0. \tag{5}$$

Let $m = 2$ and let $r_1 \leq r_2$. The hypothesis in (5) means that $1/s_j^0$ must satisfy $0 < r_1 \leq 1/s_j^0 \leq r_2$. Then $(\lambda_{1j}, \lambda_{2j}) = \left(\dfrac{r_2 - 1/s_j^0}{r_2 - r_1}, \dfrac{1/s_j^0 - r_1}{r_2 - r_1} \right)$ are weights for which that hypothesis is satisfied. (5) then implies

$$(r_2 - 1/s_j^0) f(r_1, s_j^0) + (1/s_j^0 - r_1) f(r_2, s_j^0) = r_2 - r_1,$$

so that $f(r_1, s_j^0)$ is linear in r_1 and $f(r_2, s_j^0)$ is linear in r_2. The constant term in $f(r_1, s_j^0)$ is

$$\frac{r_2 - (1/s_j^0) f(r_2, s_j^0)}{r_2 - (1/s_j^0)} . \tag{6}$$

Now let $r_1 = \ldots = r_m = r_0$ and let $r_0 \to 0$. Then $\sum\limits_i \lambda_{ij} r_i s_j^0 \to 0$ and the $<$ implication of (3) means that $\lim\limits_{r_0 \to 0} f(r_0, s_j^0) \leqq 0$. The continuity of f and condition (2) imply that this limit is zero. But then also the function $f(r_1, s_j^0)$ of the last paragraph $\to 0$ with r_1 and the constant term (6) of this function must always vanish, i.e.

$$f(r_2, s_j^0) = r_2 s_j^0.$$

By a parallel argument $f(r_1, s_j^0) = r_1 s_j^0$, so we have $f(r, s_j^0) = r s_j^0$ for any positive r. Indeed for all $r_i, s_j > 0$

$$f(r_i, s_j) = r_i s_j$$

and we have proved

THEOREM 13. There exists no continuous function f on pairs (r_i, s_j) of positive numbers which satisfies conditions (2) to (4), viz. that (i) $f(r_i, s_j) \neq r_i s_j$, (ii) $f(r_i, s_j)$ be nonnegative, (iii) the sequences $(\sum\limits_i l_{ij}, \sum\limits_i r_i s_j l_{ij}, \sum\limits_i f(r_i, s_j) l_{ij})$ be monotonic for all semipositive vectors $(l_{1j}, \ldots, l_{mj})$.

3 A CONSTRAINED MINIMUM DISTANCE METHOD

We have failed to find a satisfactory projection L^P of L, L^* in which l_{ij}^P has the form $l_{ij} f(r_i, s_j)$, where $f(r_i, s_j)$ does not involve elements of L or L^* other than the (i, j)th.

The exponential projection $\langle r \rangle^t L \langle s \rangle^t$, however, violates just one of the conditions (2) to (4), namely the monotonicity one (3). That is, it violates only certain *a priori* inequality constraints on its column sums. This suggests the following procedure for projecting L, L^*: (i) sharpen the *a priori* inequality constraints to equational ones; (ii) find, subject to these equational constraints, a matrix in some sense 'nearest' to the exponential one. For we already know how to do (ii); and since we may hope that the solution will be near the exponential projection, we may also hope that it will share some of the virtues of this projection that were described in section 1.

Let us postpone considering the problems that arise in executing (i) until the next section, and meanwhile assume them to be solved. First, then, we tackle stage (ii) of the above procedure.

We begin with a digression. Let us drop for the moment our convention that L denotes an input–output coefficient matrix. Instead, let L denote any matrix to whose projection we may appropriately attach both conditions (2) to (4) and, in addition, a condition on row sums analogous to (3). In this case a fairly trivial problem results. When both row- and column-sum constraints have been transformed from inequality to equational form the constrained minimization problem (ii) we are left with is, for the appropriate criterion function, a least-squares, Friedlander or biproportional constrained matrix problem. In particular, consider the case when the distance-like function is $\tilde{\phi}$ of section 4 of Chapter 6, so that a biproportional problem results. The projection is the solution, if one exists, of the biproportional problem $(\langle r \rangle^t L \langle s \rangle^t, u^P, v^P)$, where u^P, v^P are the vectors defining the equational constraints on the row and column sums. By the uniqueness theorem (Corollary 1) this solution equals $L^B(u^P, v^P)$ and so is independent of r, s. Indeed it is dependent on what is observed at $t = 1$ only to the extent that (u, v) enters into the determination of (u^P, v^P). Only to this extent may it be regarded as a projection of a time-series for $t = 0, 1$. We have in general quite lost the property of $\langle r \rangle^t L \langle s \rangle^t$ of being obtained from L by the transformation that maps L into L^*, raised to some power.

Suppose, secondly, that the criterion is $\tilde{\chi}^2$, giving a Friedlander problem as the constrained minimization problem as in section 3 of Chapter 6. Then a unique solution exists, not necessarily nonnegative, and of the form

$$\langle r \rangle^t L \langle s \rangle^t + \langle \xi \rangle \left(\langle r \rangle^t L \langle s \rangle^t \right) + \left(\langle r \rangle^t L \langle s \rangle^t \right) \langle \eta \rangle,$$

which may be written

$$\langle r \rangle^t \left(L + \langle \xi \rangle L + L \langle \eta \rangle \right) \langle s \rangle^t.$$

The commutativity here shown of the biproportionality and Friedlander transformations permits the following interpretation of the Friedlander multipliers ξ, η. They transform the base year matrix into a matrix $(L + \langle \xi \rangle L + L \langle \eta \rangle)$ whose pre- and post-multiplication by $\langle r \rangle^t$, $\langle s \rangle^t$ yield a matrix with row- and column-sums u^P, v^P.

When L is, as before, an input–output coefficient matrix, monotonicity constraints apply to column sums alone. In this case we are faced, after replacing the inequality constraints by equational ones, with a problem of the kind discussed in section 6 of Chapter 6, that is, we need to minimize with respect to projections L^P a 'potential' function of $(\langle r \rangle^t L \langle s \rangle^t, L^P)$ subject only to the column sum constraints

$$iL^P = v^P,$$

where it may be assumed that

$$v^P > 0.$$

We have seen that, when the potential is either $\tilde{\chi}^2$ or $\tilde{\phi}$, the unique solution is L^P given by

$$iL^P = v^P,$$

$$L^P = (\langle r \rangle^t L \langle s \rangle^t) \langle \sigma \rangle,$$

and $L^P \geq 0$. $L^P = L^*$ for all permissible L only if $r = i$. L^P therefore satisfies condition (i) of section 1. The projection depends upon r, though not directly upon s. However, for given L, r is a function of both u and v. Thus L^P depends upon both u and v through r as well as upon v through its influence on v^P, and may certainly be regarded as a genuine projection of L, L^*.

Recapitulating, L^P has the following properties: (i) for $l_i \geqslant 0$, $l^j \geqslant 0$, $i = 1, ..., m$; $j = 1, ..., n$; $u, v, v^P > 0$, it is nonnegative; (ii) it is not identical with L; (iii) it satisfies an equational (monotonicity) condition on its column sums; (iv) it depends upon u, v; (v) it is as 'near' to the exponential projection as is consistent with (iii).

4   PROJECTING INTERMEDIATE INPUT RATIOS

We have now to go back to consider the problems that arise in part (i) of the procedure for projecting an input–output matrix proposed in the last section. In effect, (i) means that we have to commit ourselves to a projection of the vector of industries' ratios of intermediate inputs to total inputs at constant prices. The methods of doing so that suggest themselves give rise to the same kinds of difficulty as we encountered in trying to project the whole of a matrix according to simple functional forms. Linear projections may contain negatives, which are unacceptable. Exponential projections are necessarily positive, but impart upward bias to a weighted mean of industries' intermediate input ratios, in the sense that if such a weighted mean is constant for $t = 0, 1$, it in general exceeds this constant value in the projection. We must now also concede that the individual column sum projections should be bounded from above, as well as from below by zero. However, economic theory, even when it does pay attention to the contribution of intermediate inputs to output [27], has little to say about the magnitudes of appropriate upper bounds—any more than the usual production theory has much to say about bounds on per unit inputs of labour or capital. Econometric studies touch the question only glancingly [15, 50]. In the following description of a method of projecting intermediate input ratios—the outcome of discussions with Professor J. A. C. Brown—we accordingly leave the upper bounds arbitrary. In illustrative calculations presented in Chapter 11 we shall use upper bounds of one.

Denote by c, c^* the sum of the elements of a particular column of L, L^* respectively, i.e. the (actual or estimated) value of the column sum at $t = 0, 1$ respectively. Let the upper bound for this sum over time be $k \geq 1$. Then define the values τ, τ^* of a variable θ by

$$\text{prob}\,(x \leqq \tau) = \frac{c}{k}, \quad \text{prob}\,(x \leqq \tau^*) = \frac{c^*}{k}, \qquad (7)$$

where x is a standardized normal variate. Our projection c^P of the sum of elements of the column for a time $t > 1$ is then

$$k \operatorname{prob}[x \leqq \tau^P],$$

where $\tau^P = \tau + t(\tau^* - \tau)$. This projection method, which is illustrated in figure 2, has the following interpretation.

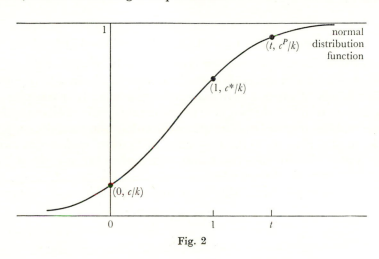

Fig. 2

The column sum is moving over time away from the value zero towards the value k (or between these values in the reverse direction) at a speed which is to be determined by observing its value at times $t = 0, 1$. A large increment $c^* - c > 0$ shows that the 'time' argument θ which determines according to (7) the value taken on by the sum, is increasing fast with respect to 'calendar' time t over the interval $(0, 1)$, and is taken to mean that θ will increase as fast over the interval $(1, t)$. Specifically, c/k is given as a probit function of θ and θ as a linear function of calendar time. The probit function is the same for every column sum, but the slope of θ as a function of calendar time is left to be determined for any column sum by the pair of observations (c, c^*) made on that column sum. A decrement $c^* - c < 0$ indicates, of course, that column-sum time θ moves in the reverse direction to calendar time.

The projection c^P obtained by this method is clearly bounded below away from 0 and bounded above away from k.

If $c \geq k/2$ and $c^* > c$ or if $c \leq k/2$ and $c^* < c$ (i.e. if the column sum is departing from the value $k/2$) this sigmoid projection method yields slower further movement away from $k/2$ than would a simple linear projection. Similarly, movement towards $k/2$ is speeded up by sigmoid projection.

No projection of intermediate input ratios based on only two observations can be more than a shot in the dark. The sigmoid method has the virtue of satisfying both upper and lower *a priori* bounds without resort to excessive conservatism. It is easy enough to keep within bounds by extrapolating with enough caution. The sigmoid-projected change, by contrast, may be expected even to exceed the linear one as often as not, viz. whenever the observed movement in an intermediate input ratio is towards the value $k/2$.

5   PROJECTION OF MAKE AND MIX MATRICES

So far in this chapter our explicit concern has been almost exclusively with input–output matrices. But much of what has been said is relevant to other kinds of nonnegative economic matrices. In particular, the analysis in section 3 of the problem of projecting a pair of biproportional matrices subject to exact constraints on the column sums of the projected matrix, applies directly to the projection of Markov matrices as soon as the projected column sum constraint vector v^P is taken to be the unit vector i. Thus if A, $A*$ are Markov matrices such that $A* = \langle r \rangle A \langle s \rangle$, the $\tilde{\chi}^2$-nearest or $\tilde{\phi}$-nearest Markov matrix to $\langle r \rangle^t A \langle s \rangle$ is A^P where

$$A^P = \langle r \rangle^t A \langle s \rangle^t \langle \sigma \rangle,$$

$$iA^P = i.$$

Another fruitful application of the method of section 3 is to the 'make' matrices introduced in section 6 of Chapter 3. A make matrix is a matrix whose (i,j)th element shows the amount of commodity j produced by the multi-product industry i. It will be recalled from Chapter 3 that there is a stage in the Cambridge Growth Project calculation of an overall projection of the economy described in [15] at which a projection of the commodity gross outputs, q^P say, has already been obtained and the next step is to obtain the gross outputs of industries as g^P say. In other words, one has an estimate of the column sums, and wishes to estimate the row sums, of the make matrix of the projection year.

Suppose that, as in the Cambridge Growth Project calculations, the make matrix for $t = 1$ has been estimated as a matrix, $M*$ say, biproportional to the make matrix M for $t = 0$, and suppose too, with only a slight loss of generality, that $M*$ can be written as

$$M* = \langle r \rangle M \langle s \rangle.$$

Then the method of section 3 gives as the nonnegative matrix that is 'nearest' to the exponential projection $\langle r \rangle^t M \langle s \rangle^t$ subject to its column sums' being equal to q^P, the matrix

$$M^P = \langle r \rangle^t M \langle s \rangle^t \langle \sigma \rangle, \tag{8}$$

where
$$iM^P = q^P. \tag{9}$$

Hence we obtain the projection of industries' gross outputs

$$g^P = M^P i.$$

A *mix matrix* is a matrix formed from a make matrix by taking coefficients either by columns or by rows. For a make matrix M, the mix matrix $\mathscr{C}M$ shows, in its columns, the 'industry mixes' of products; $\mathscr{R}M$ shows, in its rows, the product mixes of industries. A difficulty of interpretation arises when we examine the pairs of mix matrices associated with M, M^* and M^P respectively. Natural estimates of the pair of mix matrices for $t = 1$ are

$$(\mathscr{C}M)^* = \mathscr{C}M^* = \mathscr{C}(\langle r \rangle M \langle s \rangle) = \langle r \rangle (\mathscr{C}M) \langle s' \rangle,$$

$$(\mathscr{R}M)^* = \mathscr{R}M^* = \mathscr{R}(\langle r \rangle M \langle s \rangle) = \langle r' \rangle (\mathscr{R}M) \langle s \rangle,$$

where r', s' are some positive vectors. We also have the following obvious projections of the pair of mix matrices:

$$(\mathscr{C}M)^P = \mathscr{C}(M^P) = \langle r \rangle^t (\mathscr{C}M) \langle s'' \rangle, \tag{10}$$

$$(\mathscr{R}M)^P = \mathscr{R}(M^P) = \langle r'' \rangle (\mathscr{R}M) (\langle s \rangle^t \langle \sigma \rangle), \tag{11}$$

where r'', s'' are certain positive vectors.

Now the elements of the ith rows of $\mathscr{C}M$, $(\mathscr{C}M)^*$ are shares of the ith industry in the production of commodities $1, \ldots, n$. Hence the ith element r_i of r may be interpreted as a measure of the extent to which the ith industry has tended over the time interval $(0, 1)$ to increase its domination of all lines of commodity production, perhaps through a process of vertical integration. It is then natural to want for our projection of $\mathscr{C}M$ a matrix as 'nearly' as possible of the form $\langle r \rangle^t (\mathscr{C}M) \langle x \rangle$ subject to its being a Markov matrix. The projection $(\mathscr{C}M)^P$ given in (10) accomplishes exactly this.

Similarly, the jth element s_j of s may be interpreted as the extent to which the jth commodity has assumed increased importance in all industries during $(0, 1)$—for example, because all (many) industries have increasingly found it profitable to manufacture their own packages in plants subsidiary to those producing their principal products. If we like this interpretation a natural requirement for our projection of $\mathscr{R}M$ is that it should as 'nearly' as possible have the form $\langle y \rangle (\mathscr{R}M) \langle s \rangle^t$ subject to its being the transpose of a Markov matrix. This requirement is obviously *not* in general fulfilled by the projection $(\mathscr{R}M)^P$ given in (11).

It can soon be shown that, in general, a projection of the pair of mix matrices in which each has the appropriate property specified above is incompatible with the constraint q^P on the column sums of the make matrix of the projection year. For any consistent projections $(\mathscr{C}M)^P$, $(\mathscr{R}M)^P$, g^P must satisfy

$$(\mathscr{C}M)^P \langle q^P \rangle = \langle g^P \rangle (\mathscr{R}M)^P = M^P,$$

whence
$$(\mathscr{C}M)^P q^P = M^P i = g^P,$$
$$[(\mathscr{R}M)^P]' g^P = (M^P)' i = q^P,$$

so that
$$[(\mathscr{R}M)^P]' (\mathscr{C}M)^P q^P = q^P. \tag{12}$$

That is, q^P must be an eigenvector corresponding to eigenvalue 1 of $[(\mathscr{R}M)^P]' (\mathscr{C}M)^P$. But $(\mathscr{R}M)^P$, $(\mathscr{C}M)^P$ are determined independently of q^P by the requirements defined in the last two paragraphs, and so therefore is the set of eigenvectors of $[(\mathscr{R}M)^P]' (\mathscr{C}M)^P$ corresponding to 1.

What is suggested by the above is to search for a pair $[(\mathscr{R}M)^P, (\mathscr{C}M)^P]$ of nonnegative matrices as near as possible according to some suitable function to a pair of the form $[\langle y \rangle (\mathscr{R}M) \langle s \rangle^t, \langle r \rangle^t (\mathscr{C}M) \langle x \rangle]$, subject to $(\mathscr{R}M)^P i = i$, $i(\mathscr{C}M)^P = i$ and to the constraint (12). But the economic interpretations of r, s seem too weak to make this search worthwhile. It seems preferable to regard the biproportional method simply as a convenient way of calculating a make matrix M^* conforming with observed gross outputs of commodities and industries and satisfying certain simple *a priori* restrictions, then to determine a projection as near as possible to the natural but interpretation-free extrapolation $\langle r \rangle^t M \langle s \rangle^t$ while conforming with whatever relevant information is available about the projection year. If this information consists of q^P it is the projection M^P given by (8), (9) that results.

We have now completed our investigation of the biproportional model of temporal change in input–output matrices—and make matrices. We have shown the workability of the associated estimation model by establishing the uniqueness, the existence under weak conditions, and the robustness of biproportional estimates. We have seen, too, that biproportional input–output estimates conform with the *a priori* economic requirements of 'stability' over time and insensitivity to estimation-year gross output and price variations. We have shown reasons for preferring these input–output estimates to 'least-squares', Friedlander, and two-stage biproportional estimates, among others. Finally, we have seen how one may make use of the information provided by the biproportional estimation model as a basis for extrapolation. The next chapter illustrates the versatility of the biproportional constrained matrix model by using it to solve the problem of programming a Markov chain structure described in section 6 of Chapter 3.

CHAPTER 10

A BIPROPORTIONAL METHOD OF MARKOV PROGRAMMING

1 INTRODUCTION

The theory of biproportional matrices developed in Chapters 4 to 6 related to matrices restricted to be nonnegative. This restriction was originally inspired by the input–output use to which the theory was to be put. But accounting matrices such as input–output matrices—and the international matrices and make matrices to which we saw the theory might also be applied—are by no means the only important class of nonnegative economic matrices. Of wide importance is the class of square matrices A appearing in dynamic processes of the type

$$x(t+1) = Ax(t). \tag{1}$$

The economic literature is full of examples of this type of process in which A is essentially nonnegative. In one such example A is indeed an input–output matrix and the $x(t)$ are successive 'rounds' of intermediate demands[33]. The 'rounds' may be taken in either a real or a computing sense. But other examples abound (see e.g. [33, 42]).

An important subclass of dynamic processes of the form (1) is that in which the elements of each column of A sum to one and columns become interpretable as probability vectors. If $x_j(t)$ denotes the probability that, at time t, a 'system' is in its jth possible 'state', $j = 1, ..., m$, then a_{ij} stands for the conditional probability that, if in state j at t, it will be in state i at $t+1$. The fact that, for each j, $\sum_{i=1}^{m} a_{ij} = 1$, i.e. that a^j is a probability vector, means that $\{1, ..., m\}$ represents an exhaustive and mutually exclusive classification of states for the system. Such a process is known as a Markov process. Correspondingly A is called a Markov matrix if

$$A \text{ is square,}$$

$$A \geqq 0,$$

$$iA = i.$$

The characteristic property of a Markov process is that the system's probability of being in state i at $t+1$ depends only upon its state at t, and does not depend upon its earlier history.

Well-known economic examples of Markov processes belong to the study of the generation of the size distribution of income[1, 14]. In these studies the states represented by the indices $1, ..., m$ are an exhaustive set of income intervals and the elements of A are the probabilities that an income-receiver will move from one income interval to another between t and $t+1$. The generation of the size-distribution of firms in an industry has been represented analogously (e.g. [11]).

To pass from the concept of a Markov probability process to talk of the frequency distribution of a population over a set of contemporaneous states, some care is necessary. The Markov process relates to a single system or individual, but we want to say something about what happens to a population of individuals. To get anywhere, it must be assumed that every individual is subject to the same laws of independent behaviour, i.e. to the numerically same Markov process. We may then regard the numbers in different states at $t+1$ as determined by a set of independent multinomial trials at t, one for each individual. In this case the transition probability a_{ij} is also the expected value of the *fraction* of those in j at t who will be in i at $t+1$. Moreover the probability for an individual of a multi-step transition from state j to state i gives the expected value of the corresponding fraction. As the numbers in the population are imagined to grow large, the fractions converge in probability to the corresponding probabilities. We shall have in mind such an interpretation in terms of probability limits when, in the discussion that follows, we talk of the proportions of a population that 'do' or 'will' find themselves in different states.

To illustrate the results of this chapter we take an example that has to do with the supply of various grades of labour. i runs over a set of indices representing an exhaustive and nonoverlapping set of these grades. It might consist of:

i	grade
1	unskilled manual
2	semi-skilled manual
3	skilled manual
4	clerical, administrative
5	technical
6	engineering
7	scientific
8	managerial

The matrix A represents the effect of some programme of post-educational training. For example, a_{53} gives the probability that, as a result of this training, a skilled manual worker at time t will become a technical worker by time $t+1$. The Markovian assumption that this probability is independent of the worker's history is unlikely to be exactly fulfilled. One who has risen from the semi-skilled to the skilled category in one period may be likelier to rise a further grade in the next period than a semi-skilled worker who has been one all his working life. But it has enough approximative appeal for the model to serve as illustration for the results that follow.

The training whose effectiveness is represented by A is to be thought of as the kind carried out through apprenticeship, day-relief schemes, workers' educational colleges, correspondence courses, 'universities of the air', and so on. A Markovian model is not readily applicable to the study of the effects of full-time school-and-college education, for a reason connected with the asymptotic properties of Markov processes. These properties, and this reason, will be discussed in the next two sections.

2   ASYMPTOTIC PROPERTIES OF MARKOV PROCESSES

A nonnegative square matrix A is called *indecomposable* if it cannot, by the same permutation of its rows and columns, be cast into the form

$$\begin{bmatrix} A_{11} & 0 \\ A_{21} & A_{22} \end{bmatrix},$$

where A_{11}, A_{22} are square partitions. A is called *acyclic* if it cannot be so permuted into the form

$$\begin{bmatrix} 0 & A_{12} \\ A_{21} & 0 \end{bmatrix},$$

where the null partitions are square. The following results are well known (see e.g. [22, 42]):

(i) If A is a Markov matrix and is indecomposable and acyclic then there is a uniquely proportioned characteristic vector w corresponding to the characteristic root 1, i.e. such that

$$Aw = w.$$

(ii) w may be taken to be strictly positive, i.e.

$$w > 0.$$

(iii) For any semipositive vector x

$$\lim_{t \to \infty} A^t x = kw$$

for some positive number k.

w is known as the dominant characteristic vector of A. We note the fact—which we shall employ later in this chapter—that if A is strictly positive it satisfies the condition of (i) and has a dominant characteristic vector w with the properties described.

The Markov processes we are studying obey (1), from which we obtain $x(t) = A^t x(0)$. Hence (iii) implies that, subject to the condition of (i), $x(t)$ asymptotically approaches the 'characteristic direction' defined in (i), (ii). That is, the proportions of the studied population in states $1, \ldots, m$ approach fixed positive proportions as $t \rightarrow \infty$. In the training model $x(0)$ may be interpreted as the grade distribution of a group of workers beginning their training; $x(t)$ represents the grade distribution of the same group of workers t years later. The above theorems tell us that under certain conditions on the adult education matrix A, the proportions in this grade distribution will approach fixed ones given by the dominant characteristic vector of A, whatever the value of the initial grade distribution $x(0)$.

The hierarchical character of the grade distribution in our example throws some doubt on the appropriateness of the condition in (i). If it were true that, say, no non-manual worker were ever trained into a manual worker then a_{ij} would vanish for $i < 4, j \geqq 4$. We would then have to consider the asymptotic behaviour of $x(t)$ for the case in which A is decomposable. However, it is very plausible that, for instance, non-manual workers do become manual workers by accident if not by educational design: entrepreneurs go out of business, technical workers are made redundant, and so on. In short, a nondecomposable A may reasonably be regarded as a representation of the partly random structure which currently generates labour supplies, if not of the intended effects of institutional adult education. From now on it is in this way that we shall interpret the matrix A—which we shall for brevity continue to refer to as a 'training matrix'.

The information on supplies of various grades of labour of a particular age-group which the outlined model provides is likely to be less useful for most planning purposes than corresponding information aggregated over age-groups. This must be counted a weakness of the model, considered as a planning tool. It seems from the discussion in the next section, however, that the attempt to handle age-aggregated grade-distributions introduces certain demographic questions which may rule out planning applications altogether.

3   A MARKOVIAN APPROACH TO FULL-TIME EDUCATION

We can now explain why a Markov-type model is ill-suited to describe the effects of regular school–college education. Although we know from (iii) that $x(t)$ approaches kw asymptotically for any initial semipositive vector $x(0)$, we can say little about $x(t)$ for any given t unless we know that this t is 'large enough'. Whether it is clearly depends on how near $x(0)$ is to being in the equilibrium proportions given by w. In the training model there is no strong reason to suppose the grade distribution of a particular group of workers at the start of their training will be very remote from the asymptotic one: school-and-college will already have trained the group into something like the long-run proportions. But in the case of school-and-college education itself, any natural categorization into achievement states is such that the state distribution of a group entering the system (five-year-olds say) is necessarily remote from the state distribution the group would reach if it were subjected to the same educational process for many years. For a very long extension of the programme would give at least that proportion of, say, highly-trained graduates that we would find in the group say 20 years after the start of their education. That a value of t of the order of 20 cannot be considered 'large' in the schooling process may also be seen by observing that in the last few years of these 20 sizeable shifts in the distribution are still going on. Now the actual school-and-college educational programme whose effects we would wish to describe persists for only 15–20 years: a Markov model can therefore yield little information on these effects.

In an unpublished paper Stone has proposed a dynamic model meeting this difficulty. In Stone's model pupils (students, trainees) are distinguished by age-group as well as by achievement state. The transition matrix playing the role of A shows the proportions of the numbers in each age-achievement cell that will be found in the next period in each such cell. It represents population factors (reproduction and death rates for various age-groups) as well as educational ones. In the educational model sketched above, in which we considered the progress of an identified group of persons, it was irrelevant to look at a span of time exceeding the length of a standard educational programme. But in Stone's model, which deals with the entire population of a country whose identity changes with births and deaths, it makes sense to ask what happens if the dynamic process persists over very long time intervals.

This model could not, however, be used to illustrate the results of this chapter. These results will show how one may change the asymptotic distribution of states, i.e. the dominant characteristic vector of the matrix A, by changing the structure represented in A. The elements of a training matrix may usefully be regarded as instruments of policy, for the accidental effects discussed in section 2 are likely to be both small, and easily recognized by their 'anti-hierarchical' positions in the matrix. But the elements of Stone's matrix depend jointly on the structure of training and on demographic parameters outside the domain of educational planning.

The model of Correa and Tinbergen of the educational system [19] differs from ours and Stone's in the first place by its specific and small dimensions, and, in the second place, by its emphasis of the way the educational system is embedded in the broader economy—to the neglect of detail within the structure of the education process. Only two educational grades are distinguished, and indeed only two variables are instruments of purely educational planning, viz. the teacher–pupil ratios at these two grades. The Markovian structure of pupils' movements between grades is ultra-simple: a student either passes to the next grade or to the labour market. The proportion that proceeds to the upper grade is not taken to be instrumental. But even if it were, the low dimensions of the model would make the problem of separating out the values of instrumental parameters much more tractable than it is in Stone's model. Bénard's linear programming model[8] is larger than Correa and Tinbergen's, but like it in abstracting from questions of altering the values of parameters that represent the inner workings of education.

4   Programming a Markov structure

The central problem of this chapter is: given a Markov matrix A, find a Markov matrix B in some sense as close as possible to A while having a prescribed dominant characteristic vector v. The closeness condition is imposed because in applications a cost is likely to be incurred in altering the structure represented in A to that represented in B and to be a typically increasing function of the distance from A to B. Thus the closeness condition may be read as a cost-minimizing one. Why we are willing to incur any cost at all has been explained already. The new structure B would, subject to certain conditions, yield the desired proportions of a prescribed vector asymptotically. In terms of the training model, we would be assured that, perhaps by some stage in the middle of their working lives, each generation of workers would be available for employment in specified skill-proportions. In particular, scientists and engineers would be in supply in large enough numbers relative to the numbers of workers of other grades belonging to their generation. The conditions on B are those laid down in (i) for results (i) to (iii) on the asymptotic behaviour of $x(t)$; a solution B to the structure-programming problem must be neither decomposable nor cyclic.

A straightforward way of tackling the problem is as a mathematical programme, that of minimizing $f(A, B)$ subject to $iB = i$, $Bv = v$, $B \geqq 0$, where f is a function expressing the cost of replacing A by B. We might take f to be $\sum_{i,j} c_{ij}|b_{ij} - a_{ij}|$, in which case the problem can be reduced to a linear programme in the way described in section 8 of Chapter 3; or f might be quadratic.

Another possible approach is by the constrained matrix methods of Chapters 3 to 6. In particular, we may exploit our knowledge of the solution procedure and other properties of the biproportional matrix model. The use of constrained matrix methods is suggested by the following result, which connects Markov matrices having prescribed characteristic vectors corresponding to the characteristic root 1 with matrices having given row and column sums.

THEOREM 14. Let v be a strictly positive vector. Then the matrix B is nonnegative and satisfies

$$iB = i, \tag{2}$$

$$Bv = v \tag{3}$$

if and only if $\qquad B\langle v \rangle = C$

for some nonnegative matrix C satisfying

$$iC = v, \tag{4}$$

$$Ci = v. \tag{5}$$

PROOF. (a) Necessity. $iC = iB\langle v \rangle = i\langle v \rangle$, using (2). $Ci = B\langle v \rangle i = Bv = v$, using (3). (b) Sufficiency. $iB = iC\langle v \rangle^{-1} = v\langle v \rangle^{-1} = i$, using (4). $Bv = C\langle v \rangle^{-1}v = Ci = v$, from (5). |

The restriction on v to be strictly positive is needed if (4), (5) are to be sufficient for (2), (3). For if some v_j were zero, the column c^j would vanish whatever the value of b^j, and *a fortiori* whatever its sum.

We are now in a position to exploit known results on the biproportional constrained matrix problem. From Corollaries 1 and 2 (the uniqueness and existence results), we immediately get the following.

THEOREM 15. There exists a unique nonnegative matrix B satisfying (3) and biproportional to a given nonnegative square matrix A if and only if

$$A_{I'J} = 0 \quad \text{implies} \quad \sum_I v_i \geqq \sum_J v_j, \tag{6}$$

where I', J are subsets of indices of rows and columns.

The first inequality of Corollary 2 being $\sum_{I'} v_i \leqq \sum_{J'} v_j$, it is automatically satisfied whenever the second is. The matrix B is of course given by

$$B = A^B(v, v) \langle v \rangle^{-1}.$$

In the training model application, what is the basis for requiring that the desired vector v be strictly positive? On the face of it, the restriction means that we want a positive proportion of unskilled workers in the labour force of the indefinite future: yet asymptotically we might expect automation to force this proportion towards zero. The answer is that we are not, in fact, programming for so remote a time. On the contrary, for our results to be useful the asymptotic state under the revised educational structure B ought to be approximated within a decade or two. In so short a span of time we would hardly expect the vanishing of the demand for unskilled manual workers or for any other of our eight categories of workers.

5 Dynamic properties of the programmed structure

We must next enquire whether the 'topological' characteristics required of A in (i) are preserved in B; specifically, whether decompositions or cyclicities can be present in one or not in the other. We shall then be able to say something about the asymptotic behaviour of the new structure, knowing that of the old.

First, it is clear that zero elements of A remain zero in B. Hence the transformation cannot cure 'pathological' traits in A. The best that could be hoped is that B is no worse than A. We know from Corollary 4 (p. 56) that this is the case whenever the conditions in (6) are satisfied as strict inequalities. The following example shows, however, that the hope is not always fulfilled. A matrix A of the form

$$
\begin{array}{c c}
& \begin{array}{c c c c c} 1 & 2 & 3 & 4 & 5 \end{array} \\
\begin{array}{c} 1 \\ 2 \\ 3 \\ 4 \\ 5 \end{array} &
\left[\begin{array}{c c c c c}
+ & + & + & + & + \\
+ & + & + & + & + \\
0 & + & 0 & + & 0 \\
0 & + & 0 & + & 0 \\
0 & + & 0 & + & +
\end{array}\right]
\end{array}
$$

is easily checked to be indecomposable (and acyclic). But if for instance

$$v = (10,\ 20,\ 20,\ 5,\ 12)$$

A^B must have the form

$$
\left[\begin{array}{c c c c c}
+ & 0 & + & 0 & 0 \\
+ & 0 & + & 0 & 0 \\
0 & + & 0 & + & 0 \\
0 & + & 0 & + & 0 \\
0 & 0 & 0 & 0 & +
\end{array}\right]
$$

which is decomposable according to {1, 2, 3, 4} and {5}. It is clear that such examples are unlikely to occur in practice, as they depend upon the fortuitous equality of sums of the v_j taken over different subsets of the indices j. They depend, too, as Corollary 4 shows, on the vanishing of certain partitions of A. If such a case did arise the process B would no longer have the crucial independence property expressed in (i) to (iii): the distribution towards which it leads would no longer be the same for all initial ones. *A fortiori*, the process could not be counted on to lead towards the desired vector v. One way out would be to amend this vector. But the change might have to be unacceptably great, for continuity considerations show that for small changes in v the corresponding B, though giving asymptotic convergence to v, might do so only slowly. Another way would be to disturb the matrix A by substituting positive values for elements of the null partitions $A_{I'J}$ which are not zero by their very nature.

Similar remarks apply in the case in which the structure of A and the value of v lead to a cyclicity in A^B not present in A.

So far we have been content to see whether B possesses the dynamic property described in section 2. That is, we have asked only whether $B^t x(0)$ converges to a certain vector: we have scarcely considered the speed with which this convergence takes place. Yet this question may be of crucial practical importance. If, in the training model, the time unit is a year and $B^t x(0)$ approximates the dominant eigenvector of B only after t is of the order of, say, 50, the optimum grade distribution is quite unattainable and we must recognize that the new régime B can do no more than improve the initial distribution. In a more general treatment of the training problem we would set out by looking for a B which not only did its job cheaply in the sense of departing little from A, but also did it quickly—did it, that is, within either a fixed or a minimal span of time. More generally still, we would attempt to minimize the sum of changeover costs and running costs. Here, however, we shall limit ourselves to a few minor observations.

It is not at all obvious that the attempt to limit jointly the costs of changing A into B and the cost of maintaining B over a period would lead to a régime which produced quick results but was expensive to set up. The outcome could as well look like the one contemplated in the last paragraph, with a new structure that is cheap to achieve but relatively slow to converge.

Given an initial distribution $x(0)$, the time $2t$ in which B generates a particular distribution $B^{2t} x(0)$ may be halved by adopting the structure B^2 in place of B; and this statement has an obvious generalization. At best, however, the substitution of B^2 for B would be a haphazard way of economizing time. What is more, B^2 might be unacceptably far from A. In particular, B^2 in general has positive values for elements that are zero in B and A: some of these elements may be necessarily zero in any plausible training matrix.

As $B^t x(0)$ approaches v the 'steps' between $B^t x(0)$ and $B^{t+1} x(0)$ become progressively smaller. On the other hand, the cost of running an educational programme whose matrix stays constant may be presumed to be constant too. In some sense the marginal net productivity of education is diminishing. There must be some cut-off point t beyond which continued education ceases to be profitable. In the numerical example presented in Chapter 11 it takes a working lifetime for a batch of workers to get near their asymptotic distribution. But intuitive inspection of the sequence of $B^t x(0)$'s suggests that their education would become socially unprofitable not later than the middle of their working lives. Thus Chapter 11's example suggests the useful conclusion that

A should be changed to *B* and *B* applied for, say, 20 years, rather than the useless one that *B* should be applied until the asymptotic distribution is approximated but the workers composing it are all dead.

Three features stand out in the kind of Markov programming problem we have been considering. First, it explicitly concerns itself only with what happens 'in the end'. Secondly, its unwavering aim at a single grade distribution of the labour force argues a latent utility function that is extremely convex round this chosen direction. Thirdly, it looks for a 'one-shot' decision. In the last two respects—but not in the first— Howard's 'dynamic programming' of Markov processes[40] is diametrically opposed: he considers periodically repeated choices among alternative Markov processes, and maximizes a 'return' which, in our terms, is linear in the numbers changing their states in various ways (j, i). The only kind of utility of the state distribution that can be fitted into this formulation is linear too, that is, the function is the *least* curved of convex functions. At first sight Howard's admission of repeated choices seems like an important improvement. But it turns out that at least for a linear return function, optimal long-run policy foregoes the extra opportunities that Howard offers it: this policy, he shows, consists of the repeated selection of a single matrix. Howard's problem does effectively generalize the present one in another way—the return function can take account not only of the benefit but also of the cost of a transition from state j to state i: that is, it is capable of expressing the expenses of running various possible régimes. It neglects, however, the costs of setting them up. Moreover, it prevents us from simultaneously making the benefit of being in state i independent of which state j the system has just left, while making the cost of getting there vary with j.

6   BIPROPORTIONAL AND 'ISODOMINANT' MARKOV MATRICES

This section is a short digression. In the next we shall look, finally, at the question of the 'distance' from the initial régime of the new régime determined by the biproportional model.

Let us call two Markov matrices 'isodominant' if they share a dominant characteristic vector. There is a simple relationship between biproportionality and isodominance among strictly positive matrices of a given size. Consider any strictly positive matrix *A* of order *m* and any strictly positive *m*-vector *v*. Then we know from Theorem 15 that there exists one and only one matrix *B* such that

$$B > 0, \quad iB = i, \quad Bv = v, \quad B = \langle r \rangle A \langle s \rangle,$$

for the strict positivity of *A* guarantees the fulfilment of condition (6), that the biproportionality of *A* and *B* is of the stated form, and so finally that *B* too is strictly positive.

In particular, let $v = i$. Then the above result implies that (i) for any positive matrix A there is one and only one *doubly stochastic* matrix biproportional to A (and it too is strictly positive); (ii) no two positive doubly stochastic matrices are biproportional. (B is called doubly stochastic if $B \geqq 0$, $iB = i$, $Bi = i$.)

Let a positive doubly stochastic matrix of order m be denoted by S. We have shown that any positive Markov matrix B is determined by specifying one and only one pair (S, v) and requiring that B be biproportional to S and have v as its dominant characteristic vector.

7   THE DISTANCE OF B FROM A

If condition (6) is satisfied, the biproportionality method enables us to find a Markov matrix B having a given characteristic vector corresponding to characteristic root 1. Except in freak cases this vector will possess the properties given in (i) to (iii). But we still need to check whether B is in some sense close to the given matrix A. We showed in Chapter 6, it will be recalled, that in the class of nonnegative matrices D satisfying the marginal constraints $Di = u$, $iD = v$, $A^B(u, v)$ minimizes the distance-like function $\tilde{\phi}(A, D) = \sum_{i, j} \tilde{\phi}(a_{ij}, d_{ij})$, where

$$
\tilde{\phi}(a_{ij}, d_{ij}) = \begin{cases} d_{ij} \log \dfrac{d_{ij}}{e a_{ij}} & \text{if } a_{ij} > 0,\ d_{ij} > 0, \\ \psi(a_{ij}, d_{ij}) & \text{otherwise,} \end{cases}
$$

and where ψ is defined as in (9) of Chapter 6 (p. 78). The acceptability of $\tilde{\phi}$ as a distance-like minimand was supported by the fact that ϕ approximates a positive linear transformation of χ^2 when d_{ij} is close to a_{ij}.

In the present context what we are interested in is not the distance between A and $A^B(v, v)$, upon which the above result can throw direct light, but the distance between A and $B = A^B(v, v) \langle v \rangle^{-1}$. However, it is easy to show by the same methods used in Chapter 6 that in the class of matrices B satisfying
$$
B \geqq 0, \quad Bv = v, \quad iB = i,
$$

$B = A^B(v, v) \langle v \rangle^{-1}$ minimizes $\sum_{i, j} \tilde{d}(a_{ij}, b_{ij})$ where

$$
\tilde{d}(a_{ij}, b_{ij}) = \begin{cases} d(a_{ij}, b_{ij}) = v_j b_{ij} \log \dfrac{b_{ij}}{e a_{ij}} & \text{if } a_{ij} > 0,\ b_{ij} > 0, \\ \psi(a_{ij}, b_{ij}) & \text{otherwise.} \end{cases}
$$

For consider the Lagrangian

$$
L = \sum_{S_1} d(a_{ij}, b_{ij}) + \sum_i \alpha_i (v_i - \sum_j v_j b_{ij}) + \sum_j \beta_j (1 - \sum_i b_{ij}),
$$

where $S_1 = \{(i,j)\,|\,a_{ij} > 0,\ b_{ij} > 0\} = \{(i,j)\,|\,a_{ij} > 0, a_{ij}^B > 0\}.$

We get
$$\frac{\partial L}{\partial b_{ij}} = v_j \log \frac{b_{ij}}{a_{ij}} - v_j \alpha_i - \beta_j,$$

which vanishes when
$$\log \frac{b_{ij}}{a_{ij}} = \alpha_i + \frac{\beta_j}{v_j}.$$

We know from Corollary 6 that there exist vectors $r, s > 0$ such that for all (i,j) in S_1, $a_{ij}^B = r_i a_{ij} s_j$. Setting $\alpha_i = \log r_i$, $\beta_j = v_j \log s_j / v_j$ we obtain

$$b_{ij} = r_i a_{ij} s_j \frac{1}{v_j} \quad \text{for } (i,j) \text{ in } S_1.$$

That $B = A^B(v, v) \langle v \rangle^{-1}$ simultaneously minimizes $\sum_{S_1'} \psi(a_{ij}, b_{ij})$ in the required class of matrices is easily shown arguments of the type used in Chapter 6.

The function $\sum_{S_1} d(a_{ij}, b_{ij})$ is $\phi(A, B) = \sum_{S_1} \phi(a_{ij}, b_{ij})$ reweighted in favour of columns corresponding to large elements in the desired state distribution. This may be a good weighting: if the proposed change from w to v is not great, the weighting ensures against large changes in those sectors of the existing structure which handle large parts of the population. If $\sum_{S_1} d(a_{ij}, b_{ij})$ is linear in the number 'processed' by the jth sector and χ^2 in the structural coefficients a_{ij}, it roughly minimizes the cost of structural changes.

In the next chapter we shall present a numerical example of the training model of sections 1 and 2 to illustrate the working of the biproportional method of programming a Markov structure.

CHAPTER 11

NUMERICAL RESULTS

1 INTRODUCTION

In this chapter we present numerical applications of the constrained matrix models whose theoretical properties have been the subject of Chapters 3 to 10. Sections 2 and 3 give results for constrained input–output estimation problems: 2 deals with the biproportional and 3 with the Friedlander estimate. Section 4 uses an illustrative model to compare the standard (one-stage) biproportional input–output estimation model with its two-stage variant of Chapter 8. Section 5 is devoted to input–output projection problems: both unconstrained—exponential and linear—projection, and projection subject to fixed column sums. Finally, section 6 gives illustrative results for the training model of Chapter 10.

The process (A, u, v) for solving a biproportional problem described in section 2 of Chapter 4 was programmed in 1961 by J. M. Bates, J. A. C. Brown and L. J. Slater of the Cambridge Growth Project for the University of Cambridge's computer EDSAC 2. The main features of EDSAC 2 are described in, for example, [24]. All the biproportional results presented in this chapter have been obtained from the Bates–Brown–Slater EDSAC programme. In all the applications of the model, the process (A, u, v) has reached a matrix that satisfies the marginal constraints according to a rather stringent criterion after at most a few hundred iterations. 100 iterations took about twenty minutes of EDSAC time for a 31-order matrix A. RAS calculations at Cambridge are now done on the more powerful Titan I—a version of the Ferranti Atlas—on which a floating-point multiplication takes about one micro-second to EDSAC's ten. A typical 31-order input–output solution takes fewer than 20 iterations and less than a minute.

Schneider's experience [62] was comparable and similar. He used the same algorithm, programmed by the Harvard Economic Research Project for an IBM 7094 under the name of the 'Distribute' programme. The stopping criterion is the convergence of each calculated flow rather than merely agreement of calculated and given marginals: each flow was determined, however, to only 3 significant digits. Schneider's 24-order problem took 1·1 minutes of computing time. Tilanus [70] carried out as RAS solution for a 35-order problem on a Bull Gamma ET (which takes 0·03 seconds for a floating-point multiplication). Agreement of calculated and given marginals to within 0·1 million guilders (the Netherlands flow tables are recorded in millions of guilders) took 20 iterations and

$2\frac{1}{2}$ hours. The length of this calculation is, for Tilanus, a strong reason for preferring to predict intermediate outputs by the corrective factors described in section 9 of Chapter 3 to doing so via an RAS update of the coefficient matrix. But even the former calculation took an hour of computing time on the small Bull machine; and the argument clearly loses all force when more powerful computing equipment is available.

Convergence is much faster in input–output than in make matrix applications. This phenomenon is no doubt due in part to the high degree of diagonality of make matrices. For a matrix A whose mass is in some sense evenly spread along its columns and rows, each s_j^1 is the reciprocal of a central value of the r_i's: this follows from the formula of section 4 of Chapter 4,

$$s_j^{t+1} = 1 \bigg/ \sum_{i=1}^{m} r_i^{t+1} \left(\frac{a_{ij}^{2t}}{v_j}\right),$$

applied for $t = 0$, and the analogous formula for r_i^{t+1}, applied for $t = 1$. The r_i^t's may, then, be expected to close down rapidly on a number as t increases. On the other hand, if A is nearly diagonal the weights are such that s_1^1, say, is the reciprocal of a number near to r_1^1 and r_1^2 is the reciprocal of a number near to s_1^1 and so is itself near to r_1^1. Supposing r_1^1 to be an extreme value of the r_i^1's shows that the r_i^t's may only slowly close down on a number.

The Friedlander solution presented in section 3 was EDSAC-computed. The problem was solved by the method based on matrix inversion described in Chapter 5. The solution was carried out step by step on an existing EDSAC programme for standard matrix operations. The advantage of solving the Friedlander by matrix inversion rather than by a method such as Friedlander's own—an iterative row- and column-adjustment method analogous to the biproportional process [32] —is that, by the link established in section 6 of Chapter 5, the same algorithm may be used to calculate the partials with respect to (u, v) of the (r, s) solving the biproportional problem (A, u, v).

2   INPUT–OUTPUT ESTIMATES: BIPROPORTIONAL ESTIMATION

Table 2 shows an estimate of an input–output matrix for Britain in 1960 obtained by a biproportional transformation of a corresponding table for 1954 subject to given intermediate output and input constraints for 1960. The 1954 matrix and the 1960 transaction marginals are the same as those published in [26]. [26] gives details of their sources and specifies the industrial classification exactly. The definition of an input–output table is that which was given in section 3 of Chapter 3 and which, except in Chapter 7, we have had in mind throughout the book. All the input–output tables given in this chapter are expressed in the prices of 1960.

The matrix shown in Table 2 was estimated by the modified biproportional model used by Paelinck and Waelbroeck and briefly described in section 4 of Chapter 3. We begin by partitioning the matrix $L(1)$ which is to be estimated into a part for which an outside estimate is available and the complementary part. Let us call the first of these parts the 'exogenous' part. The method is then to estimate the complementary, 'endogenous' part, by an appropriate application of the standard biproportional model. That is, we fit the 'endogenous' part of the observed matrix L to marginals which are the observed marginals for $t = 1$ minus their 'exogenous' parts. Let us write

$$L(1) = L_N(1) + L_X(1),$$

where $L_N(1)$ and $L_X(1)$ are, respectively, the endogenous and exogenous terms of $L(1)$, i.e. its endogenous and exogenous parts each filled out with zeros. Let $L_X(1)$ be exogenously estimated as est $L_X(1)$; then the exogenous component $L_X(1)\langle q\rangle$ of the transactions matrix at $t = 1$ is estimated as $[\text{est}\,L_X(1)]\langle q\rangle$. Let us denote by L_N the endogenous component of L. Then we estimate $L_N(1)$ as

$$L_N^* = L_N^B\{u - [\text{est}\,L_X(1)]\,q,\ v - i[\text{est}\,L_X(1)]\,\langle q\rangle\}\langle q\rangle^{-1},$$

and $L(1)$ as $L_N^* + \text{est}\,L_X(1)$. We shall call such an estimate of $L(1)$ a *quasi-biproportional* estimate.

The data L, u, v—viz. the 1954 input–output matrix and the 1960 transaction marginals—are exactly those published in [26]. L is displayed in Table 1. The estimation of Table 2 differs from that in [26] only in that we have added the single cell $(5, 5)$ (intra-Drink, tobacco) to the exogenous part. In the estimation in [26], where this cell was handled endogenously, r_5 came out at 0·06—a surprisingly low value relatively to the other r's. It was apparent from posterior analysis that this value had arisen mainly from error in element $(5, 5)$ of the 1954 transactions matrix, originating when the 5th row and column had had to be adjusted in going from the industrial classification used in the official 1954 input–output table [72] to that used in the Cambridge Growth Project. To this extent r_5 and s_5 were statistical corrective factors rather than measures of substitution and fabrication tendencies. Because element $(5, 5)$ was overwhelmingly dominant in its row r_5 had to perform a particularly large corrective function. The most proper course would now have been to re-estimate the 1954 transactions matrix. A roughly equivalent and much less laborious course was to regard the estimate of 1960's transaction $(5, 5)$ obtained in [26] as exogenous in a new calculation. The r_5 and s_5 obtained in the new calculation would then be restricted to the non-diagonal parts of row 5 and column 5, but would be relatively undistorted by the special type of statistical error we have just described.

Table 1. *Input–output coefficient matrix for Britain in 1954. Intermediate input ratios in 1954*

Industry	$j \ldots$ i	1	2	3	4	5	6	7	8	9	10	11	12	13	14	15	16
Agriculture, etc.	1	0·017	—	—	0·177	0·032	—	—	0·003	—	—	—	—	—	—	—	—
Coal	2	0·009	—	0·017	0·005	0·007	0·541	—	0·017	0·011	0·007	0·004	0·003	0·002	0·003	0·002	0·003
Mining n.e.s.	3	0·001	—	0·003	0·001	—	—	0·013	0·012	0·001	—	0·030	0·002	—	—	—	—
Food processing	4	0·182	—	—	0·078	0·020	—	—	0·009	—	—	—	—	—	—	—	—
Drink, tobacco	5	—	—	—	0·001	0·230	—	—	0·001	—	—	—	—	—	—	—	0·001
Coke ovens, etc.	6	—	—	0·005	—	—	0·087	0·019	0·025	0·063	—	—	0·001	0·001	—	—	0·006
Mineral oil refining	7	0·033	—	0·013	0·002	0·004	—	0·048	0·021	0·008	0·005	0·001	0·002	0·001	0·001	0·006	0·006
Chemicals n.e.s.	8	0·080	0·011	0·021	0·051	0·008	0·004	0·016	0·246	0·007	0·006	0·002	0·019	0·012	0·025	0·004	0·006
Iron, steel (primary)	9	—	—	0·001	—	—	—	—	0·003	0·313	0·375	—	0·083	0·096	0·131	0·034	0·129
Iron, steel (secondary)	10	—	—	—	—	—	—	—	0·015	—	0·102	—	0·006	0·008	0·005	0·001	0·008
Nonferrous metals	11	—	—	—	0·002	0·003	—	0·007	0·020	0·005	0·035	0·193	0·056	0·015	0·028	0·047	0·028
Engineering, electrical	12	0·025	0·037	0·042	0·012	0·015	—	—	—	0·019	0·011	0·010	0·160	0·082	0·069	0·057	0·031
Shipbuilding, etc.	13	0·005	—	—	0·001	—	—	—	—	—	—	—	—	0·255	—	—	—
Motors, cycles	14	0·008	—	0·004	—	—	—	—	—	—	—	—	—	—	0·212	0·005	—
Aircraft	15	—	—	—	—	—	—	—	—	—	—	—	—	—	—	0·281	—
Locomotives, etc.	16	—	—	—	—	—	—	—	—	—	—	—	—	—	—	—	0·046
Metal goods n.e.s.	17	0·026	0·007	0·003	0·015	0·015	—	0·004	0·023	0·013	0·002	0·001	0·048	0·050	0·119	0·029	0·031
Textiles	18	0·006	0·005	0·001	0·006	—	—	—	0·006	—	0·001	0·001	0·007	0·004	0·011	0·003	0·004
Leather, clothing	19	0·001	0·002	—	—	—	—	—	0·001	—	—	—	0·001	0·001	0·004	0·001	0·001
Building materials	20	0·003	0·003	—	—	—	—	0·003	0·003	0·009	—	0·002	0·004	—	0·005	0·001	0·001
Pottery, glass	21	—	—	—	0·006	0·106	0·001	—	0·009	—	—	—	0·008	0·017	0·005	—	0·001
Timber, furniture, etc.	22	0·002	0·014	0·004	0·004	0·013	—	—	0·005	0·001	0·004	0·001	0·010	0·001	0·014	0·002	0·008
Paper, publishing	23	0·002	0·001	0·012	0·028	0·025	—	—	0·023	—	0·001	—	0·010	0·001	0·002	0·010	—
Other manufacturing	24	0·008	0·014	0·002	0·003	—	—	0·003	0·003	0·003	—	—	0·007	0·001	0·047	0·002	0·005
Construction	25	0·033	0·030	0·005	0·003	0·005	—	—	0·004	0·012	0·005	0·001	0·004	0·004	0·003	0·003	0·002
Gas	26	0·007	—	—	0·004	—	0·059	0·005	0·002	0·010	0·005	0·005	0·004	0·001	0·004	0·002	0·002
Electricity	27	0·004	0·015	0·012	0·001	0·003	0·004	0·001	0·014	—	0·008	0·011	0·006	0·006	0·006	0·006	0·004
Water	28	0·001	—	—	—	0·001	—	—	0·001	—	—	—	—	—	—	0·001	—
Transport, communications	29	0·075	0·025	0·157	0·054	0·034	0·088	0·008	0·051	0·047	0·019	0·033	0·028	0·012	0·022	0·008	0·009
Distribution	30	0·037	0·014	0·033	0·023	0·018	0·039	0·002	0·018	0·037	0·009	0·039	0·012	0·007	0·014	0·005	0·004
Services n.e.s.	31	0·048	0·020	0·033	0·060	0·049	0·019	0·013	0·064	0·034	0·030	0·059	0·039	0·045	0·062	0·039	0·035
Intermediate input ratio		0·613	0·230	0·368	0·538	0·498	0·846	0·142	0·599	0·593	0·625	0·393	0·520	0·621	0·792	0·549	0·359

Table 1 (continued)

Industry	$j \cdots$	17	18	19	20	21	22	23	24	25	26	27	28	29	30	31
Agriculture, etc.	1	–	0·004	0·016	–	0·001	0·021	–	–	–	–	–	–	–	–	–
Coal	2	0·002	0·011	0·002	0·077	0·039	0·002	0·014	0·008	–	0·330	0·292	0·014	0·038	0·006	0·005
Mining n.e.s.	3	0·001	–	–	0·053	0·039	–	0·002	0·002	0·010	–	–	–	0·001	–	–
Food processing	4	–	0·001	–	–	–	–	0·001	–	–	–	–	–	0·003	–	–
Drink, tobacco	5	–	–	–	–	–	0·001	–	–	–	–	–	–	0·002	–	–
Coke ovens, etc.	6	0·001	–	–	0·004	0·001	–	–	0·004	0·001	–	0·001	0·001	0·007	0·003	0·003
Mineral oil refining	7	0·003	0·001	0·001	0·004	0·012	0·002	0·001	0·002	0·007	0·019	0·004	0·010	0·025	0·008	–
Chemicals n.e.s.	8	0·007	0·025	0·005	0·023	0·048	0·014	0·030	0·097	0·026	0·012	0·006	0·023	0·005	0·005	0·002
Iron, steel (primary)	9	0·131	–	–	0·008	–	0·001	–	0·004	0·033	0·016	0·003	0·043	0·006	–	–
Iron, steel (secondary)	10	0·043	–	–	–	–	–	–	0·003	0·011	0·015	0·003	0·006	–	–	–
Nonferrous metals	11	0·089	0·001	–	0·001	0·001	–	0·001	0·001	0·018	0·001	0·001	0·004	–	0·003	–
Engineering, electrical	12	0·014	0·020	0·009	0·030	0·039	0·011	0·019	0·021	0·028	0·034	0·064	0·007	0·008	0·003	0·015
Shipbuilding, etc.	13	–	–	–	–	–	–	–	–	–	0·001	–	–	0·036	–	–
Motors, cycles	14	0·001	–	–	0·002	0·002	0·002	–	0·003	0·002	–	–	–	0·016	0·012	0·006
Aircraft	15	–	–	–	–	–	–	–	–	–	–	–	–	0·004	–	–
Locomotives, etc.	16	–	–	–	–	–	–	–	–	–	–	–	–	0·042	–	–
Metal goods n.e.s.	17	0·131	0·003	0·021	0·009	0·013	0·031	0·003	0·013	0·019	0·007	0·004	0·001	–	0·002	0·004
Textiles	18	0·002	0·379	0·280	0·005	–	0·054	0·008	0·110	0·001	0·001	–	–	0·004	0·015	0·001
Leather, clothing	19	–	0·004	0·160	0·001	0·001	0·005	0·002	0·002	0·001	–	0·001	–	0·002	0·001	0·001
Building materials	20	0·001	–	–	0·069	0·011	–	–	0·003	0·100	0·008	0·008	0·004	–	0·001	0·001
Pottery, glass	21	0·004	–	–	–	0·063	0·006	0·002	–	0·011	–	0·008	–	–	–	–
Timber, furniture, etc.	22	0·010	–	0·006	0·005	0·012	0·148	–	0·013	0·019	–	0·003	–	–	0·004	0·001
Paper, publishing	23	0·005	0·003	0·009	0·048	0·013	0·001	0·246	0·027	0·006	0·003	0·002	0·002	0·002	0·013	0·078
Other manufacturing	24	0·010	0·001	0·021	0·002	0·001	0·012	0·002	0·066	0·002	–	0·003	–	0·009	0·007	0·002
Construction	25	0·002	0·005	0·004	0·001	0·005	0·001	0·004	0·005	0·114	0·002	0·002	0·004	0·041	0·002	0·002
Gas	26	0·007	0·001	0·001	0·002	0·022	0·001	0·001	0·002	–	0·022	–	0·001	0·001	0·016	0·008
Electricity	27	0·007	0·006	0·003	0·021	0·019	0·006	0·005	0·011	0·001	0·004	0·011	0·029	0·004	0·014	0·008
Water	28	–	0·001	–	0·004	0·001	–	–	0·001	–	0·002	0·004	0·033	–	0·004	0·002
Transport, communications	29	0·033	0·027	0·030	0·060	0·044	0·040	0·040	0·030	0·027	0·070	0·072	0·016	0·031	0·005	0·003
Distribution	30	0·014	0·028	0·018	0·030	0·022	0·032	0·024	0·018	0·011	0·024	0·024	0·002	0·004	0·001	0·001
Services n.e.s.	31	0·051	0·036	0·064	0·092	0·065	0·055	0·066	0·044	0·034	0·026	0·044	0·021	0·009	0·004	0·011
Intermediate input ratio		0·569	0·557	0·650	0·551	0·473	0·445	0·476	0·490	0·482	0·597	0·560	0·221	0·300	0·125	0·154

A dash represents an element less than 0·0005.   Intermediate input ratios may differ from column sums because of rounding errors.

Source: [26].

Table 2. Quasi-biproportional estimate est $L_X(1) + \langle r \rangle\, L_N \langle s \rangle$ of input–output matrix for Britain in 1960.
r, s. Intermediate input ratios

i	Industry	r_i	$j\dots$ 1	2	3	4	5	6	7	8	9	10	11
			$s_j\dots$ 0·544	0·813	0·854	0·925	1·039	1·043	1·510	0·722	0·787	0·754	0·805
1	Agriculture, etc.	0·498	0·005	—	—	0·082	0·017	—	—	0·001	—	—	—
2	Coal	0·359	0·002	—	0·005	0·002	0·003	[0·524]	—	0·004	[0·005]	[0·003]	0·001
3	Mining n.e.s.	1·203	0·001	—	0·003	0·001	—	—	0·024	0·010	0·001	—	0·029
4	Food processing	1·848	0·183	—	—	0·133	0·038	—	—	0·012	—	—	—
5	Drink, tobacco	0·111	—	—	—	—	[0·018]	—	—	—	—	—	—
6	Coke ovens, etc.	0·822	0·019	—	0·004	—	—	0·075	0·024	0·105	0·041	—	0·001
7	Mineral oil refining	1·032	0·069	0·014	0·011	0·002	0·004	—	0·075	0·016	[0·013]	[0·006]	0·002
8	Chemicals n.e.s.	1·586	—	0·036	0·028	0·075	0·013	0·007	0·038	0·282	0·009	0·007	0·002
9	Iron, steel (primary)	1·384	—	—	0·001	—	—	—	—	—	0·341	0·391	—
10	Iron, steel (secondary)	1·596	—	—	—	—	—	—	—	0·003	0·123	0·123	0·224
11	Nonferrous metals	1·442	—	—	—	0·001	0·004	—	—	0·016	0·038	0·038	0·011
12	Engineering, electrical	1·425	0·019	0·043	0·051	0·016	0·022	0·006	0·015	0·021	0·021	0·012	—
13	Shipbuilding, etc.	0·747	0·002	—	—	0·001	—	—	—	—	—	—	—
14	Motors, cycles	1·170	0·005	—	0·004	0·001	—	—	—	—	—	—	—
15	Aircraft	5·244	—	—	—	—	—	—	—	—	—	—	—
16	Locomotives, etc.	0·851	—	—	—	—	—	—	—	—	—	—	—
17	Metal goods n.e.s.	1·696	0·024	0·010	0·004	0·024	0·026	—	0·010	0·028	0·017	0·003	0·001
18	Textiles	1·821	0·006	0·007	0·002	0·010	—	—	—	0·008	—	0·001	0·001
19	Leather, clothing	0·564	—	0·001	—	—	—	—	—	—	—	—	—
20	Building materials	1·192	0·002	0·003	—	0·006	0·019	—	0·005	0·003	0·008	—	0·002
21	Pottery, glass	1·127	—	—	—	0·006	0·024	0·001	—	0·007	—	—	—
22	Timber, furniture, etc.	1·797	0·002	0·020	0·006	0·007	0·035	—	—	0·006	0·001	0·005	0·001
23	Paper, publishing	1·360	0·001	0·001	0·014	0·035	—	—	—	0·023	—	0·001	—
24	Other manufacturing	1·932	0·008	0·022	0·003	0·004	—	—	—	0·004	—	—	—
25	Construction	1·413	0·025	0·034	—	—	—	—	0·006	0·004	0·003	0·005	0·001
26	Gas	1·132	0·004	—	0·006	0·003	0·007	0·070	—	0·002	0·011	0·004	0·005
27	Electricity	1·779	0·004	0·022	0·018	0·007	0·006	0·007	0·013	0·018	0·014	0·011	0·016
28	Water	0·326	—	—	—	—	—	—	—	—	—	—	—
29	Transport, communications	1·475	0·060	0·030	0·198	0·074	0·052	0·135	0·018	0·054	0·055	0·021	0·039
30	Distribution	1·249	0·025	0·014	0·035	0·027	0·023	0·051	0·004	0·016	0·036	0·008	0·039
31	Services n.e.s.	1·978	0·052	0·032	0·056	0·110	0·101	0·039	0·039	0·091	0·053	0·045	0·094
	Intermediate input ratio		0·519	0·290	0·450	0·621	0·415	0·915	0·272	0·645	0·636	0·685	0·468

Table 2 (continued)

i	Industry	r_i	$j\dots$ 12	13	14	15	16	17	18	19	20	21
		$s_j\dots$	0·680	0·653	0·614	0·242	1·161	0·719	0·631	0·679	0·673	0·656
1	Agriculture, etc.	0·498	–	–	–	–	–	–	0·001	0·005	–	–
2	Coal	0·359	0·001	–	0·001	–	0·001	0·001	0·002	–	[0·047]	[0·017]
3	Mining n.e.s.	1·203	0·002	–	–	–	–	0·001	–	–	0·043	0·031
4	Food processing	1·848	–	–	–	–	–	–	0·001	–	–	–
5	Drink, tobacco	0·111	–	–	–	–	–	–	–	–	–	–
6	Coke ovens, etc.	0·822	0·001	0·001	–	0·001	–	–	–	–	0·002	0·001
7	Mineral oil refining	1·032	0·001	0·001	0·001	0·002	0·001	0·002	0·001	0·001	[0·021]	[0·031]
8	Chemicals n.e.s.	1·586	0·020	0·012	0·024	0·011	0·011	0·008	0·025	0·005	0·025	0·050
9	Iron, steel (primary)	1·384	0·078	0·087	0·111	–	0·207	0·130	–	–	0·007	–
10	Iron, steel (secondary)	1·596	0·007	0·008	0·005	0·016	0·015	0·490	–	–	–	–
11	Nonferrous metals	1·442	0·055	0·014	0·025	0·020	0·047	0·092	0·001	0·009	0·001	–
12	Engineering, electrical	1·425	0·155	0·067	0·060	0·020	0·051	0·014	0·018	–	0·029	0·036
13	Shipbuilding, etc.	0·747	–	0·124	–	–	–	–	–	–	–	–
14	Motors, cycles	1·170	–	–	0·152	0·001	–	–	–	–	–	–
15	Aircraft	5·244	–	–	–	0·357	–	0·001	–	–	0·002	0·002
16	Locomotives, etc.	0·851	–	–	–	–	0·045	–	–	–	–	–
17	Metal goods n.e.s.	1·696	0·055	0·055	0·124	0·012	0·061	0·160	0·003	0·024	0·010	0·014
18	Textiles	1·821	0·009	0·005	0·012	0·001	0·008	0·003	0·435	0·346	0·006	–
19	Leather, clothing	0·564	–	–	0·001	–	0·001	–	0·001	0·061	–	–
20	Building materials	1·192	0·003	–	0·004	–	0·001	0·001	–	–	0·055	0·009
21	Pottery, glass	1·127	0·006	–	0·003	–	0·001	0·003	–	–	–	0·047
22	Timber, furniture, etc.	1·797	0·012	0·020	0·015	0·001	0·017	0·013	0·003	0·007	0·060	0·014
23	Paper, publishing	1·360	0·009	0·001	0·002	0·003	–	0·005	0·001	0·008	0·044	0·012
24	Other manufacturing	1·932	0·009	0·001	0·056	0·001	0·011	0·014	0·004	0·028	0·003	0·001
25	Construction	1·413	0·004	0·004	0·003	0·001	0·003	0·002	0·001	0·004	0·001	0·005
26	Gas	1·132	0·003	0·001	0·003	0·001	0·003	0·006	0·001	0·001	0·002	0·016
27	Electricity	1·779	0·007	0·007	0·007	0·003	0·008	0·009	0·007	0·004	0·025	0·022
28	Water	0·365	–	–	–	–	–	–	–	–	0·001	–
29	Transport, communications	1·279	0·028	0·012	0·020	0·003	0·015	0·035	0·025	0·030	0·060	0·043
30	Distribution	1·448	0·010	0·006	0·011	0·002	0·006	0·013	0·022	0·015	0·025	0·018
31	Services n.e.s.	1·297	0·052	0·058	0·075	0·019	0·080	0·073	0·045	0·086	0·122	0·084
	Intermediate input ratio		0·529	0·493	0·714	0·455	0·596	0·634	0·597	0·635	0·537	0·453

A dash represents an element less than 0·0005. Square brackets indicate an exogenous element. Intermediate input ratios may differ from column sums because of rounding errors. *Source:* (intermediate input ratios), [26].

Table 2 (continued)

i	Industry	r_i	$j \ldots$ 22	23	24	25	26	27	28	29	30	31
		$s_j \ldots$	0·607	0·734	0·691	0·838	0·755	0·440	0·756	0·836	0·984	1·142
1	Agriculture, etc.	0·498	0·006	–	–	–	–	–	–	–	–	–
2	Coal	0·359	–	[0·010]	0·002	–	[0·286]	[0·241]	0·004	0·011	0·002	0·002
3	Mining n.e.s.	1·203	–	0·002	0·002	0·010	–	–	–	0·001	–	–
4	Food processing	1·848	–	0·001	–	–	–	–	–	0·005	–	–
5	Drink, tobacco	0·111	–	–	–	–	–	–	–	–	–	–
6	Coke ovens, etc.	0·822	–	–	0·002	0·001	–	–	0·001	0·005	0·002	0·003
7	Mineral oil refining	1·032	0·001	[0·005]	0·001	0·006	[0·026]	0·004	0·008	0·022	0·008	–
8	Chemicals n.e.s.	1·586	0·013	0·035	0·106	0·035	0·014	0·002	0·028	0·007	0·008	0·004
9	Iron, steel (primary)	1·384	0·001	–	0·004	0·038	0·017	0·002	0·045	0·007	0·008	–
10	Iron, steel (secondary)	1·596	–	0·001	0·003	0·015	0·018	0·001	0·007	–	–	–
11	Nonferrous metals	1·442	–	0·005	0·001	0·022	0·001	0·001	0·004	–	–	–
12	Engineering, electrical	1·425	0·010	0·020	0·021	0·033	0·037	0·040	0·008	0·010	0·004	0·024
13	Shipbuilding, etc.	0·747	–	–	–	–	0·001	–	–	0·022	–	–
14	Motors, cycles	1·170	0·001	–	0·002	0·002	–	–	–	0·016	0·014	0·008
15	Aircraft	5·244	–	–	–	–	–	–	–	0·018	–	–
16	Locomotives, etc.	0·851	–	–	–	–	–	–	–	0·030	–	–
17	Metal goods n.e.s.	1·695	0·032	0·004	0·015	0·027	0·009	0·003	0·001	–	0·003	0·008
18	Textiles	1·821	0·060	0·011	0·138	0·002	0·001	–	–	0·006	0·027	0·002
19	Leather, clothing	0·564	0·002	0·001	0·001	–	–	–	–	0·001	–	0·001
20	Building materials	1·192	0·004	–	0·002	0·100	0·007	0·004	0·004	–	0·001	0·001
21	Pottery, glass	1·127	–	0·002	–	0·010	–	0·004	–	–	–	–
22	Timber, furniture, etc.	1·797	0·162	–	0·016	0·029	0·003	–	–	0·002	–	–
23	Paper, publishing	1·360	0·001	0·246	0·025	0·007	–	0·001	–	0·015	0·013	0·003
24	Other manufacturing	1·932	0·014	0·003	0·088	0·003	0·002	0·014	0·004	0·048	0·016	0·003
25	Construction	1·413	0·001	0·004	0·005	0·135	0·019	–	0·002	0·003	0·012	0·003
26	Gas	1·132	0·006	0·001	0·002	0·001	0·005	0·009	0·001	0·018	0·007	0·010
27	Electricity	1·779	–	0·007	0·014	–	–	0·001	0·039	0·025	0·017	0·016
28	Water	0·326	–	–	–	–	–	–	0·008	0·006	0·013	0·001
29	Transport, communications	1·475	0·036	0·043	0·031	0·033	0·078	0·047	0·018	0·038	0·007	0·005
30	Distribution	1·249	0·024	0·022	0·016	0·012	0·023	0·013	0·002	0·004	0·017	0·001
31	Services n.e.s.	1·978	0·066	0·096	0·060	0·056	0·039	0·038	0·031	0·015	0·008	0·025
	Intermediate input ratio		0·441	0·517	0·558	0·577	0·586	0·477	0·214	0·289	0·170	0·242

A dash represents an element less than 0·0005. Square brackets indicate an exogenous element. Intermediate input ratios may differ from column sums because of rounding errors. *Source:* (intermediate input ratios), [**26**].

The time series composed of the input–output matrices shown in Tables 1 and 2 shows the 'structural' stability which Chapter 6's discussion of distance properties leads us to expect. Table 2 exemplifies, too, the basic nonnegativity and zero-preservation properties of biproportional estimates. Perhaps the most surprising feature of Table 2 is the range of r's and s's.

In spite of our exogenous treatment of intra-5 transactions, r_5 remains very low. This is partly because the classification adjustment made in obtaining Table 1 resulted in some positive error in off-diagonal elements of row and column 5 as well as the large positive error in element $(5, 5)$ we have mentioned—and in the calculation of Table 2 these off-diagonal elements have been treated endogenously.

The multipliers relating to Aircraft, r_{15} and s_{15}, are rather high and rather low respectively. This is because of a low (and erroneous?) estimate of v_{15} together with one of u_{15} roughly equal to its 'constant-coefficients' value. The low value for v_{15} tends to give a low value for s_{15}. Because transaction $(15, 15)$ dominates its row, the steadiness of u_{15} then implies an r_{15} roughly reciprocal to s_{15}.

The dominance of $(5, 5)$, $(15, 15)$ and other diagonal elements of the 1954 transactions matrix of their respective rows or columns suggests a danger in writing diagonal transactions into the table at all. The basic biproportional assumption of the uniformity of 'substitution' and 'fabrication' effects along rows and columns may be especially inappropriate for the diagonal elements of observed matrices [53]. In particular, changes may occur in the observed values of these elements because of changes in the pattern of industrial ownership: if transactions statistics are collected on a between-firm basis, then mergers may reduce the recorded levels of diagonal transactions without affecting off-diagonal ones. The extent to which all this matters clearly depends on the relative sizes of diagonal and off-diagonal elements. If, as we have seen, diagonal transactions may be large in their rows or columns, such institutional factors may seriously distort the r's and s's we obtain and may lead to much worse estimates of the non-diagonal part of the matrix than we would obtain by working net of intra-industrial transactions. We may not, of course, have a choice: usually, and in the case of British data for 1960, official statistics do not provide the necessary information, namely figures for an industry's sales restricted to buyers outside the industry. There remains, however, the possibility of regarding all diagonal elements as 'exogenous' and seeking estimates of them by separate analyses.

An interesting and somewhat encouraging feature is the smaller dispersion of the s's than of the r's. The coefficients of variation are respectively 0·294 and 0·635. This fact lends some support to Stone's interpretation of the r's and s's as substitution and fabrication effects. For one would expect tendencies towards changes in the degree of fabrication to be associated with changes in the capital stock and hence to be typically smaller than substitution effects in a fairly short period such as 1954 to 1960: they would then also be likely to show a smaller dispersion over industries. Another implication of the difference in dispersions is that the r's do most of the 'work' in changing L into L^*: i.e. an appropriate normalization would show $\langle r \rangle L$ to be directionally nearer than $L\langle s \rangle$ to L^*. This provides some support for the projection L^P proposed in Chapter 9 which was arrived at by, in essence, extrapolating the effects measured by the r's and disregarding those measured by the s's.

The quasi-biproportional estimate of $L(1960)$ (Table 2) is not presented as a definitive or even a usable estimate. Even if it could be taken as a reliable value for $L(1960)$, Table 2 as it stands would, indeed, have no use whatsoever: the discussion of Tilanus's corrective factors in section 9 of Chapter 3 has shown that in the prediction of intermediate outputs—the point of input–output—the *extrapolation* of crude measures improves on the *updating* of coefficient matrices, even when the updating is exact. But in any case Table 2 is not claimed to be a reliable update. Indeed it has been substantially revised by the Cambridge Growth Project since the publication of [26] in 1963; a new version will be published in a future volume of the series *A Programme for Growth* in which [24, 25, 26] appeared. It is shown here as one of a number of theoretically interesting alternatives: Table 6 shows another—an update based on Friedlander's method.

That Table 2 should not be regarded as a trustworthy estimate of 1960's input–output coefficients is emphasized by published and unpublished scepticism from several quarters. The authors of [26] emphasize the critical dependence of the table on estimates of the marginals that are themselves suspect. Final demand estimates—the basis for the residual estimation of u—are especially subject to error for several reasons [48]: the need to transform a vector cast in terms of a 'functional' classification to one in terms of industrially defined commodities; the use of figures for distribution margins on consumer expenditures based on 1951 and 1957 data; the fragmentary character of data on government expenditures; and the need to guess figures for the export of goods that did not cross the British frontier.

Beckerman [6] casts doubts on Table 2 from another direction: he compares the gross output vector which it implies—given 1960's final demands—with that implied by 1954 coefficients. Some oddities appear, including upward changes of surprising size in the outputs of Textiles (24·0%), Paper and Publishing (31·4%), and Aircraft (25·3%). Because final demands have been held constant in the comparison, these changes may only be attributed to ascribed changes in technical coefficients: if the output changes are not plausible neither, then, are the coefficient changes. But the conclusion is not peculiarly damaging to the biproportional model. Any estimates of 1960's coefficients which—given 1960's final demands—imply the same values of 1960's gross outputs as do the biproportional estimates, would be just as implausible. Beckerman's test questions the vector of gross outputs which Table 2 makes follow from 1960 final demands: effectively, then, it questions the 'row control totals' in the RAS—or any other—constrained matrix estimate of 1960 coefficients.

Beckerman's test confirms the Cambridge Growth Project's own judgement that the marginals used in calculating Table 2 are subject to significant error. The practical evolution since 1963 of Growth Project estimates of 1960's interindustry structure springs from this judgment. Lecomber[48] has proposed a way of revising initial estimates of the marginals by applying a biproportional model to the 'four quadrant' matrix consisting of the input–output matrix bordered by a column and a row of final demands and primary inputs: i, j thus run over sets of indices extended by one. Lecomber's biproportional model is a still more flexible one than the 'quasi-biproportional' model. As in that model, we have $L(1) = L_N(1) + L_X(1)$. But it is now allowed that both $l_{ijN}(1)$ and $l_{ijX}(1)$ be positive. The second new element of flexibility comes from letting $l_{ijN}(1)$ be

$$l_{ijN}(1) = r_i(g_{ij}l_{ij})s_j,$$

in which 'gearing ratio' g_{ij} is an adjustive factor applied to l_{ij} before the latter is put through the biproportional transformation. This flexible RAS model was used in estimating the input–output matrix for 1960 that played a part in determining the British National Plan[28].

Lecomber's model can take advantage of several kinds of information other than reliable independent estimates of coefficients of the sort that the quasi-biproportional model is designed to handle. For example, suppose we know the paints component of the unit input of chemicals (commodity i) into some industry j. We might write this component $l_{ijX}(1)$, make appropriate subtractions from l_{ij} and u_i, and run an ordinary RAS. But then the non-paint component of $l_{ij}(1)$ would be determined in part by a row multiplier which, elsewhere in the ith row, described the tendency to substitute-in both non-paint chemicals and paint. This bias may be corrected in the Lecomber model by using a gearing ratio g_{ij} not equal to one. The appropriate value of g_{ij} depends on, *inter alia*, the values that independent row multipliers for paint, non-paint would take in a disaggregated RAS calculation. These values can only be guessed. In this and other applications Lecomber's model lacks a formal mechanism for transforming hard data through exact hypotheses into the figures that are needed. But it may well be that the experienced input–output analyst can make a better guess than the one that is, let it be noted, implicit in the 'ungeared' biproportional solution.

When the geared quasi-biproportional model is used to revise initial estimates of u and v the interpretation of the $l_{ijX}(1)$'s and the g_{ij}'s is rather different. Suppose that the ith input coefficient of final demand, $l_{i, n+1}(1)$ is *initially* estimated as $l^*_{i, n+1}(1)$, but is in doubt. Let r^*_i, s^*_{n+1} be initial estimates of r_i, s_{n+1} corresponding to $l^*_{i, n+1}(1)$. (We leave aside the problem of how to interpret s_{n+1}.) The surer we are of $l^*_{1, n+1}(1)$ the more exogenous would we like to make its determination: in the extreme we would set $l_{i, n+1, X}(1) = l^*_{i, n+1}(1)$. In general we set $l_{i, n+1, X}(1)$ at some fraction of $l^*_{i, n+1}(1)$. We then choose g_{ij} so that $l_{i, n+1}$ is altered just enough for the initial estimates $l^*_{i, n+1}(1)$, r^*_i, s^*_j to be consistent, i.e. just enough so that

$$l^*_{i, n+1}(1) = r^*_i g_{i, n+1} l_{i, n+1} s^*_j + l_{i, n+1, X}(1).$$

By the application of this technique to all sure and unsure exogenous estimates in the enlarged tableau, we produce a final estimate in which what were the 'marginal' elements (and are now the $(m+1)$st row and $(n+1)$st column) have been determined by the initial estimate to the extent that we are sure of it and, to the extent that we are doubtful of it, by extending the application of the biproportional hypothesis to primary input and final demand coefficients.

There is no overriding prior objection to extending the biproportional hypothesis in this way. Tilanus's classical time series analysis of Netherlands input coefficients (described in section 3 of Chapter 2) discerned no great differences between the temporal behaviour of secondary and primary input coefficients. On the other hand one would expect non-uniformity of row effects due to the aggregation of inputs to be especially pronounced for a breakdown of users into intermediate and final. Again, the effects measured by the s_j's are now less independent of the r-effects and are no longer interpretable as relative tendencies to fabricate. It would certainly be preferable not to extend the domain of the hypothesis. The extent to which informalism is carried in this application of the geared model is also worrying. Without a clear rule about how to relate subjective uncertainty measures to exogeneity factors $l_{ijX}(1)/l^*_{ij}(1)$, how will intuition fare in the solution of a large problem? By contrast, the approach of Chapter 5 (which we next illustrate) makes no demands on a delicate 'feeling for numbers' which not all possess, beyond a statement of the subjective prior variances of observation errors in the national accounting data. Neither does this approach place an extra burden on assumptions of proportionality.

Table 4 gives the covariance matrix of proportional deviations from the r's and s's of the biproportional estimation problem whose solution is shown in Table 2. The stochastic model expressing this covariance matrix in terms of that of errors of observation on net final demands (i.e. final demands less competitive imports), net outputs and gross outputs at $t = 1$ (1960) was described in section 7 of Chapter 5. It will be recalled that the expression for the covariance matrix of the (r, s) is valid only for small enough values of that of the (u, v). In the present application this condition may not be strictly fulfilled.

The r, s given in Table 2 are those that arose (indirectly) from the sample observations of net final demands, net outputs and gross outputs that 'happened'. The sample observations of net final demands and net outputs—whose totals do not have to 'balance'—are not in general the same, however, as the balancing estimates of them which imply the marginals directly entering the calculation of r, s and Table 2. For completeness we record in Table 3 these balancing estimates of net final demands and net outputs, observed gross outputs (which are also the maximum likelihood estimates of gross outputs), and the standard deviations of observation errors in all these variables. The figures for standard deviations of observation errors are entirely subjective estimates based on experience with the statistical sources.

Table 5 records variances of proportional deviations from the non-zero-valued, endogenous coefficients of the quasi-biproportional estimate of Table 2.

It was pointed out in Chapter 5 that the Cambridge Growth Project's ultimate estimates of net final demands, net outputs and gross outputs are subject not only to the errors in the raw figures collected by official statisticians that are dealt with in the model of Chapter 5, but also to errors arising subsequently in going from the C.S.O.'s to the Growth Project's industrial classification. Rather than attempt to form subjective estimates of the standard deviations of the two types of error considered separately, we have tried to estimate those of fictitious 'raw' figures that already fall into the Cambridge classification: the subjective standard deviations shown in Table 3 try to take account of both types of error. Some distortion of the actual stochastic process that generated the Growth Project u, v is involved in this procedure, as it ignores the fact that the C.S.O. figures were 'balanced' before being transformed into the Cambridge classification as well as after. But the distortion seems negligible, especially as the classification changes seriously affected only a few elements. In any case, we do not claim for Tables 3, 4 and 5 that they do more than indicate sensible orders of magnitude.

Table 4 shows only the diagonal and above-diagonal elements of the symmetric variance–covariance matrix it records.

The diagonal estimates of Table 4 show that we may place only limited confidence in our estimates (Table 2) of the multipliers r, s transforming 1954's input–output coefficients into 1960's. For the values given in Table 3 for standard deviations of observation errors in the elements of f, y, q, all but three multipliers (the r for Drink and Tobacco, the r for Leather and Clothing and the s for Distribution) have proportional variances of less than 0·16: this implies 68 % confidence limits of less

Table 3. *Maximum likelihood estimates and standard deviations of observation errors for net final demands, net outputs and gross outputs for Britain in* 1960 (£m.)

Industry	i	Net final demand		Net output		Gross output	
		M.L.E.	s.d. of obs. error	M.L.E.	s.d. of obs. error	Obs. value	s.d. of obs. error
Agriculture, etc	1	1330	62·80	747	14·00	1553	9·30
Coal	2	259	3·35	570	3·55	807	2·85
Mining n.e.s.	3	19	1·70	79	0·75	149	0·75
Food processing	4	1668	80·60	945	11·80	2332	13·80
Drink, tobacco	5	683	29·00	408	6·90	697	7·30
Coke ovens, etc.	6	59	0·95	5	1·70	232	1·40
Mineral oil refining	7	175	8·40	376	4·70	516	3·05
Chemicals n.e.s.	8	537	12·25	648	8·10	1961	11·90
Iron, steel (primary)	9	83	2·40	645	8·05	1750	10·55
Iron, steel (secondary)	10	95	4·50	86	1·35	315	2·40
Nonferrous metals	11	24	1·15	392	3·70	734	3·60
Engineering, electrical	12	2433	35·00	1783	22·30	3836	23·15
Shipbuilding, etc.	13	326	7·00	235	4·45	454	4·55
Motors, cycles	14	1293	33·15	496	9·30	1704	16·75
Aircraft	15	336	17·20	310	7·75	605	8·25
Locomotives, etc.	16	106	1·00	88	1·95	206	2·55
Metal goods n.e.s.	17	301	8·80	524	6·55	1410	9·20
Textiles	18	433	7·25	843	7·90	2092	10·45
Leather, clothing	19	959	19·30	384	4·80	1042	6·25
Building materials	20	40	1·25	199	2·50	437	2·60
Pottery, glass	21	92	1·90	118	1·50	218	1·30
Timber, furniture, etc.	22	148	7·70	310	2·90	560	2·80
Paper, publishing	23	251	8·50	699	6·55	1445	7·25
Other manufacturing	24	233	6·00	295	3·70	649	4·25
Construction	25	2307	46·15	1307	29·50	3041	24·35
Gas	26	170	1·70	169	1·05	377	1·30
Electricity	27	347	3·45	412	2·55	778	2·70
Water	28	86	1·70	77	1·95	98	1·30
Transport, communications	29	1645	66·65	2147	53·65	3032	45·50
Distribution	30	3015	75·35	2966	89·00	3579	71·80
Services n.e.s.	31	1870	87·85	3060	76·50	4043	60·70

Sources: [26], Cambridge Growth Project.

than 50 % about their 'observed' values—i.e. about the values given in Table 2. But not one multiplier has such narrow confidence limits at the 95 % level, and the very high figure for the proportional variance of r_5 suggests that we can place no confidence whatever in the estimate of that multiplier. The high variance comes from having to explain a *high* intermediate output variance by variations in a row multiplier deviation and a set of column multiplier deviations which operate on only a *small* amount of initial estimate of intermediate output. The latter, small in any case, has been cut to almost nothing by the extraction of flow (5, 5)

Table 4. Covariance matrix for proportional deviations in r, s for the quasi-biproportional input–output matrix estimate for Britain in 1960 (Table 2)

Industry	$r,s \ldots$	r_1	r_2	r_3	r_4	r_5	r_6	r_7	r_8	r_9	r_{10}	r_{11}	r_{12}	r_{13}	r_{14}	r_{15}	r_{16}
Agriculture, etc.	r_1	—	—	—	—	—	—	0·109	0·103	0·106	0·105	0·106	0·106	0·111	0·110	0·112	0·113
Coal	r_2		0·112	0·106	0·096	0·579	0·107	0·105	0·102	0·105	0·104	0·104	0·105	0·106	0·107	0·108	0·107
Mining n.e.s.	r_3			0·104	0·095	0·358	0·105	0·096	0·094	0·095	0·095	0·095	0·095	0·096	0·096	0·096	0·097
Food processing	r_4				0·110	0·189	0·095	—	—	—	—	—	—	—	—	—	—
Drink, tobacco	r_5					882·63	0·380	0·498	0·375	0·332	0·329	0·324	0·312	0·714	0·323	0·624	0·934
Coke ovens, etc.	r_6						0·107	0·107	0·103	0·106	0·105	0·105	0·106	0·108	0·109	0·109	0·109
Mineral oil refining	r_7							0·109	0·103	0·106	0·105	0·105	0·106	0·109	0·110	0·111	0·111
Chemicals n.e.s.	r_8								0·100	0·102	0·102	0·102	0·102	0·104	0·105	0·105	0·105
Iron, steel (primary)	r_9									0·105	0·105	0·105	0·105	0·107	0·108	0·109	0·108
Iron, steel (secondary)	r_{10}										0·105	0·104	0·105	0·106	0·107	0·108	0·107
Nonferrous metals	r_{11}											0·105	0·105	0·107	0·108	0·109	0·108
Engineering, electrical	r_{12}												0·106	0·107	0·108	0·109	0·108
Shipbuilding, etc.	r_{13}													0·118	0·111	0·115	0·116
Motors, cycles	r_{14}														0·122	0·112	0·112
Aircraft	r_{15}															0·150	0·118
Metal goods n.e.s.	r_{16}																0·121
Textiles	r_{17}																
Leather, clothing	r_{18}																
Building materials	r_{19}																
Pottery, glass	r_{20}																
Timber, furniture, etc.	r_{21}																
Paper, publishing	r_{22}																
Other manufacturing	r_{23}																
Construction	r_{24}																
Gas	r_{25}																
Electricity	r_{26}																
Water	r_{27}																
Transport, communications	r_{28}																
	r_{29}																
Distribution	r_{30}																
Services n.e.s.	r_{31}																

A dash represents an element less than 0·005 in absolute value.

Table 4 (continued)

Industry	$r_{,s}$	$r_{1,s}\cdots r_{17,s}$	r_{18}	r_{19}	r_{20}	r_{21}	r_{22}	r_{23}	r_{24}	r_{25}	r_{26}	r_{27}	r_{28}	r_{29}	r_{30}	r_{31}
Agriculture, etc.	r_1	—	—	—	—	—	—	—	—	—	—	—	—	—	—	—
Coal	r_2	0·105	0·106	0·107	0·106	0·103	0·106	0·107	0·108	0·109	0·110	0·108	0·110	0·104	0·106	0·105
Mining n.e.s.	r_3	0·104	0·104	0·105	0·105	0·102	0·104	0·105	0·105	0·107	0·106	0·106	0·107	0·103	0·108	0·104
Food processing	r_4	0·095	0·094	0·095	0·095	0·093	0·094	0·094	0·095	0·096	0·096	0·095	0·095	0·095	0·097	0·094
Drink, tobacco	r_5	0·322	0·303	0·253	0·328	0·320	0·331	0·249	0·363	0·413	0·240	0·297	0·209	0·327	0·181	0·280
Coke ovens, etc.	r_6	0·105	0·105	0·107	0·106	0·103	0·105	0·106	0·107	0·107	0·108	0·107	0·109	0·104	0·108	0·105
Mineral oil refining	r_7	0·105	0·106	0·107	0·106	0·103	0·105	0·106	0·108	0·108	0·109	0·108	0·110	0·104	0·106	0·105
Chemicals n.e.s.	r_8	0·101	0·102	0·103	0·103	0·100	0·102	0·103	0·103	0·104	0·104	0·103	0·105	0·101	0·105	0·101
Iron, steel (primary)	r_9	0·104	0·105	0·106	0·106	0·103	0·104	0·105	0·106	0·107	0·107	0·106	0·107	0·104	0·109	0·104
Iron, steel (secondary)	r_{10}	0·104	0·104	0·106	0·105	0·102	0·104	0·105	0·106	0·107	0·106	0·106	0·107	0·103	0·108	0·104
Nonferrous metals	r_{11}	0·104	0·104	0·106	0·105	0·102	0·104	0·105	0·106	0·107	0·107	0·106	0·107	0·104	0·109	0·104
Engineering, electrical	r_{12}	0·104	0·105	0·106	0·106	0·103	0·104	0·106	0·106	0·107	0·108	0·107	0·108	0·104	0·108	0·104
Shipbuilding, etc.	r_{13}	0·106	0·106	0·108	0·107	0·104	0·106	0·107	0·109	0·111	0·109	0·108	0·109	0·105	0·109	0·106
Motors, cycles	r_{14}	0·107	0·108	0·109	0·108	0·105	0·107	0·109	0·110	0·110	0·112	0·110	0·113	0·106	0·107	0·106
Aircraft	r_{15}	0·107	0·107	0·109	0·108	0·105	0·107	0·108	0·110	0·112	0·110	0·109	0·110	0·106	0·109	0·107
Locomotives, etc.	r_{16}	0·107	0·104	0·105	0·104	0·101	0·103	0·105	0·105	0·113	0·110	0·109	0·110	0·105	0·109	0·107
Metal goods n.e.s.	r_{17}	0·103	0·105	0·109	0·105	0·102	0·104	0·106	0·106	0·106	0·106	0·105	0·107	0·103	0·105	0·105
Textiles	r_{18}			0·178	0·106	0·103	0·106	0·106	0·108	0·106	0·108	0·107	0·108	0·103	0·106	0·105
Leather, clothing	r_{19}				0·107	0·103	0·103	0·106	0·107	0·107	0·108	0·107	0·109	0·105	0·109	0·105
Building materials	r_{20}					0·100	0·105	0·103	0·103	0·109	0·108	0·103	0·104	0·105	0·106	0·105
Pottery, glass	r_{21}						0·104	0·105	0·106	0·104	0·104	0·106	0·108	0·101	0·106	0·105
Timber, furniture, etc.	r_{22}							0·109	0·107	0·106	0·107	0·106	0·107	0·103	0·106	0·104
Paper publishing	r_{23}								0·108	0·107	0·110	0·108	0·107	0·104	0·106	0·106
Other manufacturing	r_{24}									0·108	0·110	0·108	0·109	0·105	0·106	0·106
Construction	r_{25}									0·117	0·110	0·109	0·111	0·107	0·111	
Gas	r_{26}										0·114	0·111	0·111	0·106	0·105	0·106
Electricity	r_{27}											0·110	0·110	0·107	0·111	0·106
Water	r_{28}												0·148	0·106	0·111	
Transport, communications	r_{29}														0·102	0·106
Distribution	r_{30}															0·142	0·104
Services n.e.s.	r_{31}															0·105	0·105

Table 4 (continued)

Industry	r, s	s_1	s_2	s_3	s_4	s_5	s_6	s_7	s_8	s_9	s_{10}	s_{11}
Agriculture, etc.	r_1	—	—	—	—	—	—	—	—	—	—	—
Coal	r_2	−0·102	−0·106	−0·105	−0·089	−0·100	−0·106	−0·106	−0·104	−0·106	−0·106	−0·106
Mining n.e.s.	r_3	−0·100	−0·105	−0·104	−0·088	−0·099	−0·105	−0·105	−0·103	−0·105	−0·104	−0·105
Food processing	r_4	−0·100	−0·095	−0·095	−0·085	−0·092	−0·095	−0·095	−0·095	−0·095	−0·095	−0·095
Drink, tobacco	r_5	−0·278	−0·324	−0·317	−0·386	−0·081	−0·297	−0·376	−0·447	−0·318	−0·325	−0·305
Coke ovens, etc.	r_6	−0·101	−0·106	−0·105	−0·089	−0·100	−0·106	−0·106	−0·104	−0·106	−0·106	−0·105
Mineral oil refining	r_7	−0·102	−0·106	−0·105	−0·089	−0·100	−0·106	−0·106	−0·104	−0·106	−0·106	−0·105
Chemicals n.e.s.	r_8	−0·099	−0·102	−0·102	−0·087	−0·007	−0·003	−0·102	−0·101	−0·102	−0·102	−0·102
Iron, steel (primary)	r_9	−0·101	−0·105	−0·105	−0·089	−0·099	−0·106	−0·105	−0·104	−0·105	−0·105	−0·105
Iron, steel (secondary)	r_{10}	−0·100	−0·105	−0·104	−0·088	−0·099	−0·105	−0·104	−0·103	−0·105	−0·105	−0·105
Nonferrous metals	r_{11}	−0·101	−0·105	−0·105	−0·088	−0·099	−0·106	−0·105	−0·103	−0·105	−0·105	−0·105
Engineering, electrical	r_{12}	−0·101	−0·105	−0·105	−0·089	−0·099	−0·106	−0·105	−0·104	−0·105	−0·105	−0·105
Shipbuilding, etc	r_{13}	−0·103	−0·107	−0·106	−0·090	−0·101	−0·107	−0·107	−0·105	−0·107	−0·107	−0·107
Motors, cycles	r_{14}	−0·103	−0·108	−0·107	−0·090	−0·101	−0·108	−0·108	−0·106	−0·108	−0·108	−0·107
Aircraft	r_{15}	−0·103	−0·109	−0·107	−0·091	−0·102	−0·108	−0·109	−0·106	−0·108	−0·108	−0·108
Locomotives, etc	r_{16}	−0·103	−0·108	−0·107	−0·090	−0·101	−0·108	−0·108	−0·106	−0·108	−0·108	−0·107
Metal goods n.e.s.	r_{17}	−0·100	−0·104	−0·104	−0·088	−0·098	−0·104	−0·104	−0·102	−0·104	−0·104	−0·104
Textiles	r_{18}	−0·100	−0·105	−0·104	−0·088	−0·099	−0·105	−0·104	−0·103	−0·105	−0·104	−0·104
Leather, clothing	r_{19}	−0·101	−0·106	−0·105	−0·089	−0·100	−0·106	−0·106	−0·104	−0·106	−0·106	−0·106
Building materials	r_{20}	−0·101	−0·105	−0·105	−0·089	−0·100	−0·106	−0·106	−0·104	−0·106	−0·106	−0·106
Pottery, glass	r_{21}	−0·099	−0·103	−0·102	−0·087	−0·097	−0·103	−0·102	−0·101	−0·103	−0·102	−0·102
Timber, furniture, etc.	r_{22}	−0·100	−0·105	−0·104	−0·088	−0·099	−0·105	−0·104	−0·103	−0·104	−0·104	−0·104
Paper, publishing	r_{23}	−0·101	−0·105	−0·105	−0·089	−0·099	−0·106	−0·105	−0·104	−0·105	−0·105	−0·105
Other manufacturing	r_{24}	−0·102	−0·106	−0·105	−0·089	−0·100	−0·106	−0·106	−0·104	−0·106	−0·106	−0·106
Construction	r_{25}	−0·104	−0·109	−0·108	−0·091	−0·102	−0·109	−0·109	−0·107	−0·109	−0·109	−0·108
Gas	r_{26}	−0·102	−0·107	−0·106	−0·090	−0·101	−0·108	−0·107	−0·105	−0·107	−0·107	−0·106
Electricity	r_{27}	−0·101	−0·106	−0·105	−0·089	−0·100	−0·107	−0·106	−0·105	−0·106	−0·106	−0·106
Water	r_{28}	−0·102	−0·107	−0·106	−0·090	−0·101	−0·108	−0·108	−0·106	−0·107	−0·107	−0·106
Transport, communications	r_{29}	−0·100	−0·104	−0·105	−0·088	−0·098	−0·105	−0·104	−0·102	−0·104	−0·104	−0·104
Distribution	r_{30}	−0·103	−0·107	−0·107	−0·090	−0·101	−0·109	−0·105	−0·104	−0·108	−0·107	−0·109
Services n.e.s.	r_{31}	−0·100	−0·104	−0·104	−0·088	−0·099	−0·104	−0·104	−0·103	−0·104	−0·104	−0·104

A dash represents an element less than 0·005 in absolute value.

Table 4 (continued)

Industry	r, s	s_{12}	s_{13}	s_{14}	s_{15}	s_{16}	s_{17}	s_{18}	s_{19}	s_{10}	s_{21}
Agriculture, etc.	r_1	—	—	—	—	—	—	—	—	—	—
Coal	r_2	−0·106	−0·107	−0·107	−0·111	−0·106	−0·106	−0·106	−0·105	−0·106	−0·105
Mining n.e.s.	r_3	−0·104	−0·105	−0·105	−0·107	−0·105	−0·104	−0·104	−0·104	−0·104	−0·104
Food processing	r_4	−0·095	−0·095	−0·095	−0·096	−0·095	−0·094	−0·094	−0·094	−0·095	−0·095
Drink, tobacco	r_5	−0·313	−0·416	−0·321	−0·553	−0·366	−0·318	−0·302	−0·272	−0·302	−0·310
Coke ovens, etc.	r_6	−0·105	−0·106	−0·106	−0·108	−0·106	−0·105	−0·105	−0·105	−0·105	−0·105
Mineral oil refining	r_7	−0·106	−0·106	−0·106	−0·110	−0·106	−0·105	−0·105	−0·105	−0·105	−0·105
Chemicals n.e.s.	r_8	−0·102	−0·102	−0·103	−0·105	−0·102	−0·102	−0·105	−0·105	−0·102	−0·102
Iron, steel (primary)	r_9	−0·105	−0·106	−0·106	−0·108	−0·105	−0·105	−0·105	−0·104	−0·105	−0·104
Iron, steel (secondary)	r_{10}	−0·105	−0·105	−0·105	−0·107	−0·105	−0·104	−0·104	−0·104	−0·104	−0·104
Nonferrous metals	r_{11}	−0·105	−0·105	−0·105	−0·108	−0·105	−0·105	−0·104	−0·104	−0·105	−0·104
Engineering, electrical	r_{12}	−0·105	−0·106	−0·106	−0·108	−0·105	−0·105	−0·105	−0·104	−0·105	−0·104
Shipbuilding, etc.	r_{13}	−0·107	−0·109	−0·107	−0·113	−0·107	−0·106	−0·106	−0·106	−0·106	−0·106
Motors, cycles	r_{14}	−0·108	−0·108	−0·110	−0·111	−0·108	−0·108	−0·107	−0·107	−0·107	−0·107
Aircraft	r_{15}	−0·108	−0·110	−0·109	−0·143	−0·109	−0·108	−0·107	−0·107	−0·108	−0·107
Locomotives, etc.	r_{16}	−0·108	−0·110	−0·108	−0·116	−0·108	−0·107	−0·107	−0·107	−0·107	−0·107
Metal goods n.e.s.	r_{17}	−0·104	−0·104	−0·105	−0·107	−0·104	−0·104	−0·104	−0·104	−0·104	−0·103
Textiles	r_{18}	−0·104	−0·105	−0·105	−0·107	−0·105	−0·104	−0·104	−0·106	−0·104	−0·104
Leather, clothing	r_{19}	−0·106	−0·106	−0·107	−0·108	−0·106	−0·106	−0·108	−0·086	−0·106	−0·105
Building materials	r_{20}	−0·106	−0·106	−0·106	−0·108	−0·106	−0·105	−0·105	−0·105	−0·105	−0·105
Pottery, glass	r_{21}	−0·102	−0·103	−0·103	−0·105	−0·102	−0·102	−0·102	−0·102	−0·102	−0·102
Timber, furniture, etc.	r_{22}	−0·104	−0·105	−0·105	−0·107	−0·104	−0·104	−0·104	−0·104	−0·104	−0·104
Paper, publishing	r_{23}	−0·105	−0·105	−0·106	−0·107	−0·105	−0·105	−0·105	−0·105	−0·105	−0·105
Other manufacturing	r_{24}	−0·106	−0·106	−0·107	−0·109	−0·106	−0·106	−0·106	−0·106	−0·106	−0·105
Construction	r_{25}	−0·108	−0·109	−0·109	−0·113	−0·109	−0·108	−0·108	−0·108	−0·108	−0·106
Gas	r_{26}	−0·107	−0·107	−0·108	−0·109	−0·107	−0·108	−0·107	−0·107	−0·107	−0·106
Electricity	r_{27}	−0·106	−0·106	−0·107	−0·109	−0·106	−0·106	−0·106	−0·106	−0·106	−0·105
Water	r_{28}	−0·107	−0·107	−0·108	−0·109	−0·107	−0·107	−0·108	−0·107	−0·107	−0·107
Transport, communications	r_{29}	−0·104	−0·104	−0·104	−0·106	−0·104	−0·104	−0·103	−0·103	−0·104	−0·103
Distribution	r_{30}	−0·106	−0·106	−0·106	−0·107	−0·106	−0·106	−0·105	−0·105	−0·107	−0·106
Services n.e.s.	r_{31}	−0·104	−0·105	−0·105	−0·106	−0·104	−0·104	−0·104	−0·104	−0·104	−0·104

Table 4 (continued)

Industry	$r, s \cdots s_{22}$ (r, s)	s_{23}	s_{24}	s_{25}	s_{26}	s_{27}	s_{28}	s_{29}	s_{30}	s_{31}
Agriculture, etc.	r_1 —	—	—	—	—	—	—	—	—	—
Coal	r_2 −0·103	−0·104	−0·104	−0·105	−0·104	−0·104	−0·104	−0·107	−0·111	−0·107
Mining, n.e.s.	r_3 −0·093	−0·095	−0·095	−0·095	−0·095	−0·095	−0·095	−0·097	−0·097	−0·096
Food processing	r_4 −0·442	−0·275	−0·324	−0·336	−0·303	−0·301	−0·324	−0·993	−0·118	−0·188
Drink, tobacco	r_5 −0·104	−0·106	−0·105	−0·106	−0·105	−0·105	−0·106	−0·109	−0·114	−0·110
Coke ovens, etc.	r_6 −0·104	−0·105	−0·105	−0·106	−0·105	−0·105	−0·106	−0·112	−0·117	−0·108
Mineral oil refining	r_7 −0·100	−0·102	−0·102	−0·103	−0·102	−0·102	−0·102	−0·105	−0·110	−0·105
Chemicals n.e.s.	r_8 −0·103	−0·105	−0·105	−0·106	−0·105	−0·105	−0·105	−0·108	−0·112	−0·108
Iron, steel (primary)	r_9 −0·103	−0·104	−0·104	−0·105	−0·104	−0·104	−0·105	−0·107	−0·111	−0·107
Iron, steel (secondary)	r_{10} −0·103	−0·105	−0·104	−0·105	−0·105	−0·104	−0·105	−0·108	−0·111	−0·108
Nonferrous metals	r_{11} −0·103	−0·105	−0·105	−0·106	−0·105	−0·105	−0·105	−0·108	−0·112	−0·109
Engineering, electrical	r_{12} −0·103	−0·105	−0·105	−0·106	−0·105	−0·105	−0·105	−0·108	−0·112	−0·109
Shipbuilding, etc.	r_{13} −0·105	−0·106	−0·106	−0·108	−0·106	−0·106	−0·107	−0·117	−0·113	−0·109
Motors, cycles	r_{14} −0·106	−0·108	−0·108	−0·108	−0·107	−0·107	−0·108	−0·112	−0·121	−0·112
Aircraft	r_{15} −0·106	−0·108	−0·108	−0·109	−0·108	−0·108	−0·108	−0·119	−0·114	−0·110
Locomotives, etc.	r_{16} −0·106	−0·107	−0·107	−0·109	−0·107	−0·107	−0·108	−0·121	−0·115	−0·110
Metal goods n.e.s.	r_{17} −0·102	−0·104	−0·104	−0·105	−0·104	−0·104	−0·104	−0·107	−0·111	−0·107
Textiles	r_{18} −0·103	−0·104	−0·104	−0·105	−0·104	−0·104	−0·105	−0·107	−0·116	−0·108
Leather, clothing	r_{19} −0·105	−0·106	−0·107	−0·106	−0·106	−0·106	−0·106	−0·109	−0·114	−0·109
Building materials	r_{20} −0·104	−0·105	−0·105	−0·107	−0·106	−0·105	−0·106	−0·109	−0·112	−0·109
Pottery, glass	r_{21} −0·101	−0·102	−0·102	−0·103	−0·102	−0·102	−0·102	−0·105	−0·109	−0·105
Timber, furniture, etc.	r_{22} −0·103	−0·104	−0·104	−0·105	−0·104	−0·104	−0·104	−0·104	−0·114	−0·108
Paper, publishing	r_{23} −0·103	−0·107	−0·105	−0·105	−0·105	−0·105	−0·106	−0·107	−0·115	−0·116
Other manufacturing	r_{24} −0·104	−0·106	−0·106	−0·106	−0·106	−0·106	−0·106	−0·110	−0·118	−0·110
Construction	r_{25} −0·106	−0·108	−0·108	−0·110	−0·108	−0·108	−0·109	−0·115	−0·115	−0·111
Gas	r_{26} −0·105	−0·108	−0·107	−0·107	−0·107	−0·106	−0·108	−0·110	−0·127	−0·114
Electricity	r_{27} −0·104	−0·107	−0·106	−0·106	−0·106	−0·105	−0·107	−0·109	−0·122	−0·112
Water	r_{28} −0·105	−0·108	−0·108	−0·107	−0·107	−0·107	−0·103	−0·110	−0·130	−0·115
Transport, communications	r_{29} −0·102	−0·104	−0·103	−0·104	−0·104	−0·104	−0·104	−0·105	−0·110	−0·106
Distribution	r_{30} −0·105	−0·106	−0·105	−0·106	−0·108	−0·107	−0·105	−0·107	−0·093	−0·106
Services n.e.s.	r_{31} −0·102	−0·104	−0·104	−0·105	−0·104	−0·104	−0·104	−0·106	−0·110	−0·105

A dash represents an element less than 0·005 in absolute value.

Table 4 (continued)

Industry	$r, s \cdots s_1$ r, s	s_1	s_2	s_3	s_4	s_5	s_6	s_7	s_8	s_9	s_{10}	s_{11}	s_{12}	s_{13}	s_{14}	s_{15}	s_{16}
Agriculture	s_1	0·101	0·101	0·101	0·087	0·096	0·101	0·101	0·100	0·101	0·101	0·101	0·101	0·101	0·101	0·103	0·101
Coal	s_2		0·106	0·105	0·089	0·100	0·106	0·105	0·104	0·106	0·105	0·105	0·105	0·106	0·106	0·108	0·105
Mining n.e.s.	s_3			0·105	0·088	0·099	0·105	0·104	0·103	0·105	0·105	0·105	0·104	0·105	0·105	0·107	0·105
Food processing	s_4				0·076	0·084	0·089	0·088	0·087	0·089	0·088	0·089	0·088	0·089	0·089	0·090	0·088
Drink, tobacco	s_5					0·095	0·100	0·099	0·098	0·099	0·099	0·099	0·099	0·099	0·100	0·101	0·099
Coke ovens, etc.	s_6						0·107	0·105	0·104	0·106	0·105	0·105	0·105	0·105	0·105	0·107	0·105
Mineral oil refining	s_7							0·106	0·103	0·105	0·104	0·104	0·104	0·105	0·105	0·107	0·104
Chemicals n.s.e.	s_8								0·102	0·104	0·103	0·103	0·103	0·104	0·104	0·106	0·103
Iron, steel (primary)	s_9									0·106	0·105	0·105	0·105	0·105	0·106	0·108	0·105
Iron, steel (secondary)	s_{10}										0·105	0·105	0·105	0·105	0·105	0·108	0·105
Nonferrous metals	s_{11}											0·105	0·105	0·105	0·105	0·107	0·105
Engineering, electrical	s_{12}												0·105	0·105	0·106	0·109	0·106
Shipbuilding, etc.	s_{13}													0·107	0·106	0·106	0·106
Motors, cycles	s_{14}														0·106	0·106	0·108
Aircraft	s_{15}															0·138	0·108
Locomotives, etc.	s_{16}																0·106
Metal goods n.e.s.	s_{17}																
Textiles	s_{18}																
Leather, clothing	s_{19}																
Building materials	s_{20}																
Pottery, glass	s_{21}																
Timber, furniture, etc.	s_{22}																
Paper, publishing	s_{23}																
Other manfacturing	s_{24}																
Construction	s_{25}																
Gas	s_{26}																
Electricity	s_{27}																
Water	s_{28}																
Transport, communications	s_{29}																
Distribution	s_{30}																
Services n.e.s.	s_{31}																

Table 4 (continued)

Industry	$r, s \ldots s_{17}$ / r, s	s_{18}	s_{19}	s_{20}	s_{21}	s_{22}	s_{23}	s_{24}	s_{25}	s_{26}	s_{27}	s_{28}	s_{29}	s_{30}	s_{31}
Agriculture, etc. s_1	0·101	0·100	0·100	0·101	0·100	0·099	0·101	0·100	0·101	0·101	0·101	0·101	0·103	0·105	0·103
Coal s_2	0·105	0·105	0·105	0·105	0·105	0·103	0·105	0·105	0·106	0·105	0·105	0·105	0·108	0·112	0·108
Mining n.e.s. s_3	0·104	0·104	0·104	0·104	0·104	0·103	0·104	0·104	0·105	0·105	0·105	0·104	0·107	0·110	0·107
Food processing s_4	0·088	0·088	0·088	0·088	0·088	0·087	0·088	0·088	0·089	0·088	0·088	0·088	0·090	0·093	0·090
Drink, tobacco r_5	0·099	0·099	0·099	0·099	0·099	0·097	0·099	0·099	0·100	0·099	0·099	0·099	0·101	0·104	0·102
Coke ovens, etc. s_6	0·105	0·105	0·105	0·105	0·105	0·103	0·105	0·105	0·105	0·105	0·105	0·105	0·107	0·112	0·108
Mineral oil refining s_7	0·104	0·104	0·104	0·104	0·104	0·102	0·104	0·104	0·105	0·104	0·104	0·104	0·108	0·113	0·107
Chemicals n.e.s. s_8	0·103	0·103	0·103	0·103	0·103	0·102	0·103	0·103	0·104	0·103	0·103	0·103	0·106	0·110	0·106
Iron, steel (primary) s_9	0·105	0·105	0·104	0·105	0·104	0·103	0·105	0·105	0·106	0·105	0·105	0·105	0·108	0·111	0·108
Iron, steel (secondary) s_{10}	0·105	0·104	0·104	0·105	0·104	0·103	0·105	0·104	0·105	0·105	0·105	0·105	0·108	0·112	0·108
Nonferrous metals s_{11}	0·105	0·104	0·104	0·105	0·104	0·103	0·105	0·104	0·105	0·105	0·105	0·105	0·107	0·110	0·107
Engineering, electrical s_{12}	0·105	0·104	0·104	0·105	0·104	0·103	0·105	0·104	0·105	0·105	0·105	0·105	0·107	0·112	0·108
Shipbuilding, etc. s_{13}	0·105	0·105	0·105	0·105	0·103	0·103	0·105	0·105	0·106	0·105	0·105	0·105	0·110	0·112	0·108
Motors, cycles s_{14}	0·105	0·105	0·105	0·105	0·105	0·104	0·105	0·105	0·106	0·105	0·105	0·105	0·108	0·114	0·109
Aircraft s_{15}	0·107	0·107	0·107	0·107	0·107	0·105	0·107	0·107	0·108	0·107	0·107	0·108	0·117	0·114	0·110
Locomotives, etc. s_{16}	0·105	0·104	0·104	0·105	0·104	0·103	0·105	0·105	0·106	0·105	0·105	0·105	0·109	0·112	0·108
Metal goods n.e.s. s_{17}	0·105	0·104	0·104	0·105	0·104	0·103	0·105	0·104	0·105	0·105	0·105	0·105	0·107	0·114	0·108
Textiles s_{18}		0·104	0·104	0·104	0·104	0·103	0·104	0·105	0·105	0·104	0·104	0·104	0·107	0·113	0·107
Leather, clothing s_{19}			0·109	0·104	0·104	0·103	0·104	0·104	0·105	0·104	0·104	0·104	0·107	0·111	0·107
Building materials s_{20}				0·105	0·104	0·103	0·105	0·104	0·105	0·105	0·105	0·105	0·107	0·111	0·108
Pottery, glass s_{21}					0·104	0·102	0·104	0·104	0·105	0·104	0·104	0·104	0·107	0·111	0·107
Timber, furniture, etc. s_{22}						0·102	0·103	0·103	0·103	0·103	0·103	0·103	0·105	0·110	0·106
Paper, publishing s_{23}							0·106	0·104	0·105	0·105	0·105	0·105	0·107	0·112	0·111
Other manufacturing s_{24}								0·104	0·105	0·104	0·104	0·105	0·107	0·113	0·108
Construction s_{25}									0·107	0·106	0·106	0·106	0·109	0·112	0·108
Gas s_{26}										0·105	0·105	0·105	0·107	0·111	0·108
Electricity s_{27}											0·105	0·105	0·107	0·110	0·107
Water s_{28}												0·117	0·108	0·114	0·108
Transport, communications s_{29}													0·122	0·115	0·110
Distribution s_{30}														0·160	0·117
Services n.e.s. s_{31}															0·128

Table 5. Variances of proportional deviations in the elements of the quasi-biproportional input–output matrix estimate (Table 2)

Industry	i	j...1	2	3	4	5	6	7	8	9	10	11	12	13	14	15	16
Agriculture, etc.	1	0·101	—	—	0·076	0·095	—	—	0·102	—	—	—	—	—	—	—	—
Coal	2	0·009	—	0·007	0·010	0·007	[-]	—	0·006	[-]	[-]	0·005	0·005	—	0·004	—	0·006
Mining n.e.s.	3	0·005	—	0·001	0·004	—	—	—	—	—	—	—	0·001	—	—	—	—
Food processing	4	0·011	—	—	0·016	0·021	—	—	0·022	—	—	—	—	—	—	—	—
Drink, tobacco	5	—	—	—	—	[-]	—	—	—	—	—	—	—	—	—	—	—
Coke ovens, etc.	6	—	—	0·002	—	0·002	[-]	0·001	0·001	0·001	—	0·002	0·002	0·002	0·001	—	—
Mineral oil refining	7	0·006	—	0·004	0·007	0·004	—	0·003	0·003	[-]	—	—	—	0·004	—	0·027	0·003
Chemicals n.e.s.	8	0·003	0·002	0·001	0·002	0·001	—	0·002	—	0·002	[-]	0·004	0·002	0·003	—	0·028	0·002
Iron, steel (primary)	9	—	0·001	—	—	—	—	—	—	0·001	0·001	—	—	—	—	0·027	0·001
Iron, steel (secondary)	10	—	—	—	0·005	—	—	—	0·001	—	—	—	—	—	0·001	—	0·001
Nonferrous metals	11	0·005	—	—	0·005	0·002	—	—	0·001	0·001	—	0·001	0·001	0·002	0·001	0·027	0·001
Engineering, electrical	12	0·013	0·002	0·001	0·004	0·003	—	0·002	—	0·002	—	—	—	0·002	—	0·028	0·002
Shipbuilding, etc.	13	0·017	—	0·013	0·018	—	—	—	—	—	—	—	—	0·001	—	—	—
Motors, cycles	14	—	—	—	—	—	—	—	—	—	—	—	—	0·007	0·008	0·038	—
Aircraft	15	—	—	—	—	—	—	—	—	—	—	—	—	—	—	0·002	—
Locomotives, etc.	16	0·004	—	—	—	—	—	—	—	—	—	—	—	—	—	—	0·011
Metal goods n.e.s.	17	0·006	0·001	0·002	0·003	—	—	0·001	0·001	0·001	—	—	—	0·002	−0·001	0·027	0·001
Textiles	18	—	0·001	—	0·005	—	—	—	0·001	—	0·002	0·002	—	0·002	0·001	0·029	0·001
Leather, clothing	19	0·006	0·072	—	—	—	—	—	—	—	—	—	—	—	0·070	—	0·072
Building materials	20	—	0·001	—	—	0·001	0·001	0·001	0·001	0·001	—	—	—	—	0·001	—	0·001
Pottery, glass	21	0·005	—	—	—	0·001	—	—	—	—	—	—	0·001	—	—	—	0·002
Timber, furniture, etc.	22	0·008	—	0·001	0·004	0·001	—	—	0·003	0·002	0·001	0·001	0·001	0·001	—	0·028	0·002
Paper, publishing	23	0·005	0·005	0·004	0·007	0·006	—	—	0·002	—	0·004	—	0·004	0·006	0·003	0·033	—
Other manufacturing	24	0·005	0·002	0·003	0·006	—	—	0·005	0·005	0·005	0·004	0·006	0·001	0·003	0·005	0·028	0·002
Construction	25	0·010	0·005	0·006	0·011	0·008	0·005	—	0·006	0·006	0·005	0·007	0·006	0·006	0·005	0·029	0·005
Gas	26	0·011	—	—	0·010	0·005	0·003	—	0·002	0·004	0·003	0·003	0·005	0·007	0·004	0·034	0·006
Electricity	27	0·009	0·004	0·005	0·008	0·005	0·003	0·004	—	—	—	—	0·003	0·005	0·002	0·030	0·004
Water	28	—	—	—	—	—	—	—	—	—	—	—	—	—	—	—	—
Transport, communications	29	0·007	0·004	0·001	0·006	0·005	0·003	0·004	0·004	0·004	0·003	0·003	0·003	0·005	0·004	0·032	0·004
Distribution	30	0·037	0·034	0·033	0·038	0·035	0·031	0·038	0·036	0·032	0·033	0·029	0·035	0·037	0·036	0·066	0·036
Services n.e.s.	31	0·006	0·003	0·002	0·005	0·002	0·004	0·003	0·001	0·003	0·002	0·002	0·002	0·002	0·001	0·031	0·003

Table 5 *(continued)*

i	Industry	$j\ldots17$	18	19	20	21	22	23	24	25	26	27	28	29	30	31
1	Agriculture, etc.	–	0·104	0·109	–	–	0·102	–	–	–	–	–	–	–	–	–
2	Coal	0·005	0·004	–	[–]	[–]	–	[–]	0·004	–	[–]	[–]	0·017	0·008	0·038	0·020
3	Mining n.e.s.	0·001	–	–	–	0·001	–	0·002	–	–	0·001	–	–	0·012	–	–
4	Food processing	–	0·026	–	–	–	–	0·026	–	–	–	–	–	0·038	–	–
5	Drink, tobacco	–	–	–	–	–	–	–	–	–	–	–	–	–	–	–
6	Coke ovens, etc.	–	–	–	0·002	0·001	–	–	–	–	–	–	–	–	–	–
7	Mineral oil refining	0·004	0·003	0·008	[–]	[–]	0·003	[–]	0·001	0·002	[–]	[–]	0·012	0·011	0·039	0·015
8	Chemicals n.e.s.	0·001	–	0·005	0·001	–	0·002	0·002	0·003	0·004	0·001	0·001	0·014	0·007	0·035	0·018
9	Iron, steel (primary)	–	–	–	–	–	0·001	–	–	0·001	–	–	0·013	0·012	0·040	–
10	Iron steel (secondary)	0·002	0·001	–	–	–	–	0·003	0·001	–	–	0·002	0·012	0·011	–	–
11	Nonferrous metals	–	–	–	–	–	0·001	0·001	0·001	0·002	–	–	0·013	–	–	–
12	Engineering, electrical	0·001	–	0·005	0·001	0·002	0·002	0·002	–	0·002	0·002	0·002	–	0·012	0·042	0·016
13	Shipbuilding, etc.	–	–	–	–	–	–	–	–	0·001	0·011	–	–	0·006	–	–
14	Motors, cycles	0·011	–	–	0·013	0·012	0·012	–	0·010	0·013	–	–	–	0·020	0·040	0·026
15	Aircraft	–	–	–	–	–	–	–	–	–	–	–	–	0·034	–	–
16	Locomotives, etc.	–	–	–	–	–	–	–	–	–	–	–	–	0·001	–	–
17	Metal goods n.e.s.	–	–	0·004	–	–	0·001	0·001	0·001	–	–	–	0·012	–	0·041	0·017
18	Textiles	0·002	0·001	0·002	0·002	0·001	0·001	0·003	–	0·002	0·002	–	–	0·013	0·033	0·017
19	Leather, clothing	–	0·066	0·115	–	–	0·070	0·072	0·068	–	–	–	–	0·082	–	0·088
20	Building materials	0·002	–	–	0·002	0·001	–	–	–	–	–	0·002	0·012	–	0·043	0·017
21	Pottery, glass	0·001	–	–	–	–	–	–	–	0·001	–	0·001	–	–	–	–
22	Timber, furniture, etc.	0·001	–	0·005	0·001	0·003	0·005	0·001	0·003	0·001	–	0·001	–	–	0·036	0·016
23	Paper, publishing	0·004	0·003	0·004	0·004	0·002	0·002	0·002	–	0·006	0·004	0·004	0·014	0·017	0·039	0·005
24	Other manufacturing	0·001	–	0·005	0·001	0·005	0·007	0·007	0·005	0·003	0·001	0·001	–	0·010	0·032	0·016
25	Construction	0·006	0·005	0·010	0·006	0·006	–	0·004	0·004	0·004	0·006	0·006	0·016	0·009	0·047	0·023
26	Gas	0·005	0·004	0·009	0·005	0·004	0·004	0·002	0·002	0·005	0·005	0·005	0·016	0·016	0·020	0·014
27	Electricity	0·003	0·002	0·007	0·003	–	–	–	–	–	0·003	0·039	0·015	0·014	0·026	0·014
28	Water	–	–	–	0·039	–	–	–	–	0·005	–	0·003	0·059	0·018	0·048	0·046
29	Transport, communications	0·003	0·004	0·009	0·003	0·004	0·004	0·004	0·004	0·005	0·003	0·003	0·018	0·018	0·046	0·022
30	Distribution	0·035	0·036	0·041	0·033	0·034	0·034	0·036	0·036	0·037	0·031	0·033	0·049	0·050	0·116	0·058
31	Services n.e.s.	0·002	0·001	0·006	0·002	0·001	0·003	0·003	0·001	0·002	0·002	0·002	0·014	0·015	0·045	0·023

A dash represents an element less than 0·0005. A dash enclosed in square brackets indicates the (zero) proportional variance of an exogenously estimated element of Table 2.

from the endogenous calculation. The rigidity of the quasi-biproportional method does not allow for the removal, with the individual flow, of part of the variability of the total intermediate output; in retrospect it seems that some such reduction would have been sensible, and that the variance attributed to u_5 is in any case too high.

On the other hand, we may place a good deal of confidence in Table 2's estimates of the input–output coefficients themselves. Table 5 shows that the great bulk of coefficients have proportional variances of less than 0·01 and hence 95 % confidence limits of less than 20 % about their 'observed' values.

These findings throw further doubt on the use of interpreting the r's and s's as independent measures of substitution and fabrication effects; while lending support to the products $r_i s_j$ as useful measures of trends in individual coefficients embodying these two 'effects' jointly. It is the negativity of the covariances of (r_i, s_j) pairs that is responsible for this distinction. This negativity is to be expected. A heuristic argument runs as follows. Consider a 'partial' error, say a positive one in u_h. It pushes r_h in the same direction. But then there must be negative errors in all the s_j's to compensate the errors which this too high r_h induces in the $a_{hj}^B, j \neq h$. Finally, the row multipliers other than r_h are forced too high to compensate the downward errors induced by the s_j's in the $a_{ij}^B, i, j \neq h$. In short, all the r's move up and all the s's down: the hth row of the Jacobian $\partial(r, s)/\partial(u, v)$ has the form $(+ \ldots + \ - \ldots -)$.

The formula for covariance of pairs of marginals (p. 72) shows that with a positive error in u_i are associated a lesser positive error in v_i and much smaller errors in other marginals. The latter are small enough to be ignored, so in considering the joint effects on r_i and s_j we need only take note of that exerted directly by error in u_h and that produced by the associated error in v_h. The positive error in u_h directly induces contrary errors in r_i and s_j—upward in r_i and downward in s_j. Indirectly, through the associated positive error in v_h, it induces further error in s_j, which this time is upward and tends to cancel the first one. The direct effect, however, is stronger than the indirect effect, and the net outcome is a tendency to oppositely directed error in r_i and s_j.

The covariance of x_i and y_j has the same sign as that of r_i and s_j and may be written more conveniently. By (35) (on p. 72) it is

$$\sum_{h, k} c_{ih}^{B0} c_{j+m, k}^{B0} \omega_{hk},$$

where ω_{hk} stands for the covariance of the hth and kth elements of $(\bar{u}, v)$, not of (u, v), and where $c_{ih}^{B0}, c_{j+m, k}^{B0}$ are elements of the Jacobian $\partial(x, y)/\partial(u, v)$. The argument of the last paragraph amounts to saying that, in evaluating the sub-sum of this sum consisting of terms in which h takes a particular value, we may approximate by

$$c_{i-1, h}^{B0} c_{j+m-1, h}^{B0} \omega_{hh} + c_{j+m-1, h+m}^{B0} \omega_{h, h+m},$$

and that the negative first term of this approximation outweighs the positive second term.

The sign pattern of the Jacobian $\partial(r, s)/\partial(u, v)$—which is the same as that of C^{B0}—and the relief in the pattern of marginal covariances, are illustrated in the following 3×3 example, which shows the steps of a calculation like the one that led to Tables 4 and 5.

Let

$$A^{B0} = \begin{bmatrix} 20 & 0 & 10 \\ 0 & 30 & 0 \\ 60 & 20 & 30 \end{bmatrix},$$

then the associated Jacobian $\partial(\bar{x}, y)/\partial(\bar{u}, v)$ is, from (22) (p. 68), the definition of C^{B0} (p. 68), (16) (p. 64) and the definition of B (p. 63),

$$\overline{C^{B0}} = \begin{bmatrix} 0.1278 & 0.0444 & -0.0333 & -0.0944 & -0.0333 \\ 0.0444 & 0.0444 & -0.0333 & -0.0444 & -0.0333 \\ -0.0333 & -0.0333 & 0.0375 & 0.0333 & 0.0250 \\ -0.0944 & -0.0444 & 0.0333 & 0.0944 & 0.0333 \\ -0.0333 & -0.0333 & 0.0250 & 0.0333 & 0.0500 \end{bmatrix}.$$

Recall that C^{B0} does not show the effects of u_1. Here we have also left out the trivial first row of C^{B0} showing the effects on r_1. Notice that $\overline{C^{B0}}$ is symmetric: the effect of a disturbance in U_k on X_h and of an equal disturbance in U_h on X_k are the same.

Let the standard deviations of observations on final demands, net outputs and gross outputs be, for example,

$$\begin{pmatrix} \sigma_1 \\ \sigma_2 \\ \sigma_3 \end{pmatrix} = \begin{pmatrix} 15 \\ 2 \\ 4 \end{pmatrix}, \quad \begin{pmatrix} \sigma_4 \\ \sigma_5 \\ \sigma_6 \end{pmatrix} = \begin{pmatrix} 5 \\ 1 \\ 6 \end{pmatrix}, \quad \begin{pmatrix} \sigma_7 \\ \sigma_8 \\ \sigma_9 \end{pmatrix} = \begin{pmatrix} 3 \\ 1 \\ 2 \end{pmatrix}.$$

Then the covariance matrix of $(\bar{u}, v)$ works out at

$$\Omega = \begin{bmatrix} 4.948 & -0.208 & 0.326 & 1.013 & 0.469 \\ -0.208 & 19.166 & 1.303 & 0.052 & 5.876 \\ 0.326 & 1.303 & 31.964 & -0.081 & -2.931 \\ 1.013 & 0.052 & -0.081 & 1.997 & -0.117 \\ 0.469 & 5.876 & -2.931 & -0.117 & 35.779 \end{bmatrix}.$$

The dominance of the leading diagonal, and of the 'three up' and 'three down' diagonals showing covariances of pairs (u_i, v_i), is evident. Finally, we get

$$\overline{C^{B0}} \Omega \, (\overline{C^{B0}})' = \begin{bmatrix} 0.149 & 0.104 & -0.089 & -0.132 & -0.097 \\ 0.104 & 0.091 & -0.079 & 0.100 & -0.088 \\ -0.089 & -0.079 & 0.073 & 0.086 & 0.074 \\ -0.132 & -0.100 & 0.086 & 0.121 & 0.094 \\ -0.097 & -0.088 & 0.074 & 0.094 & 0.104 \end{bmatrix}.$$

An encouraging feature of Table 4 is the high proportional variances of those multipliers (r_5, r_{15}, s_{15}) for whose untrustworthiness we gave reasons earlier in this section. Two other extreme multiplier values (r_{19} for Leather and clothing = 0·564 and r_{28} for Water = 0·326) turn out to show large proportional errors. That for r_{19} may, again, be partly ascribed to the extreme dominance of the single input–output coefficient (19, 19) in its row: this restricts the possibility of accounting for variation in u_{19} by variation in s's.

High absolute variances of coefficient estimates occur where high proportional variances are associated with big coefficients. On this criterion the most untrustworthy coefficients are: (1, 4) (Agriculture to Food processing), (15, 15) (intra-Aircraft), (18, 30) (Textiles to Distribution), (19, 19) (intra-Leather and clothing), (27, 30) (Electricity to Distribution), and (30, 1), (30, 3), (30, 4), (30, 6), (30, 9), (30, 11), (30, 20) (Distribution to Agriculture, Mining n.e.s., Food processing, Coke ovens, etc., Iron and steel (primary), Nonferrous metals, and Building materials). All of the larger endogenously estimated coefficients except (15, 15) have relatively small proportional variances.

It would be interesting to use Table 4 to compute the probabilities with which errors in input–output coefficient estimates would lead to specified errors in gross output estimates from given (net) final demands. A study by Berman[9] suggests that, for the bulk of coefficients, even quite large errors may be 'unimportant' in the sense that they would not lead to unacceptable errors in gross output estimates of this kind. This conclusion is in turn supported by Evans's theoretical study[29] of the effect on the 'Leontief inverse' $(I-L)^{-1}$ of errors in an input–output matrix L. But the exercise would be academic, as the Table 2 estimate is not intended to be used to provide gross output estimates. The question would be pertinent for a projection of Table 2 to a later year—but for such a projection we have no way of determining the joint distribution of coefficients.

3   INPUT–OUTPUT ESTIMATES: FRIEDLANDER ESTIMATION

Table 6 shows a 'quasi-Friedlander' estimate of an input–output matrix for Britain in 1960. By this is meant an estimate part of which is exogenous—and the same as the exogenous part of Table 2—and the remainder of which is a Friedlander estimate obtained from the endogenous part of the 1954 matrix and the 1960 transaction marginals modified exactly as in getting the 'quasi-biproportional' estimate in Table 2.

The rank correlation coefficient of the r's of the quasi-biproportional estimate and the x's of the quasi-Friedlander estimate has the extremely high value of 0·9964. Effectively, it makes no difference whether we take the r's or the x's as giving the ordering of 'substitution effects'.

Table 6. Quasi-Friedlander estimate of input–output matrix for Britain in 1960. x, y. Intermediate input ratios

Industry	i	x_i	j 1	2	3	4	5	6	7	8	9	10	11
		y_j	-1·081	-0·679	-0·622	-0·502	-0·341	-0·392	-0·205	-0·807	-0·720	-0·773	-0·698
Agriculture, etc.	1	0	-0·001	—	—	0·088	0·021	—	—	0·001	—	—	—
Coal	2	-0·031	-0·001	—	0·006	0·002	0·004	[0·524]	—	0·003	[0·005]	[0·003]	0·001
Mining n.e.s.	3	-0·671	-0·001	—	0·003	0·001	0·036	—	0·024	0·010	0·001	—	0·029
Food processing	4	1·141	0·193	—	—	0·128	[0·018]	—	—	0·012	—	—	—
Drink, tobacco	5	-0·257	—	—	—	—	—	—	—	—	—	—	—
Coke ovens, etc.	6	0·331	—	—	0·004	—	0·005	0·082	0·029	0·013	0·038	[0·006]	0·001
Mineral oil refining	7	0·525	0·015	0·014	0·012	0·002	0·013	—	0·083	0·015	[0·013]	—	0·002
Chemicals n.e.s.	8	0·961	0·070	0·036	0·028	0·074	—	0·006	0·035	0·284	0·009	0·007	—
Iron, steel (primary)	9	0·818	—	—	0·001	—	—	—	—	—	0·344	0·392	—
Iron, steel (secondary)	10	0·973	—	—	—	0·003	—	—	—	0·004	—	0·122	—
Nonferrous metals	11	0·866	—	—	—	0·001	0·005	—	—	0·016	0·006	0·038	0·225
Engineering, electrical	12	0·853	0·019	0·043	0·052	0·016	0·023	0·006	0·014	0·021	0·022	0·012	0·012
Shipbuilding, etc.	13	0·323	0·001	—	—	—	—	—	—	—	—	—	—
Motors, cycles	14	0·674	0·005	—	0·004	0·001	—	—	—	—	—	—	—
Aircraft	15	2·098	—	—	—	—	—	—	—	—	—	—	—
Locomotives, etc.	16	0·327	—	—	—	—	—	—	—	—	—	—	—
Metal goods n.e.s.	17	1·042	0·025	0·010	0·004	0·023	0·026	—	0·009	0·028	0·017	0·003	0·001
Textiles	18	1·118	0·006	0·007	0·002	0·010	—	—	—	0·008	—	0·001	0·001
Leather, clothing	19	0·252	—	0·001	—	—	—	—	—	—	—	—	—
Building materials	20	0·654	0·002	0·003	—	—	—	—	0·006	0·003	0·008	—	0·002
Pottery, glass	21	0·617	—	—	—	0·007	0·020	0·001	—	0·007	—	—	—
Timber, furniture, etc.	22	1·120	0·002	0·020	0·006	0·006	0·023	—	—	0·007	0·001	0·005	0·001
Paper, publishing	23	0·788	0·001	0·001	0·014	0·036	0·036	—	—	0·023	—	0·001	—
Other manufacturing	24	1·211	0·009	0·021	0·003	—	—	—	—	0·004	—	—	—
Construction	25	0·829	0·025	0·035	0·006	0·004	0·007	—	0·006	0·004	0·003	0·005	0·001
Gas	26	0·590	0·004	—	—	0·003	0·005	0·071	—	0·002	0·010	0·004	0·004
Electricity	27	1·135	0·004	0·022	0·018	0·007	0·001	0·007	0·012	0·019	0·014	0·011	0·016
Water	28	-0·120	—	—	—	—	—	—	0·001	—	—	—	—
Transport, communications	29	0·881	0·060	0·030	0·198	0·074	0·052	0·131	0·017	0·055	0·055	0·021	0·039
Distribution	30	0·718	0·024	0·015	0·036	0·028	0·025	0·052	0·004	0·016	0·037	0·009	0·040
Services n.e.s.	31	1·257	0·056	0·032	0·054	0·105	0·094	0·035	0·032	0·093	0·052	0·045	0·092
Intermediate input ratio			0·519	0·290	0·450	0·621	0·415	0·915	0·272	0·645	0·636	0·685	0·468

A dash represents an element less than 0·0005 in absolute value.   Square brackets indicate an exogenous element. Intermediate input ratios may differ from column sums because of rounding errors.   *Source:* (intermediate input ratios), [26].

Table 6 (continued)

i	Industry	x_i	$j \dots$ 12 $y_j \dots$ -0.882	13 -0.889	14 -0.980	15 -1.692	16 -0.179	17 -0.826	18 -0.960	19 -0.876	20 -0.885	21 -0.809
1	Agriculture, etc.	0	—	—	—	—	—	—	—	0.002	—	—
2	Coal	-0.031	—	—	—	—	—	—	—	—	[0.047]	[0.017]
3	Mining n.e.s.	-0.671	0.002	—	—	—	0.002	0.001	—	—	0.042	0.030
4	Food processing	1.141	—	—	—	—	—	—	—	—	—	—
5	Drink, tobacco	-0.257	—	—	—	-0.001	—	—	—	—	—	—
6	Coke ovens, etc.	0.331	—	—	—	—	—	0.001	—	—	0.002	—
7	Mineral oil refining	0.525	0.001	0.001	0.001	-0.001	0.001	0.002	0.001	0.001	[0.021]	[0.031]
8	Chemicals n.e.s.	0.961	0.021	0.013	0.025	0.001	0.011	0.008	0.025	0.005	0.025	0.051
9	Iron, steel (primary)	0.818	0.078	0.089	0.110	0.004	0.211	0.130	—	—	0.007	—
10	Iron, steel (secondary)	0.973	0.007	0.009	0.005	—	0.014	0.049	—	—	—	—
11	Nonferrous metals	0.866	0.055	0.015	0.025	0.008	0.047	0.093	0.001	—	0.001	—
12	Engineering, electrical	0.853	0.155	0.079	0.060	0.009	0.052	0.014	0.018	0.009	0.029	0.037
13	Shipbuilding, etc.	0.323	—	0.111	—	—	—	—	—	—	—	—
14	Motors, cycles	0.674	—	—	0.147	—	—	—	—	—	—	0.002
15	Aircraft	2.098	—	—	—	0.395	—	—	—	—	—	—
16	Locomotives, etc.	0.327	—	—	—	—	0.053	—	—	—	—	—
17	Metal goods, etc.	1.042	0.056	0.058	0.126	0.010	0.058	0.159	0.003	0.024	0.010	0.015
18	Textiles	1.118	0.009	0.005	0.013	0.001	0.008	0.003	0.439	0.348	0.006	—
19	Leather, clothing	0.252	—	—	0.001	—	0.001	—	0.001	0.060	—	—
20	Building materials	0.654	0.003	0.003	0.003	—	0.001	0.001	—	—	0.053	0.008
21	Pottery, glass	0.617	0.006	—	0.003	—	0.001	0.003	—	—	—	0.045
22	Timber, furniture, etc.	1.120	0.012	0.021	0.016	0.001	0.016	0.013	0.002	0.007	0.006	0.015
23	Paper, publishing	0.788	0.009	0.001	0.002	0.001	—	0.005	0.001	0.008	0.043	0.011
24	Other manufacturing	1.211	0.009	0.001	0.058	0.001	0.010	0.014	0.001	0.028	0.003	0.001
25	Construction	0.829	0.004	0.004	0.003	—	0.003	0.002	0.004	0.004	0.001	0.005
26	Gas	0.590	0.003	0.001	0.002	—	0.003	0.005	0.001	0.001	0.001	0.015
27	Electricity	1.135	0.008	0.007	0.007	-0.003	0.008	0.009	0.007	0.004	0.026	0.023
28	Water	-0.120	—	—	—	-0.001	—	—	—	—	—	—
29	Transport, communications	0.881	0.030	0.012	0.020	-0.002	0.015	0.035	0.025	0.030	0.060	0.043
30	Distribution	0.718	0.010	0.006	0.010	—	0.006	0.012	0.021	0.015	0.025	0.018
31	Services n.e.s.	1.257	0.054	0.062	0.079	0.022	0.073	0.073	0.047	0.088	0.126	0.088
	Intermediate input ratio		0.529	0.493	0.714	0.455	0.596	0.634	0.597	0.635	0.537	0.453

Table 6 (continued)

Industry	i	y_j … x_i	22	23	24	25	26	27	28	29	30	31
j … / y_j			−0·996	−0·0795	−0·862	−0·646	−0·764	−1·243	−0·744	−0·627	−0·435	−0·288
Agriculture	1	0	—	—	—	—	—	—	—	—	—	—
Coal	2	−0·031	—	[0·010]	0·001	—	—	—	0·003	0·013	0·003	0·004
Mining n.e.s.	3	−0·671	—	0·002	0·002	0·010	[0·286]	[0·241]	—	0·001	—	—
Food processing	4	1·141	—	0·001	—	—	—	—	—	0·005	—	—
Drink, tobacco	5	−0·257	—	—	—	—	—	—	—	—	—	—
Coke ovens, etc.	6	0·331	—	[0·005]	0·002	0·001	[0·026]	[0·061]	0·001	0·005	0·003	0·003
Mineral oil refining	7	0·525	0·001	0·035	0·001	0·006	0·014	0·004	0·008	0·022	0·009	—
Chemicals n.e.s.	8	0·961	0·014	—	0·107	0·034	0·017	0·002	0·028	0·007	0·008	0·003
Iron, steel (primary)	9	0·818	—	—	0·004	0·039	0·018	0·002	0·046	0·007	—	—
Iron, steel (secondary)	10	0·973	—	0·001	0·003	0·015	0·001	0·001	0·007	—	—	—
Nonferrous metals	11	0·866	—	0·005	0·001	0·022	0·037	0·039	0·004	—	—	—
Engineering, electrical	12	0·853	0·009	0·020	0·021	0·034	0·001	—	0·008	0·010	0·004	0·024
Shipbuilding, etc.	13	0·323	—	—	—	—	—	—	—	0·025	—	—
Motors, cycles	14	0·674	0·001	—	0·002	0·002	—	—	—	0·017	0·015	0·009
Aircraft	15	2·098	—	—	—	—	—	—	—	0·010	—	—
Locomotives, etc.	16	0·327	—	—	—	—	0·009	0·003	—	0·029	—	—
Metal goods n.e.s.	17	1·042	0·032	0·004	0·015	0·027	0·001	—	0·001	—	0·003	0·007
Textiles	18	1·118	0·061	0·011	0·138	0·001	—	—	—	0·006	0·025	0·002
Leather, clothing	19	0·252	0·001	0·001	0·001	0·001	0·007	0·003	—	0·001	—	0·001
Building materials	20	0·654	—	—	0·002	0·101	—	0·003	0·004	—	0·001	0·001
Pottery, glass	21	0·617	0·004	0·002	0·011	0·011	—	0·003	—	—	—	—
Timber, furniture, etc.	22	1·120	0·166	—	0·016	0·028	—	0·001	—	—	0·007	0·002
Paper, publishing	23	0·788	0·001	0·244	0·025	0·007	0·003	0·001	0·002	0·002	0·018	0·122
Other manufacturing	24	1·211	0·015	0·003	0·089	0·003	—	0·003	—	0·014	0·012	0·004
Construction	25	0·829	0·001	0·004	0·005	0·135	0·002	0·001	0·004	0·049	0·003	0·003
Gas	26	0·590	—	0·001	0·001	—	0·018	—	0·001	0·001	0·018	—
Electricity	27	1·135	0·007	0·007	0·014	0·001	0·005	0·010	0·040	0·006	0·024	0·015
Water	28	−0·120	—	—	—	—	—	−0·001	0·004	—	0·002	0·001
Transport, communications	29	0·881	0·035	0·044	0·031	0·033	0·078	0·046	0·018	0·039	0·007	0·005
Distribution	30	0·718	0·023	0·022	0·015	0·012	0·023	0·011	0·002	0·004	0·001	0·001
Services n.e.s.	31	1·257	0·069	0·096	0·061	0·055	0·039	0·045	0·032	0·015	0·007	0·022
Intermediate input ratio			0·441	0·517	0·558	0·577	0·586	0·477	0·214	0·289	0·170	0·240

A dash represents an element less than 0·0005 in absolute value. Square brackets indicate an exogenous element. Intermediate input ratios may differ from column sums because of rounding errors. *Source:* (intermediate input ratios), [26].

Table 6 illustrates the property of Friedlander estimates which was our main reason for rejecting them in favour of biproportional ones—namely, that their nonnegativity is not assured. On the other hand, the negative elements of Table 6 are few and are all very small. Little adjustment of the table would be needed to make it nonnegative and so satisfy all our *a priori* requirements—nonnegativity, zero preservation, and proximity to the matrix observed at $t = 0$.

The effective nonnegativity of Table 6 is a consequence of its closeness to the biproportional—and therefore nonnegative—estimate in Table 2. This closeness—which is manifest on inspection—is in turn attributable to the directional closeness of (u, v) to the marginals of the constant-coefficient transactions matrix $L\langle q \rangle$. In section 4 of Chapter 6 we saw that this directional closeness made the Friedlander estimate approximate the biproportional one. In these circumstances the similarity of the ranking of the r_i's and x_i's causes no surprise.

4   INPUT–OUTPUT ESTIMATES: TWO-STAGE ESTIMATION

In Chapter 8 it was shown that an input–output coefficients or transactions matrix at $t = 1$ generated from the corresponding matrix at $t = 0$ by a (one-stage) biproportional transformation is in general falsely estimated by the two-stage biproportional type of estimate described in that chapter. Conversely, we showed that if the $t = 1$ matrix is generated from the $t = 0$ matrix by a certain two-stage biproportional type transformation, it is in general falsely estimated by the usual (one-stage) biproportional estimate. These results are illustrated in the next tables, which follow a six-order industrial classification. The tables are not based on actual figures. Major statistical work would be needed to make use of, say, the 1954 British input–output matrix. The main difficulty is that one industry may produce, in unknown proportions, products belonging to different 'input classes': e.g. the engineering and electrical goods industry produces both material inputs and current account equipment items.

Table 7 shows the input–output transactions matrix Z at $t = 0$. Table 8 shows a (one-stage) biproportional transform $\langle r \rangle Z \langle s \rangle$ of Z into a 'true' transactions matrix at $t = 1$, and Table 9 an aggregation of this transform according to the three input classes $\{1\}, \{2, 3\}, \{4, 5, 6\}$.

Table 10 shows the biproportional adjustment to the marginals of Table 9 of the corresponding aggregation of Z: the row multipliers in this biproportionality are interpretable as substitution effects between input classes. Finally Table 11 shows the partitions of the two-stage biproportional estimate of Table 8, each of which is a biproportional adjustment of a partition of Z to a partition of u and a row of Table 10: in each of these biproportionalities the row-multipliers are interpretable as substitution effects within an input class.

Table 12 shows a biproportional transform of the aggregation of Z, and the partitions of Table 13 are biproportional transforms of the partitions of Z whose column sums are the rows of Table 12. Table 13 is then a 'true' transactions matrix for $t = 1$ that is a two-stage biproportional transform of Z. Finally, Table 14 shows the (one-stage) biproportional adjustment of Z to the marginals of Table 13.

Table 7. Transactions matrix Z at $t = 0$

	1	2	3	4	5	6
1	10	37·5	50	–	–	30
2	20	7·5	50	1	10	30
3	10	–	–	40	–	–
4	30	–	–	60	10	60
5	–	45	25	–	–	15
6	10	15	25	70	20	45

A dash indicates a zero element.

Table 8. One-stage biproportional transform of Z

		1	2	3	4	5	6
	col. mult. ... 1·1 row mult.	0·8	1·0	1·2	1·1	0·9	
1	1·0	11·0	30·0	50·0	–	–	27·0
2	1·1	24·2	6·6	55·0	1·32	12·1	29·7
3	0·6	6·6	–	–	28·8	–	–
4	1·6	52·8	–	–	115·2	17·6	86·4
5	1·3	–	46·8	32·5	–	–	17·55
6	0·9	9·9	10·8	22·5	75·6	19·8	36·45

A dash indicates a zero element.

Table 9. Aggregation of Table 8

	1	2	3	4	5	6	row sums
1	11·0	30·0	50·0	–	–	27·0	118·0
2, 3	30·8	6·6	55·0	30·12	12·1	29·7	164·32
4, 5, 6	62·7	57·6	55·0	190·8	37·4	140·4	543·9
column sums	104·5	94·2	160·0	220·92	49·5	197·1	

A dash indicates a zero element.

Table 10. *Adjustment $Z^{①}$ of aggregation of Table 7 to marginals of Table 9*

		1	2	3	4	5	6
	b ...	1·18	0·79	1·00	1·09	1·05	0·94
	a						
1	0·99	11·63	29·07	49·46	–	–	27·84
2, 3	0·94	33·26	5·54	47·15	41·98	9·84	26·54
4, 5, 6	1·26	59·61	59·59	63·38	178·94	39·66	142·71

A dash indicates a zero element.

Table 11. *Partitions of two-stage biproportional estimate $Z^{②}$ of Table 8*

		1	2	3	4	5	6
	col. mult. 1·0	1·0	1·0	1·0	1·0	1·0	1·0
	row mult.						
1	1·0	11·63	29·07	49·46	–	–	27·84
	col. mult. 0·94	0·44	0·56	4·86	0·58	0·52	
2	1·69	31·63	5·54	47·15	8·21	9·84	26·54
3	0·17	1·63	–	–	33·77	–	–
	col. mult. 0·97	0·92	1·24	1·06	1·11	0·88	
4	1·74	50·67	–	–	110·61	19·26	91·46
5	1·13	–	46·91	35·00	–	–	14·93
6	0·92	8·94	12·68	28·38	68·33	20·40	36·32

A dash indicates a zero element.

Table 12. *Biproportional transform $Z^{①}$ of aggregation of Z*

		1	2	3	4	5	6
	β ...	1·2	0·8	1·0	1·1	1·0	0·9
	α						
1	0·95	11·4	28·5	47·5	–	–	25·65
2, 3	0·90	32·4	5·4	45·0	40·59	9·0	24·3
4, 5, 6	1·20	57·6	57·6	60·0	171·6	36·0	129·6

A dash indicates a zero element.

Table 13. *Partitions of two-stage biproportional transform* $Z^{②}$ *of* Z (*biproportional transforms of partitions of* Z *whose column sums are the rows of Table* 12)

		1	2	3	4	5	6
	row mult.						
1	1·0	11·4	28·5	47·5	–	–	25·65
2	1·1	24·58	5·4	45·0	1·534	9·0	24·3
3	0·7	7·82	–	–	39·06	–	–
4	1·6	48·51	–	–	103·61	16·94	81·32
5	1·1	–	45·26	33·0	–	–	13·98
6	0·9	9·10	12·34	27·0	67·99	19·06	34·31

A dash indicates a zero element.

Table 14. (*One-stage*) *biproportional estimate of* $Z^{②}$

		1	2	3	4	5	6
	$s \dots$	1·11	0·84	1·05	1·12	1·06	0·87
r							
1	0·93	10·39	29·29	48·98	–	–	24·40
2	0·92	20·57	5·80	48·48	1·04	9·77	24·16
3	0·84	9·32	–	–	37·56	–	–
4	1·53	51·12	–	–	103·00	16·20	80·06
5	1·57	–	45·13	31·44	–	–	15·67
6	0·90	10·01	11·29	23·60	70·60	19·03	35·27

A dash indicates a zero element.

It was pointed out in Chapter 8 that a drawback of two-stage estimation is that an estimate of this type may fail to exist while a one-stage one does. Our example of Table 8 depicts a situation in which the two-stage estimate $Z^{②}$ (Table 11) exists by a hair's breadth. This is revealed in Table 11 by the very low and very high values respectively of the second-stage row and column multiplier of element $(3, 4)$. The second partition of Table 11, which contains this element, is the biproportional adjustment of

$$\begin{bmatrix} 20 & 7·5 & 50 & 1 & 10 & 30 \\ 10 & – & – & 40 & – & – \end{bmatrix}$$

to row sums $(128·92, 35·4)$ and column sums $(33·26, 5·54, 47·15, 41·98, 9·84, 26·54)$. If element $(2, 4)$ vanished instead of equalling 1 the conditions of Theorem 3 would be violated, as $41·98 > 35·4$, and no solution would exist. As things are, the solution forces element $(2, 4)$ of $Z^{②}$ much too high. The outcome is that the two-stage estimate $Z^{②}$ is a considerably worse estimate of the one-stage generated matrix shown in Table 8 than the one-stage estimate in Table 14 is of the two-stage generated matrix $Z^{②}$ in Table 13. It is apparent from inspection, moreover, that substantial errors in $Z^{②}$ are not confined to the second partition.

5   INPUT–OUTPUT PROJECTIONS

Table 15 shows a 'quasi-exponential' projection of Tables 1 and 2: that is, its part corresponding to the exogenous part of Table 2 is projected independently and an element l_{ij}^P of the remaining part is given by $l_{ij}^P = r_i^2 s_j^2 l_{ij}$, where the r_i's and s_j's are those of Table 2. The exogenous projections are taken from [26].

Table 16 shows a 'quasi-linear' projection of Tables 1 and 2. In this projection an endogenous element l_{ij}^P is given by $l_{ij}^P = (2r_i s_j - 1) l_{ij}$.

Table 17 shows a projection whose endogenous part is obtained by the method settled on in Chapter 9. That is, it is the 'nearest' matrix to the endogenous part of Table 15 whose columns sum to prescribed numbers. These numbers are the endogenous components of 'sigmoid' projections of the intermediate input ratios appearing in Tables 1 and 2. These sigmoid projections are given by the method based on the normal distribution function described in section 4 of Chapter 9, with upper bounds of one for all intermediate input ratios.

Tables 15 and 16 exhibit the properties which led us, in Chapter 9, to reject both exponential and linear projections: the 'explosive' effect of exponential projection on the column sums of Table 15 is seen both from the excess over unity of those of industries 6 and 16 and the reversal of a downward movement between 1954 and 1960 (see Tables 1, 2) in those of industries 5, 19, 20, 22, 28 and 29. Table 16 contains negative elements which, unlike those in the Friedlander estimate for 1960, are not negligible: the most serious are in row 2 (Coal) and column 15 (Aircraft). Two diagonal elements, (19, 19) (intra-Leather, clothing) and (28, 28) (intra-Water), are also large and negative.

6   THE MARKOV TRAINING MODEL

In this last section we shall give an illustrative numerical example of Chapter 10's problem of reshaping a Markovian adult educational structure so as to supply a desired distribution of labour skills asymptotically. Table 18 gives a classification of labour into grades and a matrix A representing the effects of a given educational structure over a unit time period of one year. Thus under the initial régime 90 % of the unskilled workers in a batch remain unskilled after one year's training, 5 % have

Table 15. Quasi-exponential projection of input–output matrix for Britain in 1966. Intermediate input ratios

i	Industry	j…1	2	3	4	5	6	7	8	9	10	11	12	13	14	15	16
1	Agriculture, etc.	0·001	–	–	0·038	0·009	–	–	–	[0·002]	[0·002]	–	–	–	–	–	–
2	Coal	–	–	0·002	0·001	0·001	[0·535]	–	0·001	0·001	–	0·028	0·001	–	–	–	0·001
3	Mining n.e.s.	0·184	–	0·003	0·001	–	–	0·043	0·009	–	–	–	–	–	–	–	–
4	Food processing	–	–	–	0·228	0·074	–	–	–	–	–	–	–	–	–	–	–
5	Drink, tobacco	–	–	–	–	[0·021]	–	–	0·016	–	–	–	–	–	–	–	–
6	Coke ovens, etc.	–	–	0·002	–	–	0·064	0·029	0·009	0·026	–	–	–	–	–	–	–
7	Mineral oil refining	0·010	–	0·010	0·002	0·005	–	0·116	0·012	[0·013]	[0·005]	–	–	–	–	–	0·001
8	Chemicals n.e.s.	0·060	0·018	0·039	0·110	0·022	0·011	0·092	0·323	0·011	0·009	0·001	0·022	0·013	0·024	0·001	0·020
9	Iron, steel (primary)	–	0·041	0·001	–	–	–	–	–	0·372	0·408	–	0·073	0·078	0·094	0·004	0·333
10	Iron, steel (secondary)	–	–	–	0·004	–	–	–	0·004	0·006	0·148	–	0·007	0·009	0·005	–	0·027
11	Nonferrous metals	–	–	–	0·002	0·007	–	0·032	0·016	0·024	0·041	0·260	0·054	0·013	0·022	0·006	0·078
12	Engineering, electrical	0·015	0·050	0·062	0·021	0·033	0·009	–	0·021	–	0·013	0·013	0·150	0·071	0·053	0·007	0·085
13	Shipbuilding, etc.	0·001	–	–	–	–	–	–	–	–	–	–	–	0·061	–	–	–
14	Motors, cycles	0·003	–	0·004	0·001	–	–	–	–	–	–	–	–	–	0·109	–	–
15	Aircraft	–	–	–	–	–	–	–	–	–	–	–	–	–	–	0·453	–
16	Locomotives, etc.	–	–	–	–	–	–	–	–	–	–	–	–	–	–	–	0·045
17	Metal goods n.e.s.	0·022	0·013	0·006	0·037	0·047	–	0·026	0·034	0·023	0·003	0·002	0·064	0·061	0·129	0·005	0·120
18	Textiles	0·006	0·011	0·002	0·017	–	–	–	0·010	0·008	0·002	0·002	0·011	0·006	0·014	0·001	0·018
19	Leather, clothing	–	–	–	–	–	–	0·010	–	–	–	–	–	–	–	–	–
20	Building materials	0·001	0·003	–	0·007	0·022	–	–	0·002	0·008	–	0·002	0·003	–	0·003	–	0·002
21	Pottery, glass	–	–	–	0·011	0·045	0·001	–	0·006	–	–	–	0·005	–	0·002	–	0·002
22	Timber, furniture, etc.	0·002	0·030	0·009	0·044	0·050	–	–	0·008	0·002	0·007	–	0·015	0·023	0·017	–	0·035
23	Paper, publishing	0·001	0·001	0·016	–	–	–	–	0·022	–	0·001	0·002	0·009	0·001	0·001	0·001	–
24	Other manufacturing	0·009	0·035	0·005	–	–	–	–	0·006	–	–	–	0·012	0·002	0·066	–	0·025
25	Construction	0·020	0·040	0·007	0·005	0·011	–	0·014	0·004	0·004	0·006	0·001	0·004	0·003	0·002	–	0·005
26	Gas	0·003	–	–	0·003	–	0·082	–	0·001	0·010	0·004	0·004	0·002	0·001	0·002	–	0·003
27	Electricity	0·004	0·031	0·028	0·011	0·010	0·014	0·036	0·023	0·020	0·014	0·023	0·009	0·008	0·007	0·001	0·017
28	Water	–	–	–	–	–	–	–	–	–	–	–	–	–	–	–	–
29	Transport, communications	0·048	0·036	0·249	0·101	0·080	0·209	0·040	0·058	0·063	0·023	0·047	0·028	0·011	0·018	0·001	0·026
30	Distribution	0·017	0·014	0·038	0·031	0·030	0·066	0·007	0·015	0·036	0·008	0·039	0·009	0·005	0·008	–	0·008
31	Services n.e.s.	0·056	0·052	0·094	0·201	0·207	0·081	0·116	0·131	0·083	0·067	0·150	0·071	0·075	0·091	0·009	0·185
	Intermediate input ratio	0·464	0·375	0·579	0·875	0·672	1·072	0·562	0·732	0·703	0·761	0·575	0·549	0·441	0·669	0·490	1·038

A dash represents an element less than 0·0005. Square brackets distinguish exogenously projected elements. Intermediate input ratios may differ from column sums because of rounding errors.

Table 15 (*continued*)

Industry	$i \backslash j$	17	18	19	20	21	22	23	24	25	26	27	28	29	30	31
Agriculture, etc.	1	–	–	0·002	–	–	0·002	–	–	–	–	–	–	–	–	–
Coal	2	–	0·001	–	0·018	0·006	–	0·004	–	–	[0·178]	[0·228]	0·001	0·003	0·001	0·001
Mining n.e.s.	3	0·001	–	–	0·035	0·024	–	0·002	0·001	0·010	–	0·001	0·001	0·001	–	–
Food processing	4	–	0·001	–	–	–	–	0·002	–	–	–	–	–	0·007	–	–
Drink, tobacco	5	–	–	–	–	–	–	–	–	–	–	–	–	–	–	–
Coke ovens, etc.	6	–	–	–	0·001	–	–	–	0·001	–	–	0·003	–	0·003	0·002	0·003
Mineral oil refining	7	0·002	–	–	0·031	0·035	0·001	0·004	0·001	0·005	[0·072]	[0·036]	0·006	0·019	0·008	0·008
Chemicals n.e.s.	8	0·009	0·025	0·006	0·026	0·052	0·013	0·041	0·117	0·046	0·017	0·003	0·033	0·009	0·008	0·012
Iron, steel (primary)	9	0·130	–	–	0·007	–	0·001	–	0·004	0·044	0·017	0·001	0·047	0·008	0·012	0·007
Iron, steel (secondary)	10	0·057	–	–	–	–	–	–	–	0·020	0·022	0·001	0·009	–	–	–
Nonferrous metals	11	0·095	0·001	–	0·001	0·034	–	0·001	0·004	0·026	0·001	–	0·005	0·011	0·006	0·040
Engineering, electrical	12	0·015	0·016	0·008	0·028	–	0·008	0·006	0·001	0·040	0·039	0·025	0·008	0·014	0·013	0·011
Shipbuilding, etc.	13	–	–	–	–	–	–	–	0·020	0·002	–	–	–	–	–	–
Motors, cycles	14	0·001	0·001	–	0·001	0·001	0·001	–	–	–	–	–	–	0·015	0·016	0·011
Aircraft	15	–	–	–	–	–	–	–	–	–	–	–	–	0·077	–	–
Locomotives, etc.	16	–	–	–	–	–	–	–	–	–	–	–	–	0·021	–	–
Metal goods n.e.s.	17	0·195	0·003	0·028	0·012	0·016	0·033	0·005	0·016	0·038	0·011	0·002	–	–	0·011	0·004
Textiles	18	0·003	0·499	0·428	0·008	–	0·066	0·014	0·174	0·002	0·002	0·002	–	0·009	–	0·010
Leather, clothing	19	–	–	0·023	–	–	0·001	–	–	–	–	0·002	–	–	–	0·005
Building materials	20	0·001	–	–	0·044	0·001	–	–	0·002	0·100	0·006	0·002	0·003	–	–	0·013
Pottery, glass	21	0·003	–	–	–	0·034	0·003	–	–	0·010	–	0·002	–	–	–	0·033
Timber, furniture, etc.	22	0·017	0·002	–	0·007	0·017	0·176	0·001	0·003	0·043	–	0·002	–	0·003	0·018	0·004
Paper, publishing	23	0·005	0·001	–	0·040	0·010	0·001	0·245	0·020	0·008	0·003	0·001	0·002	0·024	0·023	0·188
Other manufacturing	24	0·019	0·004	0·009	0·003	0·002	0·017	0·004	0·024	0·005	–	0·002	–	0·057	0·025	0·010
Construction	25	0·002	0·001	0·008	0·001	0·004	–	0·004	0·118	0·160	0·002	0·001	0·005	0·001	–	0·005
Gas	26	0·005	0·004	0·036	0·001	0·012	–	0·001	0·005	–	0·016	–	0·001	0·009	0·021	0·058
Electricity	27	0·011	0·008	0·004	0·030	0·026	0·007	0·009	0·017	0·002	0·007	0·007	0·052	0·047	0·043	0·033
Water	28	–	0·008	0·001	–	–	–	–	–	–	–	–	–	–	0·002	0·047
Transport, communications	29	0·037	0·023	0·030	0·059	0·041	0·032	0·047	0·031	0·041	0·087	0·030	0·020	0·047	0·004	0·025
Distribution	30	0·011	0·017	0·013	0·021	0·015	0·018	0·020	0·013	0·012	0·021	0·007	0·002	0·004	0·002	0·015
Services n.e.s.	31	0·103	0·056	0·115	0·163	0·110	0·079	0·139	0·082	0·093	0·058	0·033	0·047	0·025	0·015	0·056
Intermediate input ratio		0·720	0·661	0·716	0·538	0·447	0·459	0·569	0·656	0·709	0·562	0·385	0·245	0·368	0·255	0·403

A dash represents an element less than 0·0005.   Square brackets distinguish exogenously projected elements. Intermediate input ratios may differ from column sums because of rounding errors.

Table 16. Quasi-linear projection of input–output matrix for Britain in 1966

Industry	i	j … 1	2	3	4	5	6	7	8	9	10	11
Agriculture, etc.	1	-0.008	—	—	-0.014	0.001	—	—	-0.001	[0.002]	[0.002]	-0.002
Coal	2	-0.005	—	-0.006	-0.002	-0.002	[0.535]	—	-0.008	0.001	—	-0.028
Mining, n.e.s.	3	0.184	—	0.003	0.001	—	—	0.034	-0.009	—	—	—
Food processing	4	—	—	—	0.189	0.057	—	—	-0.015	0.018	—	—
Drink, tobacco	5	—	—	—	-0.001	[0.021]	—	—	-0.001	[0.013]	[0.005]	—
Coke ovens, etc.	6	—	—	0.002	—	—	—	—	0.005	0.010	0.008	0.001
Mineral oil refining	7	-0.004	0.017	0.010	0.002	0.005	—	0.028	0.010	—	—	—
Chemicals n.e.s.	8	0.058	0.040	0.036	0.099	0.018	0.062	0.102	0.318	—	—	—
Iron, steel (primary)	9	—	—	0.001	—	—	0.009	0.061	—	0.369	0.407	—
Iron, steel (secondary)	10	—	—	—	0.004	—	—	—	—	—	0.143	—
Nonferrous metals	11	—	—	—	-0.002	0.006	—	—	-0.004	0.006	0.041	0.255
Engineering, electrical	12	0.014	0.049	0.060	0.020	0.029	0.008	0.023	0.016	0.024	0.013	0.013
Shipbuilding, etc.	13	-0.001	—	—	—	—	—	—	0.021	—	—	—
Motors, cycles	14	-0.002	—	0.004	0.001	—	—	—	—	—	—	—
Aircraft	15	—	—	—	—	—	—	—	—	—	—	—
Locomotives, etc.	16	—	—	—	—	—	—	—	—	—	—	—
Metal goods n.e.s.	17	0.022	0.012	0.006	0.032	0.038	—	0.016	0.033	0.022	0.003	0.002
Textiles	18	0.006	0.010	0.002	0.014	—	—	—	0.010	—	0.002	0.002
Leather, clothing	19	—	—	—	—	—	—	—	—	—	—	—
Building materials	20	0.001	0.003	—	—	—	—	0.008	0.002	0.008	—	0.002
Pottery, glass	21	—	—	—	0.006	0.021	0.001	—	0.006	—	—	—
Timber, furniture, etc.	22	0.002	0.027	0.008	0.009	0.036	—	—	0.008	0.002	0.007	0.002
Paper, publishing	23	0.001	0.001	0.015	0.042	0.046	—	—	0.022	—	0.001	—
Other manufacturing	24	0.009	0.030	0.005	—	—	—	—	0.005	—	—	—
Construction	25	0.018	0.039	0.007	0.005	0.010	—	0.010	0.004	0.004	0.006	0.001
Gas	26	0.002	—	—	0.003	—	0.081	—	0.001	0.009	0.004	0.004
Electricity	27	0.004	0.028	0.025	0.009	0.008	0.011	0.022	0.022	0.018	0.013	0.020
Water	28	-0.001	—	—	—	—	—	—	-0.001	—	—	—
Transport, communications	29	0.045	0.035	0.239	0.093	0.070	0.183	0.028	0.058	0.062	0.023	0.045
Distribution	30	0.013	0.014	0.037	0.030	0.029	0.063	0.006	0.014	0.036	0.008	0.039
Services n.e.s.	31	0.055	0.044	0.078	0.160	0.152	0.059	0.065	0.119	0.072	0.059	0.129
Intermediate input ratio		0.425	0.350	0.533	0.705	0.524	0.477	0.401	0.692	0.662	0.739	0.543

A dash represents an element less than 0·0005 in absolute value. Square brackets distinguish exogenously projected elements. Intermediate input ratios may differ from column sums because of rounding errors.

Table 16 (continued)

Industry	i	j … 12	13	14	15	16	17	18	19	20	21
Agriculture, etc.	1	–	–	–	–	–	–	-0·001	-0·005	–	–
Coal	2	0·002	-0·001	-0·002	-0·002	-0·001	-0·001	-0·006	-0·001	[0·018]	[0·006]
Mining n.e.s.	3	0·001	–	–	–	–	–	0·001	–	0·033	0·023
Food processing	4	–	–	–	–	–	–	–	–	–	–
Drink, tobacco	5	–	–	–	–	–	–	–	–	–	–
Coke ovens, etc.	6	–	–	–	–	–	–	–	–	–	–
Mineral oil refining	7	0·001	–	–	-0·003	–	0·001	–	–	[0·031]	[0·035]
Chemicals n.e.s.	8	0·022	0·012	0·024	-0·001	0·016	0·009	0·025	0·006	0·026	0·052
Iron, steel (primary)	9	0·073	0·077	0·092	-0·011	0·286	0·129	–	–	0·007	–
Iron, steel (secondary)	10	0·007	0·009	0·005	–	0·022	0·056	–	–	–	–
Nonferrous metals	11	0·054	0·013	0·022	-0·014	0·066	0·095	0·001	–	0·001	0·034
Engineering, electrical	12	0·150	0·071	0·052	-0·018	0·072	0·015	0·016	0·008	0·028	–
Shipbuilding, etc.	13	–	-0·006	–	–	–	–	–	–	–	–
Motors, cycles	14	–	–	0·092	-0·002	–	–	–	–	–	–
Aircraft	15	–	–	–	0·432	–	–	–	–	–	0·001
Locomotives, etc.	16	–	–	–	–	0·045	–	–	–	–	–
Metal goods n.e.s.	17	0·063	0·061	0·129	-0·005	0·091	0·188	0·003	0·027	0·012	0·016
Textiles	18	0·010	0·006	0·014	–	0·013	0·003	0·491	0·412	0·007	–
Leather, clothing	19	–	–	-0·001	-0·001	–	–	-0·001	-0·038	–	–
Building materials	20	0·002	–	0·002	–	0·002	0·001	0·002	–	0·042	0·006
Pottery, glass	21	0·004	–	0·002	–	0·002	0·002	0·001	–	–	0·030
Timber, furniture, etc.	22	0·014	0·023	0·017	–	0·025	0·016	0·004	0·008	0·007	0·016
Paper, publishing	23	0·008	0·001	0·001	-0·003	–	0·005	–	0·008	0·040	0·010
Other manufacturing	24	0·011	0·002	0·064	–	0·017	0·018	–	0·034	0·003	0·002
Construction	25	0·004	0·003	0·002	-0·001	0·005	0·002	–	0·004	0·001	0·004
Gas	26	0·002	0·008	0·002	-0·001	0·003	0·004	-0·007	0·001	0·029	0·011
Electricity	27	0·009	–	0·007	-0·001	0·013	0·011	-0·001	0·004	-0·002	0·025
Water	28	–	–	–	-0·001	–	–	–	–	–	-0·001
Transport, communications	29	0·028	0·011	0·018	-0·002	0·021	0·037	0·023	0·030	0·059	0·041
Distribution	30	0·008	0·004	0·007	-0·002	0·008	0·011	0·018	0·013	0·020	0·014
Services n.e.s.	31	0·066	0·071	0·089	-0·002	0·126	0·094	0·054	0·108	0·153	0·104
Intermediate input ratio		0·537	0·365	0·637	0·361	0·832	0·698	0·637	0·620	0·468	0·388

Table 16 (*continued*)

i	Industry	j ... 22	23	24	25	26	27	28	29	30	31
1	Agriculture, etc.	-0·008	—	—	—	—	—	—	—	—	—
2	Coal	-0·001	[0·004]	-0·004	—	[0·178]	[0·228]	-0·006	-0·015	-0·002	-0·001
3	Mining, n.e.s.	—	0·002	0·001	—	—	—	—	0·001	—	—
4	Food processing	-0·001	0·002	—	0·010	—	—	—	0·006	—	—
5	Drink, tobacco	—	—	—	—	—	—	—	-0·002	—	—
6	Coke ovens, etc.	—	—	—	—	—	—	—	-0·003	—	0·003
7	Mineral oil refining	0·001	[0·004]	0·001	0·005	[0·072]	[0·036]	0·006	0·003	0·002	—
8	Chemicals n.e.s.	0·013	0·040	0·116	0·043	0·017	0·002	0·032	0·018	0·008	0·005
9	Iron, steel (primary)	0·001	—	0·004	0·044	0·017	0·001	0·047	0·008	0·011	—
10	Iron, steel (secondary)	—	0·001	0·004	0·018	0·021	0·001	0·008	—	—	—
11	Nonferrous metals	—	0·006	0·001	0·025	0·001	—	0·004	—	—	—
12	Engineering, electrical	0·008	0·021	0·020	0·039	0·039	0·016	0·008	0·011	0·005	0·034
13	Shipbuilding, etc.	—	—	—	—	—	—	—	-0·009	—	—
14	Motors, cycles	0·001	—	0·002	0·002	—	—	—	0·015	0·016	0·010
15	Aircraft	—	—	—	—	—	—	—	0·031	—	—
16	Locomotives, etc.	—	—	—	—	—	—	—	0·018	—	—
17	Metal goods n.e.s.	0·033	0·004	0·014	0·035	0·011	0·002	0·002	—	0·005	0·011
18	Textiles	0·065	0·013	0·167	0·002	0·002	—	—	0·008	0·039	0·003
19	Leather, clothing	-0·002	—	—	—	—	-0·001	—	—	—	—
20	Building materials	—	—	0·002	0·100	0·006	—	0·003	—	0·001	0·002
21	Pottery, glass	0·002	0·001	—	0·010	—	—	—	—	—	—
22	Timber, furniture, etc.	0·175	—	0·019	0·038	—	0·002	—	—	0·010	0·003
23	Paper, publishing	0·001	0·245	0·024	0·008	0·003	—	0·002	0·003	0·022	0·164
24	Other manufacturing	0·016	0·004	0·110	0·004	—	0·002	—	0·020	0·020	0·007
25	Construction	0·001	0·004	0·004	0·156	0·002	0·002	0·005	0·056	0·004	0·004
26	Gas	—	0·001	0·001	—	0·016	—	0·001	0·001	0·020	0·013
27	Electricity	0·007	0·008	0·016	0·002	0·007	0·006	0·049	0·008	0·035	0·024
28	Water	—	—	-0·001	—	-0·001	-0·003	-0·017	—	-0·001	-0·001
29	Transport, communications	0·032	0·047	0·031	0·040	0·086	0·021	0·020	0·045	0·010	0·007
30	Distribution	0·017	0·020	0·013	0·012	0·021	0·002	0·002	0·004	0·001	0·002
31	Services n.e.s.	0·077	0·126	0·076	0·079	0·052	0·033	0·042	0·021	0·012	0·039
	Intermediate input ratio	0·437	0·544	0·623	0·672	0·301	0·087	0·208	0·278	0·216	0·330

A dash represents an element less than 0·0005 in absolute value.   Square brackets distinguish exogenously projected elements.

Intermediate input ratios may differ from column sums because of rounding errors.

Table 17. Biproportional projection of input–output matrix for Britain in 1966 with sigmoid-projected intermediate input ratios

Industry	$i \backslash j$	1	2	3	4	5	6	7	8	9	10	11	12	13	14	15	16
Agriculture, etc.	1	0·001	—	—	0·030	0·004	—	—	0·001	[0·002]	[0·002]	—	—	—	—	—	—
Coal	2	—	—	0·001	—	—	[0·535]	—	0·009	—	—	—	—	—	—	—	—
Mining n.e.s.	3	—	—	0·003	0·001	—	—	0·004	0·015	—	—	0·027	—	—	—	—	—
Food processing	4	0·168	—	—	0·182	0·036	—	—	—	—	—	—	—	—	—	—	—
Drink, tobacco	5	—	—	—	—	[0·021]	—	—	—	—	—	—	—	—	—	—	—
Coke ovens, etc.	6	—	—	0·002	—	—	0·050	0·025	0·008	0·025	—	—	—	—	—	—	—
Mineral oil refining	7	0·010	—	0·009	0·001	0·002	—	0·099	0·011	—	[0·005]	—	—	—	—	—	—
Chemicals n.e.s.	8	0·055	0·017	0·036	0·088	0·010	0·009	0·078	0·304	[0·013]	0·008	—	0·001	0·011	0·022	0·003	0·001
Iron, steel (primary)	9	—	0·039	0·001	—	—	—	—	0·004	0·358	0·397	—	—	0·065	0·088	—	0·016
Iron, steel (secondary)	10	—	—	—	—	0·003	—	—	0·015	—	0·143	—	—	0·007	0·004	—	0·257
Nonferrous metal	11	—	—	—	—	—	—	—	0·020	0·006	0·040	0·246	0·012	0·011	0·020	—	0·021
Engineering, electrical	12	0·014	0·047	0·057	0·017	0·016	0·007	—	—	0·023	0·012	0·012	0·072	0·059	0·049	—	0·061
Shipbuilding, etc.	13	0·001	—	—	—	—	—	—	—	—	—	—	0·007	0·050	—	—	0·066
Motors, cycles	14	0·003	—	0·004	0·001	—	—	—	—	—	—	—	0·053	—	0·102	—	—
Aircraft	15	—	—	—	—	—	—	—	—	—	—	—	0·147	—	—	0·336	—
Locomotives, etc.	16	—	—	—	—	—	—	—	—	—	—	—	—	—	—	—	0·035
Metal goods n.e.s.	17	0·020	0·013	0·006	0·030	0·022	—	0·022	0·032	0·022	0·003	0·002	0·063	0·051	0·120	0·004	0·093
Textiles	18	0·005	0·010	0·002	0·014	—	—	—	0·010	—	0·002	0·002	0·011	0·005	0·013	—	0·014
Leather, clothing	19	—	—	—	—	—	0·001	—	0·002	—	—	—	—	—	—	—	—
Building materials	20	0·001	0·003	0·009	0·005	0·011	—	0·008	0·006	0·008	—	0·002	0·003	—	0·002	—	0·001
Pottery, glass	21	—	—	0·015	0·009	0·022	—	—	0·008	—	0·007	—	0·005	—	0·002	—	0·001
Timber, furniture, etc.	22	0·002	0·028	0·005	0·035	0·024	—	—	0·021	0·002	0·001	0·002	0·015	0·019	0·016	—	0·027
Paper, publishing	23	0·001	0·001	0·007	—	—	—	—	0·005	—	—	—	0·008	0·001	0·001	0·001	—
Other manufacturing	24	0·008	0·033	—	—	—	—	0·012	0·004	—	—	—	0·012	0·001	0·062	—	0·019
Construction	25	0·018	0·038	0·026	0·004	0·005	—	—	0·001	0·004	0·006	0·001	0·004	0·003	0·002	—	0·004
Gas	26	0·002	0·030	—	0·003	—	0·065	—	0·022	0·009	0·004	0·004	0·002	—	0·002	—	0·003
Electricity	27	0·003	—	—	0·009	0·005	0·011	—	—	0·019	0·014	0·021	0·009	0·007	0·007	0·001	0·013
Water	28	—	—	—	—	—	—	—	—	—	—	—	—	—	—	—	—
Transport, communications	29	0·044	0·034	0·230	0·080	0·038	0·164	0·030	0·054	0·061	0·023	0·044	0·028	0·009	0·017	0·001	0·020
Distribution	30	0·016	0·014	0·035	0·025	0·015	0·052	0·006	0·014	0·035	0·008	0·037	0·008	0·004	0·008	—	0·006
Services n.e.s.	31	0·051	0·049	0·087	0·161	0·100	0·064	0·098	0·123	0·080	0·065	0·142	0·069	0·062	0·085	0·007	0·143
Intermediate input ratio		0·424	0·357	0·534	0·699	0·314	0·423	0·443	0·689	0·663	0·734	0·545	0·538	0·365	0·624	0·364	0·802

Table 17 (*continued*)

Industry	i	17	18	19	20	21	22	23	24	25	26	27	28	29	30	31
Agriculture, etc.	1	–	–	0·002	–	–	0·002	–	–	–	–	–	–	–	–	–
Coal	2	–	–	–	[0·018]	[0·006]	–	[0·004]	–	–	[0·178]	[0·228]	0·001	0·003	0·001	0·001
Mining n.e.s.	3	0·001	–	–	0·034	0·023	–	0·002	0·001	0·010	–	–	–	0·001	–	–
Food processing	4	–	0·001	–	–	–	–	0·002	–	–	–	–	–	0·005	–	–
Drink, tobacco	5	–	–	–	–	–	–	–	–	–	–	–	–	–	–	–
Coke ovens, etc.	6	–	–	–	0·001	–	–	–	0·001	–	–	–	–	0·002	0·002	0·002
Mineral oil refining	7	0·002	–	–	[0·031]	[0·035]	–	[0·004]	0·001	0·005	[0·072]	[0·036]	0·005	0·014	0·007	–
Chemicals n.e.s.	8	0·009	0·024	0·005	0·025	0·050	0·001	0·040	0·097	0·043	0·018	0·003	0·028	0·001	0·011	0·006
Iron, steel (primary)	9	0·125	–	–	0·007	–	0·012	–	0·003	0·042	0·018	0·001	0·040	0·006	–	–
Iron, steel (secondary)	10	0·055	–	–	–	–	0·001	–	0·003	0·019	0·023	0·002	0·007	–	–	–
Nonferrous metals	11	0·092	0·001	–	0·001	–	–	0·001	0·003	0·025	0·001	–	0·004	–	–	–
Engineering, electrical	12	0·014	0·016	0·007	0·027	0·033	0·008	0·005	0·082	0·038	0·041	0·027	0·007	0·009	0·005	0·035
Shipbuilding, etc.	13	–	–	–	–	–	–	0·020	0·017	–	–	–	–	0·011	–	–
Motors, cycles	14	0·001	0·001	–	0·001	0·001	0·001	–	–	0·002	–	–	–	0·012	0·014	0·009
Aircraft	15	–	–	–	–	–	–	–	–	–	–	–	–	0·058	–	–
Locomotives, etc.	16	–	–	–	–	–	–	–	–	–	–	–	–	0·016	–	–
Metal goods n.e.s.	17	0·188	0·003	0·024	0·011	0·016	0·031	0·005	0·013	0·036	0·012	0·002	0·001	–	0·005	0·002
Textiles	18	0·003	0·482	0·371	0·007	–	0·063	0·014	0·144	0·002	0·002	0·002	–	0·007	0·042	0·004
Leather, clothing	19	–	–	0·020	–	–	0·001	–	–	–	–	–	–	–	–	–
Building materials	20	0·001	–	–	0·043	0·006	–	–	0·002	0·094	0·007	0·002	0·003	–	–	0·002
Pottery, glass	21	0·003	–	–	–	0·033	0·003	0·001	0·017	0·009	–	–	–	–	–	–
Timber, furniture, etc.	22	0·016	0·002	0·008	0·007	0·016	0·168	0·240	0·020	0·041	–	–	–	–	0·018	–
Paper, publishing	23	0·005	0·001	0·007	0·039	0·010	0·001	0·004	0·097	0·007	0·003	0·001	0·004	0·002	0·020	0·004
Other manufacturing	24	0·109	0·004	0·031	0·003	0·002	0·016	0·004	0·004	0·005	–	0·002	0·014	0·018	0·011	0·164
Construction	25	0·002	–	0·003	0·001	0·004	–	0·001	0·004	0·151	0·002	–	0·001	0·043	0·022	0·009
Gas	26	0·004	–	0·001	0·001	0·012	–	0·001	0·001	–	0·016	–	–	0·001	0·003	0·005
Electricity	27	0·011	0·007	0·004	0·029	0·025	0·007	0·008	0·001	–	0·008	0·007	0·044	0·007	0·017	0·012
Water	28	–	–	–	–	–	–	–	–	–	–	–	0·002	–	0·002	0·029
Transport, communications	29	0·036	0·023	0·026	0·057	0·040	0·031	0·046	0·026	0·039	0·090	0·033	0·017	0·036	0·038	0·007
Distribution	30	0·011	0·017	0·011	0·021	0·014	0·018	0·020	0·011	0·011	0·022	0·008	0·002	0·003	0·001	0·002
Services n.e.s.	31	0·100	0·054	0·100	0·158	0·106	0·076	0·136	0·068	0·088	0·060	0·036	0·040	0·019	0·013	0·049
Intermediate input ratio		0·696	0·637	0·620	0·474	0·392	0·437	0·550	0·624	0·668	0·325	0·131	0·207	0·278	0·224	0·352

A dash represents an element less than 0·0005.   Square brackets distinguish exogenously projected elements.
Intermediate input ratios may differ from column sums because of rounding errors.

become semi-skilled, 3 % skilled, and so on. Table 19 gives an initial grade distribution $x(0)$ for a particular generation of workers, this generation's grade distribution $A^t x(0)$ after 5, 10, 20 and 40 years of training under the régime A, and its asymptotic distribution w under A. Table 20 shows the matrix B representing the educational programme re-scheduled according to the model of Chapter 10: B is, in the sense defined in that chapter, the 'nearest' matrix to A which will lead to the desired skill distribution asymptotically. The desired distribution v is shown in the last column of Table 21. The first five columns of Table 21 show the batch's initial skill distribution $x(0)$ and its distributions $B^t x(0)$ after 5, 10, 20 and 40 years' training under the new educational system B.

Table 18. *Initial educational structure A*

Grade	i	$j \dots 1$	2	3	4	5	6	7	8
Unskilled manual	1	0·90	0·05	0·03	0·01	0·01	–	–	–
Semi-skilled manual	2	0·05	0·85	0·02	0·02	–	–	–	–
Skilled manual	3	0·03	0·05	0·85	–	0·03	0·01	0·02	–
Clerical, administrative	4	–	0·02	0·03	0·85	0·02	0·03	0·02	0·02
Technical	5	0·02	0·03	0·05	0·03	0·85	0·02	0·02	–
Engineering	6	–	–	–	0·03	0·02	0·02	0·85	0·03
Scientific	7	–	–	–	–	0·05	0·02	0·85	0·03
Managerial	8	–	–	0·02	0·04	0·02	0·06	0·04	0·92

A dash represents a zero element.

Table 19. *Time pattern of percent skill distribution under educational structure A*

Grade	i	$A^t x(0)$					w
		$t \dots 0$	5	10	20	40	
Unskilled manual	1	30	24·8	21·3	17·0	13·6	12·1
Semi-skilled manual	2	20	15·5	12·9	10·0	7·8	6·8
Skilled manual	3	10	12·7	13·1	12·0	10·2	9·2
Clerical, administrative	4	10	9·9	10·1	10·7	11·4	11·6
Technical	5	10	12·8	13·6	13·3	12·2	11·4
Engineering	6	10	8·2	8·2	9·6	11·6	12·5
Scientific	7	5	5·9	7·0	8·7	10·1	10·6
Managerial	8	5	10·1	13·8	18·7	23·4	25·7

Table 20. *Final educational structure B*

Grade	i	$j...$ 1	2	3	4	5	6	7	8
Unskilled manual	1	0·851	0·033	0·018	0·023	0·007	0·007	–	–
Semi-skilled manual	2	0·073	0·865	0·019	0·024	–	–	–	–
Skilled manual	3	0·048	0·056	0·882	–	0·035	0·011	0·026	–
Clerical, administrative	4	–	0·017	0·024	0·851	0·018	0·025	0·019	0·026
Technical	5	0·028	0·029	0·045	0·034	0·861	0·019	0·022	–
Engineering	6	–	–	–	0·037	0·022	0·883	0·060	0·048
Scientific	7	–	–	–	–	0·045	0·017	0·843	0·039
Managerial	8	–	–	0·012	0·030	0·013	0·038	0·029	0·887

A dash represents a zero element.

Table 21. *Time pattern of percent skill distribution under educational structure B*

Grade	i	$t...$ 0	5	10	20	40	v
				$B^t x(0)$			
Unskilled manual	1	30	18·1	12·8	9·0	7·4	7
Semi-skilled manual	2	20	18·2	15·3	11·4	8·8	8
Skilled manual	3	10	16·8	18·8	18·3	16·2	15
Clerical, administrative	4	10	9·7	10·2	11·1	11·8	12
Technical	5	10	14·2	16·0	16·4	15·5	15
Engineering	6	10	10·3	11·3	13·9	16·9	18
Scientific	7	5	5·7	7·3	8·5	9·7	10
Managerial	8	5	7·3	8·7	11·8	14·2	15

It must be stressed that the training model and the present numerical example of it are intended mainly as illustrations of a multi-purpose model of 'Markov programming'; but it is worth commenting briefly on the figures in Tables 18–21. Little needs to be said about Table 18. As we pointed out in Chapter 10, positive entries in cells representing demotions may be read as accidental rather than intended events. On the other hand, one can imagine a far-sighted educational system actually encouraging a scientist, say, to take a routine manual job to give him spare time for some non-remunerative creative activity or to relieve him of mental stress.

Table 19 shows that, under A, a batch of workers comes nearly half-way to its asymptotic state after 10 years and two-thirds of the way after 20 years. The Euclidean distances between $x(0)$ and w, $A^{10}x(0)$ and w, and $A^{20}x(0)$ and w are 31·1, 17·8 and 10·4 respectively.

Table 20 shows that the reprogrammed structure B needs to depart little from A in order to produce asymptotically a vector that differs substantially from the asymptotic vector under A. The (absolutely) largest per cent changes are 60% in (6, 8) (managers into engineers), 60% in (3, 1) (unskilled into skilled), 46% in (2, 1) (unskilled into semi-skilled), 40% in (5, 1) (unskilled into technical), −40% in (1, 3) (skilled into unskilled), and −37% in (8, 6) (engineers into managers). The 'training' of managers into engineers may be interpreted as the persuasion of executives with engineering degrees to return to their speciality, and the negative change for the engineers into managers cell as the discouragement of practising engineers from seeking executive posts. None of the cited elements exceeds 0·06 in the matrix A. The changes point up the fact that the original structure generates far too many unskilled workers and far too many managers.

Table 21 shows that convergence to the asymptotic state proceeds slightly faster under B than under A. The Euclidean distances between $x(0)$ and v, $B^{10}x(0)$, and v, and $B^{20}x(0)$ and v are 30·3, 14·0 and 7·6 respectively. One conjectures that continued education would cease to be socially profitable by $t = 20$. After this length of time the old structure A had brought the batch, at $A^{20}x(20)$, only to within a distance of 14·3 of the desired distribution v. This distance is halved by the structure B.

REFERENCES

[1] J. Aitchison and J. A. C. Brown, *The Lognormal Distribution*, University of Cambridge, Department of Applied Economics, Monograph no. 5, Cambridge University Press (Cambridge), 1957.

[2] K. J. Arrow, H. B. Chenery, B. Minhas and R. Solow, 'Capital-labor substitution and economic efficiency', *Review of Economics and Statistics*, vol. 18, 1961, pp. 225–50.

[3] K. J. Arrow and M. Hoffenberg, with the assistance of H. Markowitz and R. Shephard, *A Time Series Analysis of Inter-Industry Demands*, North-Holland (Amsterdam), 1959.

[4] S. Arrow, 'Comparisons of input–output and alternative projections, 1929–39', The RAND Corporation, Paper P–239, 14 April 1951.

[5] H. Barnett, 'Specific industry output projections', in National Bureau of Economic Research, Conference on Research in Income and Wealth, *Long-Range Economic Projection*, Studies in Income and Wealth, vol. 16, Princeton University Press (Princeton), 1954.

[6] W. Beckerman, 'The pattern of growth of output, employment and productivity', in W. Beckerman *et al.*, *The British Economy in 1975*, Cambridge University Press (Cambridge), 1965.

[7] J. Bénard, 'Réseau des échanges internationaux et planification ouverte', *Economie Appliquée*, vol. 16, 1963, pp. 249–76.

[8] J. Bénard, 'Un modèle d'affectation optimale des ressources entre l'économie et l'education', *Bulletin du CEPREL*, no. 6, July 1966, pp. 1–69.

[9] E. B. Berman, 'A program for the examination of coefficient variation in the inter-industry context', Interindustry Item no. 47, U.S. Bureau of Mines, 1953.

[10] F. Bingen, 'Simplification de la demonstration d'un théorème de M. W. M. Gorman', note, Université Libre de Bruxelles, duplicated, 1965.

[11] C. P. Bonini and H. A. Simon, 'The size distribution of business firms', *American Economic Review*, vol. 48, 1958, pp. 607–17.

[12] J. C. Boot, *Quadratic Programming*, North-Holland (Amsterdam), 1964.

[13] B. Cameron, 'The production function of Leontief models', *Review of Economic Studies*, vol. 20, 1952–3, pp. 62–9.

[14] D. G. Champernowne, 'A model of income distribution', *Economic Journal*, vol. 63, 1953, pp. 318–51.

[15] H. B. Chenery and P. G. Clark, *Interindustry Economics*, Wiley (New York), 1959.

[16] H. B. Chenery and T. Watanabe, 'International comparisons of the structure of production', *Econometrica*, vol. 26, 1958, pp. 487–521.

[17] C. Christ, 'A review of input–output analysis', in National Bureau of Economic Research, Conference on Research in Income and Wealth, *Input–Output Analysis: an Appraisal*, Studies in Income and Wealth, vol. 18, Princeton University Press (Princeton), 1955.

[18] J. Cornfield, W. D. Evans and M. Hoffenberg, 'Full employment patterns: 1950', *Monthly Labor Review*, vol. 64, January–June 1947, pp. 163–90, 420–32.

[19] H. Correa and J. Tinbergen, 'Quantitative adaptation of education to accelerated growth', *Kyklos*, vol. 15, 1962, pp. 776–86.

[20] H. Cramér, *Mathematical Methods of Statistics*, Princeton University Press (Princeton), 1946.

[21] G. Dantzig, 'Upper bounds, secondary constraints and block triangularity in linear programming', *Econometrica*, vol. 23, 1955, pp. 174–83.

[22] G. Debreu and I. N. Herstein, 'Nonnegative square matrices', *Econometrica*, vol. 21, 1953, pp. 597–607.

[23] W. E. Deming and F. F. Stephan, 'On a least-squares adjustment of a sampled frequency table when the expected marginal totals are known', *Annals of Mathematical Statistics*, vol. 11, 1940, pp. 427–44.

[24] Department of Applied Economics, University of Cambridge, *A Computable Model of Economic Growth*, A Programme for Growth, no. 1, Chapman and Hall (London), 1962.

[25] Department of Applied Economics, University of Cambridge, *A Social Accounting Matrix for 1960*, A Programme for Growth, no. 2, Chapman and Hall (London), 1962.

[26] Department of Applied Economics, University of Cambridge, *Input–Output Relationships 1954–1966*, A Programme for Growth, no. 3, Chapman and Hall (London), 1963.

[27] E. D. Domar, 'On the measurement of technological change', *Economic Journal*, vol. 71, 1961, pp. 709–29.

[28] Economic Commission for Europe, United Nations, *Macro-Economic Models for Planning and Policy-Making* (Geneva), 1967.

[29] W. D. Evans, 'The effect of structural matrix errors on inter-industry relations estimates', *Econometrica*, vol. 22, 1954, pp. 461–80.

[30] L. R. Ford and D. R. Fulkerson, *Flows in Networks*, Princeton University Press (Princeton), 1962.

[31] M. Fréchet, 'Sur les tableaux dont les marges et des bornes sont données', *Review of the International Statistical Institute*, vol. 28, 1960, pp. 10–32.

[32] D. Friedlander, 'A technique for estimating a contingency table, given the marginal total and some supplementary data', *Journal of the Royal Statistical Society*, Series A, vol. 124, 1961, pp. 412–20.

[33] D. Gale, *The Theory of Linear Economic Models*, McGraw-Hill (New York), 1960.

[34] A. S. Goldberger, *Econometric Theory*, Wiley (New York), 1964.

[35] A. S. Goldberger, A. L. Nagar and H. S. Odeh, 'The covariance matrix of reduced-form coefficients and of forecasts for a structural econometric model', *Econometrica*, vol. 29, 1961, pp. 556–73.

[36] W. M. Gorman, '"Estimating trends in Leontief matrices": a note on Mr Bacharach's paper', note, Nuffield College, Oxford, duplicated, 1963.

[37] L. M. Graves, *The Theory of Functions of Real Variables*, McGraw-Hill (New York), 1946.

[38] M. Hatanaka, *The Workability of Input–Output Analysis*, Fachverlag für Wirtschaftstheorie und Ökonometrie (Ludwigshafen am Rhein), 1966.

[39] M. L. Helzner, 'A study of coefficient variation of selected inputs into the steel industry', Interindustry Item No. 48, U.S. Bureau of Mines, 1954.

[40] R. Howard, *Dynamic Programming and Markov Processes*, Technology Press: Wiley (Cambridge, New York), 1960.

[41] Japan, Economic Planning Agency, *Econometric Models for Medium-Term Economic Plan 1964–68* (Tokyo), 1965.

[42] S. Karlin, *Mathematical Methods and Theory in Games, Programming, and Economics*, vol. 1, Pergamon (London), 1959.

[43] M. G. Kendall, *The Advanced Theory of Statistics*, vol. 2, Griffin (London), 1946.

[44] E. S. Kirschen and R. de Falleur, *Analyse Input–Output de l'Economie Belge en 1953*, Department d'Economie Appliquée, Université Libre de Bruxelles (Brussels), 1958.

[45] L. R. Klein, *A Textbook of Econometrics*, Row, Peterson (Evanston), 1953.

[46] A. F. Kouevi, 'Essai d'application prospective de la méthode RAS au commerce international', *Bulletin du CEPREL*, no. 5, 1965, pp. 71–120.

[47] A. Lamfalussy, 'Intra-European trade and the competitive position of the E.E.C.', paper read to the Manchester Statistical Society, 13 March 1963.

[48] R. Lecomber, 'A generalisation of R.A.S.', Growth Project Paper no. 196, Department of Applied Economics, University of Cambridge, duplicated, 1964.

[49] W. W. Leontief, *The Structure of American Economy 1919–1929*, Oxford University Press (New York), 1941.

[50] W. W. Leontief, 'Structural change', in W. W. Leontief *et al.*, *Studies in the Structure of the American Economy*, Oxford University Press (New York), 1953.

[51] E. Malinvaud, 'Aggregation problems in input–output models', Chapter 8 of ed. T. Barna, *The Structural Interdependence of the Economy*, proceedings of the 2nd International Conference on Input–Output Analysis, Varenna, 1954 (New York, Milan), 1956.

[52] B. Marin-Curtoud, 'Les modèles prévisionnels des réseaux d'échanges internationaux et leur structure', *Bulletin du CEPREL*, no. 5, 1965, pp. 1–69.

[53] T. I. Matuszewski, P. R. Pitts and J. A. Sawyer, 'L'adjustment periodique des systèmes de relations interindustrielles, Canada, 1949–58', *Econometrica*, vol. 31, 1963, pp. 90–110.

[54] T. I. Matuszewski, P. R. Pitts and J. A. Sawyer, 'Linear programming estimates of changes in input coefficients', *Canadian Journal of Economics and Political Science*, vol. 30, 1964, pp. 203–10.

[55] H. Neisser, review of [49], *American Economic Review*, vol. 31, 1941, pp. 608–10.

[56] M. Nerlove, review of [3], *American Economic Review*, vol. 50, 1960, pp. 182–6.

[57] Office Statistique des Communautés Européennes, *Tableaux 'Entrées–Sorties' pour les Pays de la Communauté Economique Européenne* (Brussels), 1964.

[58] F. Omar, 'Input–output estimation', Growth Project Paper no. 227, Department of Applied Economics, University of Cambridge, duplicated, 1966.

[59] J. Paelinck and J. Waelbroeck, 'Etude empirique sur l'évolution de coefficients "input–output"', *Economie Appliquée*, vol. 16, 1963, pp. 81–111.

[60] J. Paelinck *et al.*, *Etude Comparée des Tableaux d'Entrées et de Sorties des Communautés Européennes*, Centre d'Etudes et de Recherches Universitaire de Namur (Namur), 1966.

[61] A. Phillips, 'Stability of technical coefficients', University of Pennsylvania, Input–Output Project, 1953.

[62] H. M. Schneider, *An Evaluation of Two Alternative Methods for Updating Input–Output Tables*, B.A. dissertation, Harvard College, duplicated, 1965.

[63] O. Schreier and E. Sperner, trans. M. Davis and M. Hausner, *Introduction to Modern Algebra and Matrix Theory*, Chelsea (New York), 1951.

[64] P. Sevaldson, 'Changes in input–output coefficients', in ed. T. Barna *et al.*, *Structural Interdependence and Economic Development*, Macmillan (London), 1963.

[65] I. G. Stewart, 'Input–output table for the United Kingdom, 1948', *The Times Review of Industry*, London and Cambridge Economic Bulletin, New Series, no. 28, 1958, pp. vii–ix.

[66] R. Stone, *Input–Output and National Accounts*, Organisation for European Economic Co-operation (Paris), 1961.

[67] R. Stone, 'Multiple classifications in social accounting', *Bulletin de l'Institut International de Statistique*, vol. 39, no. 3, 1962, pp. 215–33.

[68] H. Theil, *Economics and Information Theory*, North-Holland (Amsterdam), 1967.

[69] P. Thionet, 'Sur certaines variantes des projections du tableau d'échanges interindustrielles', *Bulletin of the International Statistical Institute*, Proceedings of the 34th Session, Ottawa 1963, vol. 40, book 1, pp. 119–31.

[70] C. B. Tilanus, *Input–Output Experiments, The Netherlands 1948–1961*, Rotterdam University Press (Rotterdam), 1966.

[71] W. Tims and F. M. Meyer zu Schlochtern, 'Foreign demand and the development of Dutch exports', *Cahiers Economiques de Bruxelles*, no. 15, 1962, pp. 389–95.

[72] United Kingdom, Board of Trade and Central Statistical Office, *Input–Output Tables for the United Kingdom, 1954*, Studies in Official Statistics, no. 8, Her Majesty's Stationery Office (London), 1961.

[73] P. Uribe, C. G. de Leeuw and H. Theil, 'The information approach to the prediction of interregional trade flows', Report no. 6507, Econometric Institute of the Netherlands School of Economics (Rotterdam), 1965.

[74] J. Waelbroeck, 'Les échanges des pays du Marché Commun avec les pays du monde extérieur', in *Intégration Européene et Réalité Economique*, Collège de l'Europe, Tempelhof (Bruges), 1964.

[75] P. Wolfe, 'The simplex method for quadratic programming', *Econometrica*, vol. 27, 1959, pp. 382–98.